Adorno, Culture and Feminism

Adorno, Culture and Feminism

edited by

Maggie O'Neill

SAGE Publications
London • Thousand Oaks • New Delhi

Editorial arrangement, Introduction and Chapter 1 © Maggie
O'Neill 1999
Chapter 2 © Shierry Weber Nicholsen 1999
Chapter 3 © Silvia L. López 1999
Chapter 4 © Sinkwan Cheng 1999
Chapter 5 © Regina Becker-Schmidt 1999
Chapter 6 © Gudrun Axeli Knapp 1999
Chapter 7 © Juliet Flower MacCannell 1999
Chapter 8 © Barbara Engh 1999
Chapter 9 © Hilde Heynen 1999

First published 1999

 SAGE Publications Ltd
6 Bonhill Street
London EC2A 4PU

SAGE Publications Inc
2455 Teller Road
Thousand Oaks, California 91320

SAGE Publications India Pvt Ltd
32, M-Block Market
Greater Kailash – I
New Delhi 110 048

British Library Cataloguing in Publication data

A catalogue record for this book is available from the British
Library.

ISBN 0 7619 5216 0 ✓
ISBN 0 7619 5217 9 (pbk)

Library of Congress catalog card number 98–61887

Typeset by Photoprint, Torquay
Printed in Great Britain by The Cromwell Press Ltd,
Trowbridge, Wiltshire

To Marie and Bill, Steve, Patrick and James

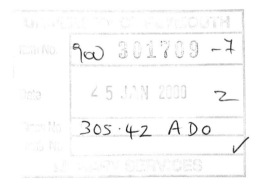

Contents

The Contributors

Regina Becker-Schmidt is Professor of Social Psychology at the University of Hanover, Germany, and has also been a visiting professor of feminist theory at the University of Vienna, University of Linz, University of Connecticut, University of Advanced Studies of Vienna and Roskilde University, Denmark. Regina received her doctorate from the Institute for Social Research, Frankfurt-on-Main and her research interests are focused upon gender relations and the constitution of gender difference as well as the social psychology of technology. Regina teaches critical theory, psycho-analysis, social psychology and political psychology and has authored and co-authored (with Gudrun Axeli Knapp) a number of books concerning working-class women, gender relations and social formation, technological development and androcentrism. These include *Arbeitsleben-Lebensarbeit*; *Geschlechtertrennung-Geschlechterdifferenz*; *Arbeiterkinder*; *Das Geschlechterverhältnis als Gegenstand der Sozialwissenschaften*; and *Zeitbilder der Technik*.

Sinkwan Cheng is a Research Associate in the English and Comparative Literature Department at the University of California, Irvine, USA. She has published seven articles and reviews in various areas including psycho-analysis, French and German critical theory, post-colonial and cultural studies, twentieth-century British and Asian American literature, as well as legal and political philosophy. Her dissertation was awarded a distinction by the Department of Comparative Literature at the State University of New York, Buffalo in the summer of 1995, and, at the invitation of Henry Sussman, is currently being revised for possible inclusion in his 'Psycho-analysis and Culture' series. She also won an Excellence in Teaching Award at SUNY, Buffalo, in a campus-wide competition.

Barbara Engh is Lecturer in Cultural Studies at the University of Leeds, UK. Her essay on music and critique in the work of Roland Barthes ('Loving it: music and criticism in Roland Barthes') appears in Ruth Solle's *Musicology and Difference: Gender and Sexuality in Music Scholarship*, and an essay 'Adorno and the Sirens: tele-phono-graphic bodies' appears in *Embodied Voices: Representing Female Vocality in Western Culture* (1994). At present Barbara is writing a book on phonography, entitled *After 'His Master's Voice': Post-phonographic Aurality*.

Hilde Heynen is Associate Professor in the Department of Architecture, Urban Design and Planning at the Katholieke Universiteit Leuven, Belgium.

She has published articles in *Assemblage, Archis* and other periodicals. She is the author of *Architecture and Modernity: A Critique* (1999). Hilde's research currently concentrates on issues of architecture, gender and the city.

Gudrun Axeli Knapp is Professor at the Psychological Institute, University of Hanover, Germany. Axeli's research interests are in the sociology of gender relations and social psychology of gender differences; feminist theory and methodology. She has published articles on feminist theory in various journals and books and is co-editor of *Traditionen Brüche. Entwicklungen feministischer Theorie* (1992), *Das Geschlechterverhältnis als Gegenstand der Sozialwissenschaften* (1995) and of the volume on *Interdisciplinarity of l'Homme*, the Austrian journal for feminist history (1995). The most recent publication edited by her is *Kurskorrekturen: Feminismus zwischen kritischer Theorie und Postmoderne* (1998).

Silvia L. López is Assistant Professor of Spanish at Carleton College, Northfield, Minnesota, USA. Her research interests are in critical theory and Latin American literature. She has published on Central American literature, Latin American cultural theory and on Walter Benjamin. Her current work focuses upon social and cultural modernity at the turn of the century in Latin America.

Juliet Flower MacCannell is Professor Emerita of Comparative Literature, University of California, Irvine, USA and Research Professor at University of California, Berkeley, Department of Rhetoric. Juliet has published fifty scholarly articles and several books whose subjects range from Rousseau and Stendhal to Atwood, Duras, Hannah Arendt, and matters of evil, fascism, violence and beauty, as well as contemporary psychoanalytic theories of culture. She recently founded a research group for psychoanalysis and the arts, Encore 2, which is planning to publish a journal. Her best-known books are *The Regime of the Brother* (1991), *Refiguring Lacan* (1986) and *Thinking Bodies* (1994). Juliet co-edited *Feminism and Psychoanalysis: A Critical Dictionary* (1992) and translated Hélène Cixous's *The Terrible but Unfinished Story of Norodom Sihanouk, King of Cambodia* (1993). She co-wrote *The Time of the Sign* with Dean MacCannell (1982). Juliet was named President of the Society for the Psychoanalytic Study of Culture and Society and in 1994 was named artist-in-residence, Moonhole, Bequia by the Engelhard Foundation and the Institute for Contemporary Art, Boston. Her new book, *Things to Come: The Hysteric's Guide to the Future Female Subject*, will be published in 1999.

Maggie O'Neill is Senior Lecturer in Sociology and Womens' Studies at Staffordshire University, UK. Maggie's research interests include critical and cultural theory, prostitution, masculinities, ethnographic field methods, especially feminist participatory action research. She has conducted extensive ethnographic action research with women and young people working as prostitutes in the UK, including comparative research with colleagues in Spain. She is currently conducting participatory action research with 'refugees' and 'asylum seekers'. Adorno's and Benjamin's notion of mimesis is a key organizing concept in her research methodology. Her publications include work on responses to child and juvenile prostitution; and a number of publications arising from ethnographic, participatory action research with female prostitutes. Her book *Prostitution and Feminism* will be published in 1999.

Shierry Weber Nicholsen is Profesor of Interdisciplinary Studies with the Graduate programme on Environment and Community at Antioch University in Seattle, USA. Her publications include translations of numerous works by Adorno and Habermas, including *Adorno's Notes to Literature* and *Hegel: Three Studies*. Shierry is also the author of *Exact Imagination/Late Work: On Adorno's Aesthetics* (1997). Her research interests include the phenomenology of aesthetic experience and ecological consciousness; and psychoanalytical perspectives on environmental consciousness.

Acknowledgements

My thanks must go, first of all, to Chris Rojek who encouraged this book project and also to Robert Rojek and Pascale Carrington, for they all supported it through to completion. Thanks to the contributors who have 'made' the book and for their patience. Thanks to Martin Jay for helpful suggestions regarding contributors as well as for encouraging the project. John O'Neill read and commented on my sections – thank you, John. Communication with Shierry Weber Nicholsen most certainly enhanced the project. Thank you to the American reader whose very helpful comments I have included in my revisions. My colleagues at Staffordshire – Barbara Kennedy, Ruth Holliday, David Bell and Janice Richardson – gave me critical and supportive comments: thank you, everyone. Thanks must also go to Conrad Lodziak who introduced me to the work of Adorno. Last, but by no means least, thanks to Jackie Clewlow for secretarial assistance, and to Barbara McCarthy and Lesley Harvey at the Staffordshire University Slide Library.

Foreword

This collection brings together a range of essays on the works and life of Theodor Adorno by feminist scholars and feminist-informed scholars, working within and between the disciplines of sociology, aesthetics, philosophy and cultural studies. The purpose of this text is to address the extent to which feminists can find sources of critique, analysis and insight in Adorno's work. The breadth and scope of the feminist scholarship represented here is of great significance not only to the literature on Theodor Adorno, his life and work, but to the growing presence and voices of women in critical social theory. The text centres on the development of feminist analysis of Adorno's works contextualized within changing historical, social and cultural processes and practices. In using Adorno, the contributors to this volume have found an aid to exploring our situatedness within wider social contexts marked by the 'mediation' between unity, difference *and* power.

Introduction

The collection of essays presented here is located at the intersection of contemporary feminist theory and socio-cultural analysis. This site is marked, in part, by both paralysis *and* creative production: the paralysis of feminist thought holding fast to ideas of universal commonalities, of universal reason; the problematics of identitarian thinking (see Regina Becker-Schmidt's chapter); *and* the relationship with what has come to be known as 'masculinist theory'. The creative production of feminist thought involves the relationship between first-wave, second-wave and contemporary feminist thought and practice, and the development of renewed methodologies and ways of working and writing as feminists in societies that are post-traditional but are marked also by the traditional; in societies that are disenchanted but are in the process of being re-enchanted; and, if we agree with Stjepan Meštrović (1997), in societies that are post-emotional but also contain possibilities of and for authenticity.

Frigga Haug contends that the marginalization of women from 'masculine spheres of production and administration' and the ways in which 'hopes for the quality of life are otherwise displaced to the margins' helps to explain the contradictory nature of women's oppression which can serve to immobilize. She reminds us that 'the ability to bring about change grows out of people's own activity' (Haug, 1992: 204). As feminists we have formed alliances across disciplinary boundaries and are working to free ourselves from the paralysis that can bind us. We can further this development in part by critically engaging with theorists such as Theodor Adorno within the historical trajectory of feminism(s) as an aid to the development of feminist thought and practice. Why? Because Adorno was concerned with (1) deconstructing identity thinking – the identity between subject and concept; (2) the relationship between psychic, social and cultural processes and practices; (3) the intersection of philosophy, politics and aesthetics; and (4) illuminating the contradictory nature of social and sexual oppression.

Adorno, Culture and Feminism seeks to show the impact/imprint of Adorno's work, for feminists, more than thirty years after his death and to ask: what is the relevance of Adorno for feminisms? His work inevitably deals with the concept of paralysis (see the essay 'Resignation' in *The Culture Industry: Selected Essays on Mass Culture*, 1991) – the pessimism contained in the utter hopelessness of challenging and changing administered society. At one and the same time he never gave up hope for transformative possibilities – the liberating potential of art and aesthetics. There are, as we shall see, resonances in Adorno's theoretical works for

feminist analysis of culture, society and aesthetics – analysis which uses
Adorno purposefully and productively as well as critically, utilizing concepts such as 'authenticity', 'the culture industry', 'commodification', 'non
identity thinking', '*Kulturkritik*', 'negative dialectics' and the 'authoritarian
personality'. But more than this, we cannot look at Adorno without also
looking at Benjamin, for the two are inextricably connected. The relationship between the two is brought home in Benjamin's letters – the exchanges
between Adorno (Teddie) and Benjamin (Detlef); and Gretel (Felizitas)
Adorno and Benjamin – and in the living impact of their mutual
influence.[1]

The role of the intellectuals who formed the Frankfurt Institute for Social
Research was far-reaching, pivoting around critical analyses of society and
culture. For Adorno, the method of negative dialectics was paramount
and the influences of Hegel, Kant, Marx, Freud, Nietzsche and Walter
Benjamin were central to the development of his thought. Indeed the origins
of 'negative dialectics' are found in Benjamin's influence, specifically
Benjamin's early works and the 'intellectual dialogue between him and
Adorno' (Buck-Morss, 1977: 64; Weber Nicholsen, 1997).

Before his death in 1969, the 'hyper-modern' (Adorno, 1984: 22) was
becoming increasingly significant in Adorno's work on aesthetics. 'Hyper-
modernism, including much of electronic music, prefers to join forces with
reified consciousness rather than stay on the side of an ideology of illusory
humanness' (Adorno, 1984: 22). The 'hyper-modern' was a sign of the take-
over of instrumental reason and the loss of mimesis (mimesis for Adorno is
associated with the non-instrumental appearance or the expression of the
sensual, the 'unsayable', of playfulness, of 'truthfulness' and of 'spirit' in
works of art – see the chapters by Regina Becker-Schmidt, Barbara Engh,
Hilde Heynen, Silvia López and Shierry Weber Nicholsen in this volume),
of hope in the present, of the *promesse de bonheur*. The hyper-modern was
a sign of the increasingly fragmentary experience of living in the world, of
living a damaged life. After Adorno's death in 1969 at the age of 66,[2] the
increasing disenchantment of the world was resonant in the development of
deconstructionism, postmodernism and post-structuralism.[3]

As the cultural sphere has been overtaken by entertainment, popular
consumption and the managers of the mass media, intellectuals have been
squeezed out and are no longer called upon to arbitrate knowledge and
culture. Intellectuals have lost their 'legislative' role and have taken on an
'interpretive role' (Bauman, 1988). Individual needs, identities and lifestyles
are tied to consumption: we fashion ourselves through consumption. We are
seduced into social conformity by fantasies and daydreams, by meanings
residing in commodities (Baudrillard, 1990, 1994). Although Adorno was
writing more than thirty years ago, the 'interpretive role', for him, resided in
critical philosophy (critical theory) and art (autonomous art). 'The mystery
of art is its demystifying power. Its social essence calls for a twofold
reflection: on the being-for-itself of art, and on its ties with society' (Adorno,
1984: 322). Furthermore, 'art is a refuge for mimetic behaviour. . . . It

represents truth in the twofold sense of preserving the image of an end smothered completely by rationality and of exposing the irrationality and absurdity of the status quo' (Adorno, 1984: 79). 'Cultural critics' on the other hand are reduced or 'degraded' 'to propagandists or censors. . . . The prerogatives of information and position permit them to express their opinion as if it were objectivity. But it is solely the objectivity of the ruling mind. They help to weave the veil' (Adorno, 1995: 20).

Taking an interpretive approach then, postmodernity (or rather 'hyper-modernity') does not mark a periodizing or epochal break, but is rather the development of submerged or marginal aspects of modernity (akin to Rojek's account of 'modernity 2' in *Decentring Leisure*, 1995) and could thus herald transformative and liberatory possibilities. Values such as choice, diversity, critique, reflexivity and agency come to the fore in hyper-modernity. The hyper-modern embraces plurality, ambiguity, ambivalence, uncertainty, the contingent, transitory, disruptive, critical and oppositional against uniform, standardized culture. Any claim to universal standards of truth, goodness and beauty is abandoned. Human knowledge is always situated but always fluid, always contested. There is no authoritative standpoint. Culture is a major site of social conflict and contestation. But what does this mean for women and for feminist thought?

Contemporary feminist thought: subjectivity, bodies and difference

Contemporary feminist thought (including post-structuralism, post-colonialism, postmodernism and post-feminisms) evolved out of critiques of the Enlightenment, modernism, structuralism and psychoanalysis. Key themes include a disavowal of binary oppositions, a focus upon deconstruction, anti-essentialism and 'the epistemological chaos of the present condition' (Lykke and Braidotti, 1996: 5). Contemporary feminists working within women's studies, philosophy, film studies, cultural studies and sociology are concerned with meanings and processes, the fluidity of subjectivity and increasingly the body and embodiment, as opposed to an earlier focus upon universals and the absence of theorizing our embodied selves. Currently the emphasis is upon the utter complexity of our experiences, our lifeworlds and our interrelations as embodied 'subject-objects', with others – with family, children, lovers – *and* what this may or may not mean for feminist politics. Our lifeworlds are contested sites of meaning, being and becoming centred around the fluidity of subjectivity and our embodied selves, our embodied 'projects of self' (Foucault, 1977; Giddens, 1992). For example, Regina Becker-Schmidt (Chapter 5 in this volume) uses Adorno's concept of 'mediation' to explore the complex and contradictory conditions of social life: *verhältnisse*. Becker-Schmidt examines the correspondence between hierarchical structures in gender orders and the state of the industrial nations described by Adorno to illustrate the complexity of the social totality and the social domination of the male gender group.

Feminist film theorists, aware of the fascination with and indeed centrality of the pedagogic role of the media in our lives, are critiquing the possibilities for trans-human spaces outside of traditional Cartesian conceptualizations. They move beyond representation, and, drawing upon Deleuze's relational figurations, explore the flows, energies and fragments involved in 'becoming': in 'becoming woman' within what is coming to be known as 'techno-cultures', 'the cyberotic and molecularity' and 'post-humanism' (Braidotti, 1997; Kennedy, 1996a, 1997).

Increasingly feminists are working in the areas of ecology and feminist science and technology (Lykke and Braidotti, 1996; Shiva, 1988). Lykke and Braidotti point to the fact that feminists working in these areas are confronting the 'epistemological haze which surrounds key social issues' at the end of the twentieth century. This focus forms an interconnecting set of axes of ' "natures", "bodies" and the forms of techno-scientific mediation that recombine them in a variety of unexpected ways' (1996: 245). The 'epistemological haze' is compounded by what Barbara Adam calls 'temporal uncertainty' (1997: 100) and the ways in which contemporary reality is characterized by a multitude of times co-existing in mutually implicating and embedded ways. For Adam, it is vital that we respond to issues of globalization and ecological crisis by developing more reflexive understandings of 'time' – presents and futures, times and spaces, natures and cultures, the material and the immaterial, the negation of rationality (Adam, 1997: 100–1). Adam suggests that social scientists must 'see multiple processes simultaneously, embrace contradictions and paradoxes, the unknowable and the known . . . [and w]ith the loss of clear boundaries, control and certainty' (1997: 101), we have to face the moral as well as the analytical issues. The question we need to ask is: what kind of feminist politics does such theorizing give rise to?

Moira Gatens writes about the important conceptual shifts between feminist theorists of the 1970s and contemporary deconstructive feminisms. The contrast between the two is illustrated through three key themes – power, body, difference. The concept of difference that Gatens proposes is one which means a multiplicity of difference and, drawing upon Foucault to explore the micropolitics of power, she investigates the ways in which power, domination and sexual difference intersect in our lived experiences – as women and as men. The imaginary body, the corporeal body, the sexed body and the political body overlap in an analysis of the operations of power. What is indisputable is that female embodiment as currently lived 'is itself a barrier to women's "equal" participation in sociopolitical life' (1996: 71). 'Difference feminism' does not concern itself with privileging biological differences – nor with constructing dualistic theories of essential difference – for to 'insist on sexual difference as the fundamental and eternally mutable difference would be to take for granted the intricate and pervasive ways in which patriarchal culture has made that difference its insignia' (1996: 73). Therefore, for Gatens, the task is to deconstruct relationships between our embodied selves, power and difference through a genealogy of sexual and social imaginaries.

Rosi Braidotti calls for explorations of the contemporary imagination, of sexual and social imaginaries in 'an age of decline of humanistic paradigms' (1997: 76) marked by 'the disaggregation of humanistic subject-positions and values; the ubiquitous presence of narcotic texts and practices; the all-pervasive political violence; the inter-mingling of the enfleshed and the technological' (1997: 76). For Braidotti, Deleuze's work offers a useful grid, particularly his theory of becoming – the philosophy of radical immanence – to help us not only to understand our cultural sensibilities but to produce transformations, to move beyond. Braidotti, like Kennedy (1996a, 1996b) reads Deleuze productively, hopefully, in concrete ways, alongside transcendental readings.[4]

On the other hand, for Janet Wolff (1989) women were written out of the literature on modernity: 'The classical misogynist duality, of woman as idealized-but-vapid/real-and-sensual-but-detested . . . is clearly related to the particular parade of women we observe in this literature on modernity' (1989: 150).[5] Wolff suggests there are three major interrelated reasons for the absence of women in the literature on modernity: the nature of sociological investigation; the partial conception of modernity; and the reality of women's place in society. Women do appear in the classical texts of sociology – but only as they relate to men. The rise of sociology as a new discipline was dominated by men, and the focus for analysis was predominantly the public sphere. The separation of the domestic sphere from the public sphere and the focus specifically upon the latter means that the literature on modernity is partial, for it misses the private sphere and also the interrelation of the public and private. Women's real 'situation in the second half of the nineteenth century was more complex than one of straightforward confinement to the home' (1989: 152–3). The task ahead, politically and practically, according to Wolff, is for sociologists and historians to recover women's experiences and fill the gaps in the classical accounts.

Barbara Marshall (1994: 148) maintains that

> feminism constitutes both a critique and a defence of modernity . . . it can fully embrace neither an unreconstructed modernism's subject nor post modernism's rejection of the subject, by virtue of the fact that women as subjects have never been accorded the coherence, autonomy, rationality or agency of the subject which undergirds an unreconstructed modernism, and which post modernism has deconstructed out of existence.

In *Feminism/Postmodernism* (1990) Linda Nicholson stresses that the post-modern turn has been an important one for feminist scholars, and is a natural *ally* as it avoids the tendency to construct theory from the position of white middle-class women.

There are no easy answers. In Nicholson's book a number of writers take issue with the interrelationships of feminism and postmodernism. Jane Flax points out the attraction of an Enlightenment world view: it is tempting for those who have been deemed incapable of reason or autonomy to insist on these powers for themselves – for, in fact, reason is an ally in feminists' struggles. But, for Flax, feminist theory belongs in the sphere of postmodern philosophy – because feminist notions of the self, of knowledge and truth are at odds with the Enlightenment and cannot fit comfortably within its boundaries. Christine de Stefano is sceptical about the postmodern turn. Her point is that since men have had their Enlightenment then they can afford to focus upon the decentring of the self, the negation of 'truth' and universality, but for women taking this stance could lead to a weakening of what is not yet strong. Furthermore, feminist politics needs a relatively unified notion of the social subject, of 'woman'.

Donna Haraway (1990, 1991) argues that postmodernism is a viewpoint of our times – a period of possibilities and foreclosures. Her cyborg metaphor is used to illuminate the mixed values of the present – the cyborg violates previously dominant distinctions between humans and animals, humans and machines, minds and bodies, materialism and idealism, rejecting hopes of unity and wholeness expressed in ideals of alienated labour, community as family. Indeed, Haraway says it is a mistake to follow universal totalizing theory, for it misses most of reality. Our dominations don't work by medicalization and normalization but by networking, communications redesign and stress management. Moreover, freed from the need to root feminist politics in identification, vanguard parties, purity or mothering, we can instead embrace the possibilities of multiple and contradictory aspects of our individual and collective identities: Haraway would rather be a cyborg than a goddess.

As I see it, there has certainly been a move, a paradigm shift, within feminist thought over the last two decades which has to be contextualized within shifts in the social organization of Western societies, the impact of globalization, of technology and digital communications, of the environmental/biological risks and hazards that we are all consciously aware of – particularly post-Chernobyl (Beck, 1992; Beck et al., 1994; Beck and Beck-Gernsheim, 1995; Clark, 1997).

We can say that metaphors of our hopes and ideals over the last three decades are centred upon 'needs' (Western Marxism, unionization, socialist feminism, Marxist feminism); 'desire' (the turn to pleasure/desire/the body in feminist theories, the impact of Foucault, French feminisms, Deleuze and Guattari); then the 'anxiety' and 'apocalypticism' of the last two decades – HIV and AIDS, the concern with the 'viral' and the interfaces between flesh and machine, the 'post-human' (see Kennedy, 1996b) environmental risks and hazards, the development of ecofeminism and feminist studies in science and technology. For John O'Neill our concern with 'needs' was replaced by concerns about 'desire', and desire has now been replaced with 'anxiety'.[6] These categories should not be read as epochal or periodizing, for needs, desires and anxiety are interrelated concerns in our everyday lived relations as well as in wider socio-historical terms.

What is very clear is that contemporary feminists (including Trinh T. Minh-ha, Elizabeth Grosz, Rosi Braidotti, Nina Lykke, Judith Butler, Elspeth Probyn, Moira Gatens, Donna Haraway, Luce Irigaray and Frigga Haug) and the contributors to this volume are challenging disciplinary boundaries, are working in spaces outside of binary thinking, and are dealing with the interrelated concerns of needs, desires and anxieties with the focus, for some, upon the body and embodiment, as well as power and difference. The great strength of new feminisms for Grosz is the 'openness to its own retranscriptions and rewritings' (1995: 80). Renewed methodologies and 'transgressions' take feminist thought outside of binary thinking, between the spaces of the linear narratives of his-(s)tory, and purposefully challenge identity thinking/identitarian thinking. This serves to prioritize certain discourses – feminist critiques of psychoanalysis, post-structuralism, and 'representation' through cultural and social imaginaries. But this is *not* to prioritize cyborg discourses over the concerns of feminists working with the actual practical lived relations of women – at grassroots level. The point about contemporary feminisms is that they deal *with* the contradictions of oppression *and* the utter complexity of our lived relations towards the close of the twentieth century – within the context of technologization, globalization and 'the permanent crisis of the totally administered society' (Piccone, 1993: 3). The totally administered society is marked by 'conformist political theory' (Piccone, 1993: 7), the transformation of the liberal state, 'mass society, pseudo culture and New Class dominations' (Piccone, 1993: 9).

Thinking about the complexity of our lived relations, as women and as feminists, we are, of course, aware of the precariousness of our positions, between the margins, outside of binary thinking at the level of politics and institutions *and* at the level of lived experience and embodied experience. The frailty and fragility of the human body, our sense of embodiment and transcendence of the body is inevitably reflected upon in our theorizing and our politics – our praxis. Adorno was very much aware of the contradictions involved in lived relations and the power of bureaucracy, the state, and cultural institutions (the culture industry). He was also very much concerned with the interrelationship and the mediation between the 'micrology' of lived experience and broader structures of power, domination and control.

Adorno's central dialectic of mimesis and constructive rationality provides an example of the importance of understanding the critical tension between emotion, feeling, spirit, subjectivity *and* our 'out there' sense of being in the world – institutions, organizations, bureaucracy, objectification. The work of Gudrun Axeli Knapp in this volume highlights the importance of mediation between subject and object in Adorno's work and the absence of reconciliation. Going beyond post-structuralist thought Knapp suggests that 'constellative micrological thinking' which draws upon the relations of mediation between the particular and the general, between subjectivity and social objectivity, contains a number of impulses, and she outlines these in Chapter 6. Critical theory's methodological and epistemological 'orientations' are for Knapp the most useful appropriations for feminist analysis. Knapp uses Regina Becker-Schmidt's work as a point of departure for exploring the contradictory societal integration of women. Given the contradictory nature of women's lived experiences, Knapp suggests that feminist analysis must develop an 'interdisciplinary integration of different theoretical perspectives' acknowledging the 'restricted ideal' of universal knowledge and grand theory and yet 'insisting on the analysis of large-scale societal constellations'.

Contemporary feminisms provide renewed methodologies and new alliances for working at the crossroads of theory, practice and politics. They manage to hold on to the tensions between women's experiences of poverty, domination and violence as well as 'becoming' woman – both analytically and morally. The breakdown of 'the feminist project', the problematics of a 'feminist successor science', should not be read as an abandonment of second-wave feminist ideals which were rooted firmly in the work of first-wave feminists, but rather as critical feminist responses to the evolving feminist project(s):

> The essence is and always has been more of a project than a description of existent reality; this insight provides us with a way to hold onto the category of woman whilst recognising ourselves to be in the process (an unending one) of defining and constructing the category. . . . In the final analysis it seems more important to struggle over what it *means* to be a woman than over whether or not to be one. (Rita Felski, cited in Modleski, 1991: 20)

See Barbara Engh's chapter in this volume for in-depth analysis of the signifier 'woman' in feminist cultural criticism and the resonances between Engh's feminist project and Adorno's project.

The work of Adorno is arguably very useful for contemporary feminists. For example: (1) his emphasis upon negativity and the need for non-identical thinking (a comparison of the work of Adorno and Deleuze via Nietzsche could usefully be developed here); (2) the focus upon aesthetics and politics and the impact of negative dialectics upon deconstructionism; (3) the focus upon micrology (drawing upon Benjamin) – upon the small scale – the minutiae of lived experience; (4) the focus upon living a damaged life, the ambiguity and ambivalence of modern and hyper-modern times; and (5) his relentless attack upon essentializing the feminine at the same time as proclaiming the utter loss of hope in the Enlightenment as progress, as the *promesse de bonheur*. These five points could be utilized to explain, account for as well as interrogate and seek to transform contemporary social life from feminist perspectives.

For Joanna Hodge (1989) this method of pushing Adorno's enquiries and concepts to the point that distinctions and boundaries begin to break down is indicative of postmodern philosophizing (rather than of modern which would seek to control such distinctions and boundaries). Hodge draws parallels with the work of Nietzsche, Heidegger, Adorno, Deleuze, Kristeva and Irigaray – the central theme is 'the questioning of the continuity and givenness of subjectivity and the parallel questioning of the continuity and givenness of historical process' (1989: 99) around the themes of subjectivity, representation and experience. Women, Hodge argues, have indeed been written out of the history of modernity, yet they are at one and the same time both in history and not in history; as women we are the repressed of both culture and philosophical history.

Carrie Hull (1997) explores Judith Butler's position in *Bodies that Matter* alongside Adorno on 'Subject and object' in *Negative Dialectics*. Hull argues that one can defend Butler's position (beyond materialism and idealism) from Adorno's 'materialist perspective' through the use of non-identity thinking, critiquing identity thinking (the concept is adequate to the object) and affirming that there is 'always something, some entity, some object beyond thought' (1997: 24). In Butler's work materiality is partly forged by what is not uttered and what falls outside of any category (Hull, 1997: 24). Additionally, Butler advocates a rethinking of identity 'so that it no longer entails a fixed, static wholeness and the corresponding rejection of what that identity purportedly does not include' (1997: 31). A reworking of the logic of non-contradiction is proposed. Hull concludes that for both Butler and Adorno, despite their differences (Adorno's materialism and Butler's post-structuralism), a similar strategy is reached, 'a new way of thinking and being . . . above identity and contradiction; it would be a togetherness in diversity' (Hull, 1997: 31).

Jessica Benjamin's (1993) powerful psychoanalytical analysis of femininity and domination draws upon Adorno and the Frankfurt School to show how masculinity and femininity become associated with the postures of master and slave, in part through our relationships to our mothers and fathers and, how the developing opposition of girl as object and boy as subject distorts the very ideal of the individual. Benjamin shows how this is reflected in the broader culture, thus preserving structures of domination. 'I will argue that the principle of rationality which social theorists since Weber have seen as the hallmark of modernity – the rationality that reduces the world to objects of exchange, calculation and control – is in fact male rationality' (1993: 184). The subordination of all aspects of life to instrumental reason subverts other values such as the values of private life and what she calls 'maternal aspects of recognition' – nurturance and attunement (the recognition of feeling) (1993: 185).

Indeed, it appears that the structure of domination is anchored so deeply into the psyche that it is impossible to envision mutual reciprocal relationships whereby both individuals are subjects and broader relations and interrelations where equality and reciprocity are possible. The answer, for Benjamin, is to analyse critically psychoanalytic thinking from a feminist approach *and* the structures of domination represented by the master(subject)–slave(object) relationship. Feminist analysis must not shy away from analysing submission, fearing our own participation in domination; nor must we construct the problem of domination as a problem of male aggression and 'female vulnerability victimized by male aggression' (1993: 9). Nor must we idealize the oppressed 'as if their culture were untouched by the system of domination, as if people did not participate in their own submission' (1993: 9) – for such simplifications reproduce structure of gender polarity while seeming to attach them. We do, however, need to be prepared to deal with mystery, uncertainty and contradiction within relationships and we need to deal with the tensions between emotion, fact and reason. Benjamin draws upon the quality Keats demanded for poetry – negative capability – and insists that a theory or politics that cannot cope with contradiction, or with the irrational, or that tries to sanitize the erotic components of human life cannot visualize an end to domination. For Benjamin, disentangling the bonds of love involves seeking mutual recognition of equal subjects leading to personal and social transformations. Indeed, feminism 'has opened up a new possibility of mutual recognition between men and women' (1993: 224).

Feminist receptions and critiques of Adorno's work should not be limited to theoretical issues, for his work can provide a means, a lens through which to examine women's contemporary lived experience and lived relations in more concrete ways. In conducting feminist participatory action research with female prostitutes I was influenced by a number of feminist writers, researchers and theorists (Maria Mies, Jalna Hanmer, Trinh T. Minh-ha, Frigga Haug, Sandra Harding, Alison Jagger, Caroline Ramazanoglu, Liz Stanley, Janet Wolff, Gillian Rose, Rita Felski) but I was also influenced by Adorno's reflections on the socio-cultural experience of living in the modern world, specifically methodologically, through negative dialectics. My ethnographic work was inspired by his reflections on coming to know the work of art through interpretation, commentary and criticism via immersion, objectification and dissociation – through 'micrology' and *Verstehen*. A 'force field' (Jay, 1993) around theory, experience and praxis developed in the process of my immersion in women's lived experiences and the subsequent tension between immersion and objectification in my ethnographic work. I developed an understanding of women's lives, specifically women's articulation of their lived relations (micrology) – of embodiment and transcending the body in order to 'make out' in sex work. Immersion in the lifeworlds of women working as prostitutes, engaging with the feelings, impressions and life experiences, witnessing the relevance for all women of these narratives and being able to work with them in transformative ways necessitates, for me, a theory of emotion/feeling/sensuousness in critical tension to reason and rationality. The dialectical relationship at work here I have called 'a politics of feeling' and my longer-term project is tied to a feminist epistemology of prostitution (see O'Neill, forthcoming).

Part I – critical social theory: aesthetics and politics

Part I provides the thematic context for each of the following specifically focused chapters that deal mainly with sociological/cultural issues and questions but which also range across the spectrum of Adorno's work on culture, politics, the media, philosophy, modernism/hyper-modernism, and the transformative potential of art and critical theory. Here (in the first four chapters) the intention is to provide a detailed outline of Adorno's central categories which will facilitate a better understanding and engagement with the chapters that follow.

In making sense of Adorno's work on social life and aesthetics, I have found it most helpful to concentrate upon three central concepts or configurations: negative *dialectics*, *Kulturkritik*, and *unintentional truth*. These three concepts are explored in some detail in Chapter 1 in order to delineate my own understanding and appreciation of Adorno's work, and also to serve as an introduction to the subsequent chapters which provide critical feminist analysis of key themes and also raise exciting possibilities for further analysis. These three configurations interrelate in Adorno's aesthetic theory and it is, in part, through his aesthetic theory that we can 'get at' his social theory.

In Chapters 2 and 3 Shierry Weber Nicholsen and Silvia López explore central motifs in Adorno's *Aesthetic Theory*. Both deal with the profound influence Benjamin's work had upon Adorno. *Aesthetic Theory* is the unfinished culmination of Adorno's life's work, which he described as representing 'the quintessence of my thought on art'. Written aporetically using the form of the 'constellation', this work is described by the editors of the 1984 edition, Gretel Adorno and Rolf Tiedemann, as being fragmentary on two levels: first in the positive sense that theory may disclose truths by disintegrating into fragments, and second in the sense that Adorno's untimely death prevented him from realizing *Aesthetic Theory*'s final law of form. In reading Adorno one must of necessity enter a dialectical relationship with the text, which is constantly challenging and revoking one's interpretation of it. Adorno's theories are interdisciplinary, yet at one and the same time he is opposed to those methodologies which seek to dissolve all boundaries, insisting upon the untruth of overcoming in thought what is still split in reality. As exemplars of negative dialectics his theories illuminate the utter complexity of the lifeworld.

Shierry Weber Nicholsen explores the interrelationship of Adorno and Benjamin's work in 'Adorno, Benjamin and the Aura: an Aesthetics for Photography?' Her chapter focuses specifically upon the notion of 'aura', photography's indexical quality, the relationship to aura and the contemporary critical potential of the aesthetic. This critical potential pivots around the struggle for preserving the capacity for critical reflection as engaged, embodied caring. Shierry Weber Nicholsen concludes by drawing upon Barthes's comments on photography to illuminate the ways in which the photograph 'in showing us a quick and oblique glimpse of intractable reality arouses our capacity to value and respect the larger physical world, which is mute, immediate, and fragile'. Shierry's chapter is supplemented by two of her own photographs.

Silvia López's contribution focuses upon 'the encoding of history' and thinking art in constellations. Art is a cipher of history: it records the traces of the totalizing process by being able to incorporate all that is excluded by bourgeois culture. In contemporary society, *Aesthetic Theory* presents untold possibilities in an age when 'venues for reflection have all been recuperated'. For Silvia, the relationship between epistemology and aesthetics is crucial. Art is not only a form of knowledge but it refuses definition, and the dialectic of mimesis and rationality articulates this most fully. Silvia suggests that the possibilities for feminism's use of these concepts and reflections are not so preposterous as we might once have thought.

The first three chapters serve to interpret and explain aspects of *Aesthetic Theory*, and the key concepts or motifs in Adorno's work. At the same time they open up debate on the relationship between Adorno's work on aesthetics, the debt to Benjamin, the usefulness of his work for feminisms and feminists via a focus upon embodiment and the politics of the gaze (for Shierry Weber Nicholsen) and the interrelationship between epistemology and aesthetics as a form of knowledge (for Silvia López). Finally in this part, Sinkwan Cheng explores Adorno's exile in exile through analysis of '*Fremdwörter* as "The Jews of Language" and Adorno's Politics of Exile'. Sinkwan Cheng focuses upon language and the frequent presence of 'foreign words' or *Fremdwörter* in Adorno's writings, thus exploring 'the damaging impact of exile on language' and Adorno's sense of homelessness and displacement – between German nationalism *and* American conformism (or the administered society). In Adorno's work *Fremdwörter* produce discontinuities that disrupt the flow of narrative, thus undermining the possibility for 'organic unity'. This is an example of non-identity thinking in action. In examining Adorno's exile in exile from the perspectives of Lacanian psychoanalysis and deconstruction Cheng unearths a contradiction in Adorno's theoretical *oeuvre* which seriously compromises his critique of totalitarianism. On the other hand, Cheng focuses upon Lacanian psychoanalysis and deconstruction to interrogate the notion of exile, the crossing of frontiers displacing nostalgia and defamiliarizing notions of 'linguistic nationality', the 'family' of people 'belonging' to the same 'language' and 'homeland'.

Part II – feminism, culture and society: the relevance of critical theory for contemporary feminisms

Part II utilizes the conceptual framework created by Part I to set in motion critical reflection on specific areas for analysis within the broad context of culture and society. Adorno's works on culture and society revolve around three central concepts: negative dialectics or non-identity thinking; *Kultur-kritik*; and unintentional truth and its relation to philosophy. Complex and fragmentary, eschewing fixed categories, the concept of 'constellation' is used to describe his way of thinking and articulating his ideas. Exploring the relationship between culture and society through Adorno's central concepts raises some key points of reflection for feminists working in the fields of cultural studies, philosophy and architecture. What is the relationship between cultural practices and social processes in late modern/postmodern/hyper-modern times? How does the concept of mediation help or hinder work on the relationship between art and society for feminist aesthetics? Each chapter in this section focuses upon a specific dimension of Adorno's work and addresses the material from the vantage point of feminist critique and analysis.

Chapters 5–7 focus upon Adorno's critical theory from the vantage points of methodology, philosophy and sociology. The dialectical relationship between these three concepts in Adorno's work is drawn out by Regina Becker-Schmidt and Gudrun Axeli Knapp. Regina Becker-Schmidt opens up with an examination of 'Critical Theory as a Critique of Society', exploring 'Theodor Adorno's Significance for a Feminist Sociology'. Gudrun Axeli Knapp continues this theme by focusing specifically upon German-speaking feminism and critical theory through the lens of Adorno's brand of critical social theory.

The relationships between methodology, sociology and philosophy in Adorno's critical social theory are important avenues to 'mine' for detailed consideration of the relevance of these works for feminisms and feminist-renewed methodologies, particularly in the debates regarding feminist praxis (the relationship between theory and practice), philosophy, feminism and post-feminism, and the possibilities of and for contemporary feminist critical theory.

Regina Becker-Schmidt informs us that reference to Adorno is seldom made in German sociology today; his attempts to 'relate societal transforma-tions to restructurings of psychical energies on a collective scale' have not been continued. Moreover, it is feminists who have productively analysed Adorno, but even so, because his image of femininity is conformist rather than progressive, his ideas must first be transferred into a feminist per-spective. Regina does this by examining, first, the relationship between equality and difference in theories of gender relations; and second, in asking what way difference in the power relations between men and women supports social domination above and beyond gender relations. Difference, identitarian logic and the correspondences between gender hierarchies and societal hegemonies are key themes. The ensuing discussion has far-reaching implications for radical feminisms, liberal feminisms and any theoretical work premised upon identitarian logic.

Gudrun Axeli Knapp continues the themes raised by Regina around identitarian logic and difference, and opens her chapter by stressing that in international feminist debates concerning equality, difference and decon-struction our specific cultural backgrounds and traditions are not being foregrounded and our arguments are formulated in too general a mode. For Gudrun Axeli Knapp recontextualization and translation are now urgent as the contours of our common experiences become blurred. Axeli explores German feminism's relationship to (reappropriation of) Adorno and critical theory alongside the usefulness of Adorno's work for current feminists' work on language, discourse, signification and post-structuralism. For those feminists reappropriating critical theory the focus upon methodological and theoretical perspectives 'can (re)gain a non-economistic, non-functionalist, historically concrete and complex notion of societal objectivity which, in the wake of belated "microsociological revolution" and of the overheated climate of changes that accompanies "postmodernism", runs the risk of being lost in feminist debates of the 1990s'.

These two chapters serve to open up debates about the usefulness of Adorno and critical theory for feminist projects, specifically focusing on the interrelationship of sociology, philosophy and methodology in German-speaking feminisms, and *for* all feminisms.

In Chapter 7 Juliet Flower MacCannell provides a brilliant analysis of 'woman' and 'the riddle of femininity' in Adorno's work. Charting a brief biographical journey, she helps the reader to locate herself within the context of Juliet's reception of/resistance to Adorno. The problematic she explores is the 'absence of recognition of a special significance to female human existence'. She acknowledges that there is indeed little fault to be found in Adorno's critical theory where women are concerned: 'His critical theory is virtually gender-blind, his aphorisms about women are almost always proto-feminist. . . . Long before the women's movement he assailed women's abuse, archaic as well as contemporary'.

However, for Juliet, Adorno does not anticipate 'woman-beyond-the bourgeoisie'. Drawing a link between Adorno's (and Horkheimer's) recep-tion of Kant to Sade, Sade to Fascism and Fascism to the female figure (indeed the figure of the Mother-maternal superego/love), Juliet interrogates Adorno for a glimpse of what he would wish for a 'truly liberated female subject'. Psychoanalysis (and Freud in particular) provides a way of seeing and speaking of the riddle of femininity in Adorno. In the end, woman beyond the here and now is without a figure – 'beyond the differentiations of the social construction of gender'. But, in the very end, interrogating Adorno on woman through Kant, Sade, Lacan and Freud lies beyond mediation and intervention of the Other; the final question is: 'Is this the resolution devoutly to be wished?'

The psychoanalytical dimension of Adorno's theory is an important and overlooked avenue for critical feminist analyses, as Juliet Flower MacCan-nell and Sinkwan Cheng's chapters in this volume show. Matt Connell (1997) is currently exploring the psychological dimension and tells us that Adorno's use of psychoanalysis enables him to speak 'for the irrational unconscious, not just against it, showing its scars to be a product of the social constraint of consciousness' (Connell, 1997: v). What Connell stresses is the fact that in studying the contradictions of consciousness (Adorno's use of Hegel and Freud) critical theory can reveal historical developments more precisely than social or economic theory alone. This particular dimension is an important one for feminists concerned with writing women into the history of modernity who are concerned to take account of the interrelationships of psychic and social processes and practices.[7]

Juliet and Sinkwan's chapters specifically, and the other chapters too, represent examples of the recovery of subjectivity and the development of creative, critical feminist thought – feminist praxis – as 'knowledge for'.

Barbara Engh explores Adorno on music and mimesis while linking the work of Luce Irigaray and Adorno to explore the signifier 'woman'. Barbara takes us on a wonderful journey through the Platonic version of 'mimesis' to *Aesthetic Theory*, the role of art, subjectivity and commodity fetishism to the magic of music and the sorcery of the feminine. In this sorcery there are traces of 'the Platonic fear of becoming woman, becoming animal'. For Barbara there is both pessimism and hope – for in remaining non-identical, in refusing to give oneself up, becoming something else is an ever-present possibility; and in remaining elsewhere, feminism may 'jam the theoretical machinery' and 'outmanoeuvre' the dominant logic.

Finally Hilde Heynen examines Adorno's relevance for a feminist theory of architecture by examining the concept of 'mimesis' and the work of Adolf Loos, drawing upon both Irigaray and Philippe Lacoue-Labarthe. Adorno's debt to Benjamin is considered, and the fact that for Adorno through mimesis art establishes a critical relation to social reality. Adorno's complex interplay of mimesis, negativity and utopia can be regarded as productive for feminist thought, making way for reflection on identity and difference whilst avoiding identity thinking; critically engaging with architecture and questioning from a feminist perspective. Taking Loos's Raumplan house as an example, Hilde subverts the identification of women with the house and domestication and transforms the meaning of the house in a 'gesture of mimetical appropriation . . . dwelling as continually permeated by its opposite . . . a dwelling in the feminine'. Hilde's chapter illuminates the links between the aesthetic and social dimensions via an interpretation of the main themes of this volume – non-identity thinking, *Kulturkritik*, and unintentional truth – focusing upon the relationship between mimesis and the feminine.

This collection is the first of its kind and draws upon a group of international feminist scholars. Sherry Weber Nicholsen suggests that although Adorno's works have been explored and reiterated to the point of 'intractable familiarity', 'the sense of familiarity masks an inaccessible core of the work that has so far proved impervious to appropriation' (1997: 1). For Weber Nicholsen, the reception of Adorno's works has remained in quite narrow bounds (with the exception of his work on music), specifically concentrating on his relationship to Marxism, to French thought, and always on finding out where he stands rather than 'imaginatively appropriating his work' (1997: 2). This collection provides both a dynamic critical under-standing of where Adorno stands, *and* examples of imaginative use of his work by feminists working within and between the contested sites of socio-cultural theory and feminisms.

Notes

1 See *The Correspondence of Walter Benjamin* (1994).

2 The last years of Adorno's life (similarly Benjamin's) were fraught with problems. On his return to Germany and Frankfurt University, the former Nazi faculty rejected his works, defining them as 'unscholarly . . . essayistic . . . and fragmentary' (Adorno, 1997: xix). Hullot-Kentor describes a situation where Adorno was grudgingly offered a *Wiedergutmachungsstuhl* (a faculty position) as reparation for his suffering through the war – not a position of merit. Furthermore, students – who had once embraced his philosophical works – rioted in his seminars, principally because he would not involve himself in the student protests of 1969: he would not accommodate and involve himself in this version of 'praxis' (Hullot-Kentor, 1997: xx). See Adorno's (1991) essay on 'Resignation' in *The Culture Industry*.

3 Indeed, Martin Jay (1984: 22) writes that there are parallels between decon-structionism and Adorno's work: both had a common appreciation of Nietszche: 'Adorno honoured him for his trenchant critique of mass culture and politics, his ruthless exposure of the bankruptcy of traditional metaphysics, and his penetrating insight into the ambiguous dialectic of the enlightenment'. See also Terry Eagleton and Michael Ryan, cited in Jay (1984).

4 As Mike Featherstone and Roger Burrows point out (1995) there are two major responses to the cyborg/cyberspace phenomenon in socio-cultural theory which focus upon relationships between the body, society and technology over the past decade. First, the interrelationship of new technology and the body produces a '*fin de millénium* pessimism, with the assumption that there are no new moves in the game and that we are confronted by a future which "has already happened" ' (1995: 1). Secondly, there are those who see utopian impulses and possibilities involved in 'moving into a reconfigured world which bears little relation to our previous speculations. . . . The writings which have emerged on cyberspace, cyberbodies and cyberpunk . . . are replete with utopian, dystopian and heterotopian possibilities' (1995: 1). Featherstone and Burrows conclude their article by stating that what is clear is that there has been a move away from systematic large-scale theory building towards complexity, difference and disorder.

5 Wolff is referring specifically to Baudelaire here.

6 From a lecture John O'Neill gave to the Sociology and Postmodernism MA group at Staffordshire University on 7 May 1997.

Nigel Clark's paper (1997) provides an interesting analysis of the anxiety of living through environmental risks and hazards. Clark uses Beck and Baudrillard to examine disasters which result in the desire to master the natural world through technical rationality. According to Beck, rationality is exceeding its limits and we must face the uncontainable consequences of a risk society because of the malfunc-tioning of instrumental rationality. We are entering a new order of undelimitable accidents. According to Baudrillard (in the West) we are currently at the stage of manufactured catastrophe, and we will soon enter a stage of pre-programmed catastrophe. The catastrophe is likely to be a superconductive event: less to do with risk of default and more to do with risks of excess – runaway energy flows and chain reactions. For Beck, nuclear reactors turn the world into a laboratory. This is encapsulated in 'I am scared' and, in response, new forms of solidarity and collective action will create a more secure technological and legal infrastructure. For

Baudrillard – whether by nuclear or biological violence – we subject ourselves to the same experimental pressures as animal species in our laboratories: there is an element of fascination in our catastrophes as they are not just unintended consequences of producing the things we want, but are events which secretly excite us. Such events are triggered by our own compulsion to generate something novel and marvellous, something which exceeds nature. We are involved in gambling – playing double or nothing with nature. Beck talks about ecological irruptions and Baudrillard talks about epidemics of simulation.

The importance of Clark's paper is the fact that here we experience a comparison between the French and German traditions in contemporary critical theory, but also the dis-enchantment and re-enchantment of the world – the further development of the contradictions involved in the 'administered society'.

7 Roslyn Bologh's feminist enquiry into Max Weber and masculine thinking may serve as a useful role model for feminists critically exploring masculine political and social thought. Drawing upon Freud's insights and Weber and Marx's humanism she speaks of the important tension between subjectivity and objectified relationships. 'The recovery of subjectivity requires replacing relations of coercion and domination with relations of erotic sociability' (Bologh, 1990: 314). Furthermore, she shows us that our subjective relationships are always mediated by objectifications:

> The aim of a genuinely sociable world would be to avoid reifying these objectifications, to avoid treating them as thing-like ends in themselves and to recover the human subjectivity (human feelings and desires) that are denied in and by those objectifications. Given the pervasive control of external objectified power and wealth in our lives, the recovery of subjectivity becomes a profound, revolutionary act. (Bologh, 1990: 314)

References

Adam, B. (1977) 'Re-vision: the centrality of time for an ecological social science perspective', in S. Lash, B. Szerszynski and B. Wynne (eds), *Risk, Environment and Modernity: Towards a New Ecology.* London, Thousand Oaks and New Delhi: Sage.

Adorno, T.W. (1984) *Aesthetic Theory*, ed. Gretel Adorno and Rolf Tiedemann, trans. Christian Lendhart. Minneapolis, MN: University of Minnesota Press.

Adorno, T.W. (1991) *The Culture Industry: Selected Essays on Mass Culture*, ed. and with an introduction by J.M. Bernstein. London: Routledge.

Adorno, T.W. (1995) *Prisms*, trans. Samuel and Shierry Weber. Cambridge, MA: MIT Press.

Adorno, T.W. (1997) *Aesthetic Theory*, ed. Gretel Adorno and Rolf Tiedemann, trans. Robert Hullot-Kentor. Minneapolis, MN: University of Minnesota Press.

Baudrillard, J. (1990) *Seduction.* London: Macmillan.

Baudrillard, J. (1994) *The Illusion of the End.* Cambridge: Polity Press.

Beck, U. (1992) *Risk Society: Towards a New Modernity.* London, Newbury Park and New Delhi: Sage.

Beck, U. and Beck-Gernsheim, E. (1995) *The Normal Chaos of Love.* Cambridge: Polity Press.

Beck, U., Giddens, A. and Lash, S. (1994) *Reflexive Modernization: Politics, Tradition and Aesthetics in the Modern Social Order.* Cambridge: Polity Press.

Benjamin, J. (1993) *The Bonds of Love: Psychoanalysis, Feminism and the Problem of Domination.* London: Virago.

Benjamin, W. (1994) *The Correspondence of Walter Benjamin 1910–1940*, ed. Gershom Scholem and Theodor Adorno, trans. Manfred Jacobson and Evelyn Jacobson. Chicago and London: University of Chicago Press.

Bologh, R.W. (1990) *Love or Greatness: Max Weber and Masculine Thinking – A Feminist Inquiry*. London, Boston, Sydney and Wellington: Unwin Hyman.

Braidotti, R. (1997) 'Meta(l)morphoses', *Theory, Culture and Society*, 14 (2): 67–80.

Buck-Morss, S. (1977) *The Origin of Negative Dialectics: Theodor W. Adorno, Walter Benjamin and the Frankfurt Institute*. Brighton: Harvester Press.

Clark, N. (1997) 'Panic ecology: nature in the age of superconductivity', *Theory, Culture and Society*, 14 (1): 77–96.

Connell, M. (1997) 'The psychological dimension of Adorno's critical theory'. PhD thesis, Nottingham Trent Library, Nottingham.

Featherstone, M. and Burrows, R. (1995) 'Cultures of technological embodiment: an introduction', *Body and Society: Cyberspace Cyberbodies Cyberpunk Cultures of Technological Embodiment*, 1 (3–4): 1–19.

Foucault, M. (1977) *Discipline and Punish*. London: Allen Lane.

Gatens, M. (1996) *Imaginary Bodies: Ethics, Power and Corporeality*. London: Routledge.

Giddens, A. (1992) *The Transformation of Intimacy*. Cambridge: Polity Press.

Grosz, E. (1995) *Space, Time and Perversion*. New York and London: Routledge.

Haraway, D. (1990) 'A manifesto for cyborgs: science, technology and socialist feminism in the 1980s', in L. Nicholson (ed.), *Feminism/Postmodernism*. London: Routledge.

Haraway, D. (1991) *Simians, Cyborgs and Women: The Reinvention of Nature*. London: Free Association Books.

Haug, F. (1992) *Beyond Female Masochism: Memory-Works and Politics*. London: Verso.

Hodge, J. (1989) 'Feminism and postmodernism: misleading divisions imposed by the opposition between modernism and postmodernism', in A. Benjamin (ed.), *The Problems of Modernity: Adorno and Benjamin*. London: Routledge.

Hull, C.L. (1997) 'The need in thinking: materiality in Theodor W. Adorno and Judith Butler', *Radical Philosophy*, 84 (July–August): 22–35.

Hullot-Kentor, R. (1997) 'Translator's introduction' to T.W. Adorno, *Aesthetic Theory*. Minneapolis, MN: University of Minnesota Press.

Jay, M. (1984) *Adorno*. London: Fontana.

Jay, M. (1993) *Force Fields: Between Intellectual History and Cultural Critique*. New York and London: Routledge.

Kennedy, B. (1996a) 'Pedagogies of the screen: cyberfeminist futures in film-noir – the jouissance in the cyborg, or why Romeo is still bleeding', in E. McWilliam and P. Taylor (eds), *Pedagogy, Technology and the Body*. New York: Lang.

Kennedy, B. (1996b) 'The fascination of the last seduction'. Paper presented at the Image of the American West conference, University of Southern Colorado, March.

Kennedy, B. (1997) 'Molecular bodies: film, faciality and *fin de siècle femmes*'. Paper presented at the Body Modification conference, TCS Centre, Nottingham Trent University, June.

Lykke, N. and Braidotti, R. (1996) *Between Monsters, Goddesses and Cyborgs: Feminist Confrontations with Science, Medicine and Cyberspace*. London: Zed Books.

Marshall, B. (1994) *Engendering Modernity: Feminism, Social Theory and Social Change*. Cambridge: Polity Press.

Meštrović, S.G. (1997) *Postemotional Society*. London, Thousand Oaks and New Delhi: Sage.

Modleski, T. (1991) *Feminism without Women: Culture and Criticism in a 'Post-feminist' Age*. New York and London: Routledge.

Nicholson, L. (1990) *Feminism/Postmodernism*. New York and London: Routledge.

O'Neill, M. (forthcoming) *Prostitution and Feminism: Towards a Politics of Feeling*. Cambridge: Polity Press.

Piccone, P. (1993) 'Beyond pseudo-culture? Reconstituting fundamental political concepts', *Telos*, 95 (Spring): 3–14.

Rojek, C. (1995) *Decentring Leisure: Rethinking Leisure Theory*. London, Thousand Oaks and New Delhi: Sage.

Shiva, V. (1988) *Staying Alive: Women, Ecology and Development*. London: Zed Books.

Weber Nicholsen, S. (1997) *Exact Imagination/Late Work: On Adorno's Aesthetics*. Cambridge, MA: MIT Press.

Wolff, J. (1989) 'The invisible flâneuse: women and the literature on modernity', in A. Benjamin (ed.), *The Problems of Modernity: Adorno and Benjamin*. London: Routledge.

Part I

CRITICAL SOCIAL THEORY: AESTHETICS AND POLITICS

1 Adorno and Women: Negative Dialectics, *Kulturkritik* and Unintentional Truth

Maggie O'Neill

> The Feminine character, and the ideal of femininity on which it is modelled, are products of masculine society. The image of undistorted nature arises only in distortion, as its opposite. . . . Glorification of the feminine character implies the humiliation of all who bear it.
>
> (Adorno, 1978: 95–6)

The work of Theodor Adorno is typically perceived by some as elitist, obscuring the interests of women within the historical context of malestream German critical theory. The central question this volume addresses is the extent to which Adorno's theoretical reflections on culture, social theory, epistemology, methodology and aesthetics can be put to use by feminist theorists as an aid (not a guide) to the development of feminist thought within the broad areas of sociology and cultural studies. What, for example, is the relationship between feminism, culture and critical theory within the context of contemporary feminist debates? What is Adorno's relevance for contemporary feminists engaged in these debates and for the development of feminist critical theory?

In 'Gender in the early Benjamin' Eva Geulen discusses the 'ambivalent status of femininity in Adorno's thought' (1994: 1). Geulen criticizes Adorno for 'aestheticizing femininity' by associating 'the utopian moment of nameless bliss with the feminine as nature'; and in doing so supporting one of the 'dominant gender ideologies of bourgeois culture' (1994: 2). Yet she acknowledges that he clearly develops a 'relentless critique of any gender-essentialism which would deny its mediation by the social whole' (1994: 1). Before turning her attention to Walter Benjamin, Geulen asks whether the 'feminist returns' to Adorno are indicative of Jameson's (1990) crucial point that in Adorno we find an 'antidote to postmodernist relativism and disintegration – namely unity and difference' (Geulen, 1994: 2).

This chapter will address the common themes running through Adorno's work in sociology, philosophy and aesthetics and provide an outline of his critical social theory and the key ideas which formed the core of his life's work. Adorno's work revolves around three interrelated concepts: negative dialectics or non-identity thinking; unintentional truth and its relation to philosophy; and *Kulturkritik*. These concepts provide the thematic threads to the book. Similarities, differences, difficulties and possibilities for feminist readings and use of Adorno's works will be explored.

Non-identity thinking, *Kulturkritik*, and the liberating/transformative potential of the unintentional truth are concepts which feminist theorists are concerned with in their work on sexuality, identity politics, socialization, aesthetics and social research, albeit using language which differs from Adorno's. The next section provides a short précis of Adorno's central ideas, specifically his critical social theory.

Negative dialectics

Susan Buck-Morss's pioneering work *The Origin of Negative Dialectics* (1977) and Gillian Rose's *The Melancholy Science* (1978) highlighted the relevance of Adorno for a generation of scholars immersed in Marxist analyses and counter-hegemonic discourses, and have continued to be key texts for the better understanding of Adorno's theory of negative dialectics and the importance of non-identity thinking. Negative dialectics is presented as an anti-system in reaction to the prevalent norms and values of society, on the grounds that they have come to legitimize a society which in no way corresponds to them – they have become lies (Rose, 1978). Adorno's aim was the explosion of reification, for concepts as ordinarily used are distorting and mask the truth (here he was influenced by Lukács's (1971) *History and Class Consciousness* and by Nietzsche's philosophy). 'Truth' and 'Identity' do not consist of a correspondence between concepts and their objects, for to engage in correspondence thinking is to engage in identity thinking never more being further from the truth. Negative dialectics looks to Marxism as method, and dialectical thinking as the core of that method. Negative dialectics is the tool for the critical analysis of society, and it aimed for the negation of the negation.

The works of Hegel and Marx in particular tell the story of the rise of human consciousness. In *The Phenomenology of Mind* Hegel (1967) describes man's path from consciousness to self-consciousness; from the master–slave dialectic to a dialectic of self-recognition and mutual recognition of egos, a dialectic of intersubjectivity. Hegel is a philosopher of cultural memory (O'Neill, 1996). The concept of the dialectic is used to describe historical/social change. The dialectical processes of change are defined through the principle of contradiction – (as used later by Marx) – which has three stages: thesis (the capacity of existing things to affirm themselves actively not passively), anti-thesis (the principle which acts to thwart the capacity of a thing to develop) and synthesis (negation of the negation). The dialectical process of assertion, contradiction and resolution in an argument in which conceptual or real world contradictions are resolved is also a process of thinking through issues creatively.

In Adorno's version Hegel's 'idealism' is countered by Marx's 'materialism' through non-identity thinking. But, *contra* Marx, Adorno's life's work never included a theory of political action: nowhere do we find a concept of a collective revolutionary subject. Indeed, for Gillian Rose Adorno's Hegelianized Marxism is reintroduced on the basis of a Nietzschean inversion (Rose, 1978: 22). Adorno claimed his project was both dialectical and materialist (Buck-Morss, 1977: 24–5).

In *Negative Dialectics* (1973) Adorno maintains that any thinking which is determined by a desire to control the world cannot qualify for the status of 'truth'. In adopting Nietzsche's idea that concepts are masks and that they hide their origins, he asserts that this is due to 'real domination' and goes on to delineate his theory of identity thinking as reification, the 'effacious reality' which stems from his interpretation of Marx's theory of value. Held explains that through identity thinking one is unable to penetrate the appearances of society and perceive the non-identical underlying it, so one cannot comprehend the nature of social relations. 'The truth and falsity of capitalist society can be assessed according to whether or not it is adequate to its concept' (Held, 1980: 220). For Held, Marx's work on exchange value and Adorno's work on culture show clearly that there is no rational identity and that negative dialectics as non-identity thinking illuminates values which are immanent to the object but which are more often than not negated by the object's actuality. For Adorno, what constitutes the truth is that which lies behind appearance. Truth is in the object and it is up to the subject (who is also an object) to grasp the truth by maintaining a critical distance, by looking for the critical oppositional.

The principle of reification in capitalist society is constituted by identity thinking: 'Language becomes a measure of the truth only when we are conscious of the non-identity of an expression with what we mean' (Adorno, 1973: 375). Reification, however, was not conceptualized purely as a fact of consciousness, and in the relationship between exchange value and use value we have a concrete example:

> The barter principle, the reduction of human labour to the abstract universal concept of average working hours, is fundamentally akin to the principle of identification. Barter is the social model of the principle, and without the principle there would be no barter; it is through barter that non-identical individuals and performances become commensurable and identical. (Adorno, 1973: 146)

Reification is posited as a social category, referring to the way consciousness is determined. But the crucial point here is that reification does not originate in consciousness. Thinking is not posited as a simple reflection of social existence, nor as mental labour distinct from manual labour. Reification is not presented as a relativist theory of consciousness: 'We can no more reduce dialectics to reification than we can reduce it to any other isolated category, however polemical' (Adorno, 1973: 190). For Adorno, thought and societal existence are interrelated processes. Ideology is rooted in the social, and not necessarily in individual consciousness.

> The trouble is with the conditions that condemn mankind to impotence and apathy and would yet be changeable by human action; is not primarily with people and the way conditions appear to people. Considering the possibility of total disaster, reification is an epiphenomenon, and even more so is the alienation coupled with reification, the subjective state of consciousness that corresponds to it. (Adorno, 1973: 190)

The onus is shifted from the consciousness of the individual or collective to an analysis of the structures of society which bind them without denying the tension between subject and object:

> The task of criticizing ideology is to judge the subjective and objective shares and their dynamics. It is to deny the false objectivity of concept fetishism by reducing it to the social subject, and to deny false subjectivity, the sometimes unrecognizably veiled claim that all being lies in the mind, by showing it up as a fraud, a parasitical nonentity, as well as demonstrating its immanent hostility to mind. . . . In the idea of objective truth, materialist dialectics turns philosophical. (Adorno, 1973: 197–8)

Adorno views the separation of subject and object as a characterization of the object, not as stemming from the subject. The object and not the subject holds the 'truth':

> An object can be conceived only by a subject but always remains something other than the subject . . . a subject however is by its very nature an object as well. . . . To be an object is part of the meaning of subjectivity; but it is not equally part of the meaning of objectivity to be a subject. (Adorno, 1973: 183)

Thus Adorno establishes priority of the object and mediation of the subject/object.

For Adorno change can only be brought about socially by changing society. Art and critical theory provide the 'change-causing gesture' which robs the present of its ideological justification, and aims at 'tearing down the veil' which prevents true knowledge of societal processes (Buck-Morss, 1977: 36–7). Truth reveals itself in the tension between subject and object, in the non-identity between 'psychological intent and its concrete objectification' (Buck-Morss, 1977: 80). The truth is in the object, and the constructive moment occurs when the mind strives to know it in thought.

Critical reflection as negative dialectics aims to guard against identity thinking. Non-identity thinking confronts the partial truth of an object with its potential truth. In this way criticism can advance the interests of the truth by identifying the false, by uncovering through immanent criticism the discontinuities and mediations among social phenomena.

Susan Buck-Morss (1977) tells us that 'immanent criticism' as materialist dialectics contains a constructive as well as a destructive moment – destructive in the juxtaposing of antithetical concepts with the reality they are supposed to describe; constructive in that the 'decaying' categories can be 'refunctioned' into tools for dialectical materialist cognition, for illuminating the unintentional truths in the particulars of cultural texts. Adorno's notion of the non-identity of the particular as a promise of utopia was taken from Ernst Bloch and used in Adorno's inaugural lecture at the University of Frankfurt in 1931. Bloch (1987) grounded the hope for the future in those non-identical traces of utopian possibility already expressed within the present. Actual or potential truths were present in the small things that slipped through the conceptual net. For Adorno, there were no philosophical first principles and, instead of constituting an argument through the usual stages, one must assemble the whole from a series of parts via the form of the constellation. Thus, the object or truth may be approximated by revealing what may be the true in the false through the use of stylistic strategies such as chiasmus and shock. At all times he is insistent upon the separation of subject and object and no power is ever invested in a revolutionary subject. It is this latter point which forms Adorno's critique of Lukács's work, and also his critique of Brecht and Benjamin's use of Brecht's work (see Adorno, 1980).

For both Adorno and Benjamin, Kafka was one author who illuminated the truth of society.

> Nowhere in Kafka does there glimmer the aura of the infinite idea; nowhere does the horizon open. Each sentence is literal and each signifies. The two moments are not merged as the symbol would have it, but yawn apart and out of the abyss between them blinds the glaring ray of fascination. Here too, in its striving not for symbol but for allegory, Kafka's prose sides with the outcasts. . . . Each sentence says 'interpret me' and none will permit it. . . . Far more than for most writers, it may be said of Kafka that not *verum* but *falsum* is *inex sui* [not the truth but the opposite is the truth]. (Adorno, 1995: 246–7; added emphasis)

Kafka's fragmentary quality of style denies closed systems. Truths regarding reality can be found in the gaps and contradictions in the text. Adorno maintains that 'What is enclosed in Kafka's glass ball is even more monotonous, more coherent and hence more horrible than the system outside' (Adorno, 1995: 261).

Central to the administered society is the relationship between the Enlightenment and technical knowledge. Enlightenment – the disenchantment of the world through instrumental reason – depicts almost total domination. If domination is almost total then what hope is there for critical theory? The only hope lies in art and interpretive philosophy – dialect-ical thinking – critical theory. 'The modernity of art lies in its mimetic relation to a petrified and alienated reality. This and not the denial of that reality is what makes art speak' (Adorno, 1984: 31). Kafka is given as an example. Kafka's works force us to be aware of the illusion in what appears to be the real – they loosen passive acceptance of the status quo.

In his search for the critical oppositional via negative dialectics Adorno stood clearly on the side of the innovative artist (Schoenberg/Kafka/Klee/ Beckett); theory was not to be subordinated to political goals. In this way art could be progressive rather than affirmative.[1]

Weber Nicholsen (1997) discusses the centrality of the aesthetic dimen-sion in Adorno's *oeuvre* and the very important link between the negative dialectical structure of his work and aesthetics. The 'non-discursive ration-ality' he offers as an alternative to 'a dominating, systematizing rationality that is the counterpart of an administered world' (1997: 3) must be considered through an understanding of his work on aesthetics. Within the administered society there is a withering of the capacity for genuine subjective experience. Art and aesthetics is premised upon genuine or authentic subjective experience as a condition for non-discursive knowledge of the object (Weber Nicholsen, 1997: 4). This conjunction of rationality and aesthetics is a very important dimension linking Adorno's social and aesthetic theories to better understand, reflect upon and transform our socio-cultural worlds (see Osborne, 1989).

The task of the artist and critic was to reveal the unintentional truths of the social world, uncover the meaning of objects, and preserve independent thinking. Adorno described Schoenberg's work as evolving from the unre-solved contradictions between subject and object:[2]

Paradigmatic artists of this century like Schoenberg, Klee and Picasso, give equal scope to the expressive-mimetic moment and the constructive one, not by finding some spurious middle ground between these two extremes but by highlighting the distance that separates them. Both poles are equally substantive or content-laden: expression is the negativity of suffering, whereas construction is the attempt to bear up under suffering of alienation by outstripping alienation in the parameters of a non-repressive application of rationality. Form and content are different, yet mediated through each other, in art no less than in philosophical thought. (Adorno, 1984: 363–4)

Furthermore, Adorno was very much against the notion of history as progress; instead he focused on the gaps and inconsistencies, the breaks in reason's logic, denying the notion of history as a continuum. There are, of course, resonances here for feminists. The notion of history as progress and the linear notion of the continuum of history has been challenged by feminist thinkers. Feminist non-identity thinking is situated in the gaps and incon-sistencies in Enlightenment thought, against 'the Master's image of prog-ress' (Minh-ha, 1991: 97). Trinh T. Minh-ha, writer and film maker, illuminates the complexity of feminist thinking and argues for a multi-cultural revision of knowledge against reductive analyses. Minh-ha does not develop discourses of 'duality' which simply reinforce binary thinking, but through 'writing the body', through the sensuousness of experience – visual, aural, textual (*through Adorno's use of mimesis*) – she relates experience/subjectivity/embodiment to feminist praxis. Minh-ha's writings and films, one could argue, are exemplars of non-identity thinking.

For example, Minh-ha writes that in Chinese mythology and Chinese poetry a multitude of expressions exist to describe feminine beauty. '*Scented mist, cloud chignon damp/Pure light, jade arm cool* . . . all hair and skin: darkness is fragrant, soft, vaporous, moist, mist- or cloud like . . . her smooth bare arm evokes the sensation of touching jade' (1991: 3). Woman is not night to man's day (as in Western literary traditions), but day in night; she does not occupy or dwell in one territory but 'criss-crosses' and so 'remains inappropriate/d – both inside and outside her own social positionings' (1991: 4). There is a break with the 'structure of hegemonic discourse and its scopic economy' (1991: 4) based upon sight (voyeur) rather than touch – the 'intercise between the visual and the tactile . . . at once within and beyond the sense of smell. Within and beyond tangible visibility . . . her (un)location is necessarily the shifting and contextual interval between arrested boundaries' (1991: 4). 'Placing oneself level with the body in writing, is among other things, putting one's finger on the obvious, on difference, on prohibition, on life' (1991: 130–1). Moreover,

> In the current situation of overcodification, of de-individualized individualism and reductionist collectivism, naming critically is to dive headlong into the abyss of un-naming. The task of inquiring into all divisions of a culture remains exacting, for the moments when things take on a proper name can only be positional, hence transitional. The function of any ideology in power is to represent the world positively unified. To challenge the regimes of representation that govern a society is to conceive of how a politics can transform reality rather than merely ideologize it. (1991: 2)

Adorno challenges the bourgeois concepts used to define history by using non-identity thinking to explore the idea of history as continuum, but for him the politics of transformation had to remain at the level of potentiality, of possibility, of hope, of critical thinking – *not* at the level of action. 'The Utopian impulse in thinking is all the stronger, the less it objectifies itself as Utopia – a further form of regression – whereby it sabotages its own realization' (Adorno, 1991: 175). For 'the individual, life is made easier through capitulation to the collective with which he identifies. He is spared the cognition of his impotence; within the circle of their own company, the few become many. It is this act – not unconfused thinking – which is resignation' (1991: 174).

Returning for a moment to Adorno on Kafka, Kafka 'depicts everything historical as condemned, just as those conditions themselves are condemned. His scenery is always obsolete' (Adorno, 1995: 257). Kafka explodes the 'space-time continuum' (Adorno, 1995: 261) and, by upsetting the natural order of history as continuum, loosens the power of history over the present, loosens the passive acceptance of the status quo. Kafka's work is a form of non-identity thinking. It celebrates the fragmentary and the critical. Kafka uses the power of negation, emptied of linear time, and forces the reader to be aware of the illusion in what appears to be the real. The power and purpose of negative dialectics is not to engage in 'pseudo-activity' (Adorno, 1991: 174), but to generate awareness of the illusion of the 'real', to uncover identity thinking, to challenge ideology as reification in order to transform reality, at the level of critical thought. This is also the power of Trinh's filmic work, to uncover identity thinking, to celebrate the fragmentary, to question passive acceptance of the status quo and the power of history over the present is to engage in feminist non-identity thinking.

Kulturkritik

> The cultural critic can hardly avoid the imputation that he has the culture which culture lacks. (Adorno, 1995: 19)

The development of the administered society, and the growth and popularity of 'mass culture' were, for Adorno, synonymous. The culture industry, or 'the entertainment business', demands little in the way of 'effort', 'pre-scribes every reaction' and in so doing helps to underpin capitalism as the administered society, and the take-over of instrumental reason (Adorno and Horkheimer, 1995: 136).

> The more total society becomes, the greater the reification of the mind and the more paradoxical its effort to escape reification on its own. Even the most extreme consciousness of doom threatens to degenerate into idle chatter. Cultural criticism finds itself faced with the final stage of the dialectic of culture and barbarism. To write poetry after Auschwitz is barbaric. . . . Critical intelligence cannot be equal to this challenge as long as it confines itself to self satisfied contemplation. (Adorno, 1995: 34)

In his work on the culture industry, Adorno stressed the mediating role that art and aesthetics play in negating the effects of the culture industry. Cultural criticism (which served only to reinforce the status quo) was replaced with dialectical criticism. Following Brecht, Adorno conceded that after Auschwitz the mansion of culture is indeed built upon 'dog-shit'. And, given the relationship between culture, the culture industry and reification, the need was for immanent, dialectical criticism – the attempt to say the 'unsayable', the 'unutterable' – to undercut cultural criticism with dialectical criticism.

> What distinguishes dialectical from cultural criticism is that it heightens cultural criticism until the notion of culture is itself negated, fulfilled and surmounted in

one. . . . The dialectical critic of culture must both participate in culture and not participate. Only then does he do justice to his object and to himself. (Adorno, 1995: 28–9, 33)

The problem here is that for Adorno the kind of politics which emerges from dialectical criticism is one which can show no commitment to transformative politics at the level of action. Critical of both Brecht and Benjamin for their 'commitment' to action, Adorno's essay on 'Commitment' in *Aesthetics and Politics* (1980) shows that suffering can be consumed through art as enjoyment and in being consumed/enjoyed it is transfigured, for something of its horror is removed (1980: 189). Adorno begins the following extract with a short quote from Sartre's play *Morts sans Sépulture*:

'Is there any meaning in life when men exist who beat people until the bones break in their bodies?' is also the question whether any art has a right to exist; whether intellectual regression is not inherent in the concept of committed literature because of the regression of society. . . . When genocide becomes part of the cultural heritage in the themes of committed literature, it becomes easier to play along with the culture that gave birth to murder. (Adorno, 1980: 188–9)

For Adorno, committed work – politically committed, such as Brecht's *Mother Courage* – demands a change of attitude; but autonomous art/great art (art which does not collapse the gap between popular art and great art, or art and life) *compels* a change of attitude (Adorno, 1980: 191). Adorno is critical of social realism because no message of political truth should be posited by the artist – art should be allowed, through form, to present the sedimented stuff of society as the *unintentional truth*. Silvia López (Chapter 3 in this volume) tells us that it is through the power of mimicry that the artist releases the expressed, that this is more than 'the tangible content of the artist's soul'; and that through art (as form) it is possible to record traces of the totalizing process, incorporating (through art as form) that which is excluded by bourgeois culture.

The 'principle that governs autonomous works of art is not the totality of their effects but their own inherent structure. They are knowledge as non-conceptual objects' (Adorno, 1980: 193). For the 'notion of a "message" in art, even when politically radical, already contains an accommodation to the world: the stance of the lecturer conceals a clandestine entente with the listeners, who could only be rescued from deception by refusing it' (Adorno, 1980: 193). The message is clear – it is only through trying to say the 'unsayable', the 'outside of language', the mimetic, the sensual, the non-conceptual that we can approach a 'politics' which undercuts identity thinking, which refuses to engage in identitarian thinking – but rather criss-crosses binary thinking/territories – and remains un-appropriated. This kind of politics and praxis strikes resonances with contemporary feminists such as Minh-ha and Braidotti for example, as well as the contributors to this volume.

Braidotti's *Nomadic Subjects* presents a theoretical figuration, in 'the nomadic mode' for contemporary subjectivity, seeking 'ways out of the phallocentric vision of the subject' (Braidotti, 1994: 1) and the feminist subject in particular. The nomad is

> a figuration for the kind of subject who has relinquished all idea, desire, or nostalgia for fixity. This figuration expresses the desire for an identity made of transitions, successive shifts, and co-ordinated changes, without and against an essential unity . . . however . . . not altogether devoid of unity. (Braidotti, 1994: 22)

Braidotti uses Adorno on the culture industry against the triumph of the image in both popular and scientific cultures to show that there is 'no adequate *simulacrum*; no image is a representation of the truth' (Braidotti, 1994: 69). For contemporary feminists, the need to question fixity, to question identitarian thinking, to celebrate nomadic subjects and escape appropriation is to be found in the kinds of politics that emerge out of the tension between our work upon subjectivities, bodies, difference and power.

The centrality of reification to Adorno's work on the culture industry as mass deception cannot be overestimated. According to Gillian Rose (1978), reification stands for the divisiveness and fragmentation of modern society, and Adorno was particularly concerned that reification should not be conceptualized as a fact of consciousness. Indeed, it is the way unlike things appear as like and the mode of thinking that considers them as equal which constitutes reification as a social phenomenon and as a process of thinking:[3] 'Absolute reification, which presupposed intellectual progress as one of its elements, is now preparing to absorb the mind entirely. Critical intelligence cannot be equal to this challenge as long as it confines itself to self-satisfied contemplation' (Adorno, 1995: 34). For Adorno, the central pivot of negative dialectics is that of the tension between ideology as reification and knowledge; and here we find a potential problem for feminists' use of Adorno.

We might ask ourselves, first of all, how relevant Adorno's work on *Kulturkritik* is in contemporary society, in view of the growth of cultural studies, the interdisciplinary work in universities across feminisms, philosophy, sociology and the humanities and the development of an industry around forms of popular culture. If we give central place to Adorno's knowledge/ideology axis then only autonomous art and dialectical criticism can see through the 'effacious reality'. Thus we are effectively denying the transformative possibilities or impulses inherent in popular art, popular culture and the lay public imagination/imaginaries. The centrality accorded to ideology/knowledge in Adorno is a sticking point for some theorists. According to Merquoir, Adorno was: 'An élitest intellectual from top to toe, he never tired of excoriating "the banausic", the vile commercial spirit of whatever art was capable of pleasing the public at large . . . only the martyrdom of form could reflect, if not mirror, the misery of modern man' (Merquoir, 1986: 137). Moreover, 'the more one plunges into *kulturkritik*, the less able one is to retrieve a decent theory of the historical process' (Merquoir, 1986: 138).

Certainly, Steven Crook, in his introduction to *adorno the stars down to earth*, concludes that 'Adorno *does* still matter' (Crook, 1994: 28), particularly his work on authoritarian irrationalism, first and foremost because it raises unsettling questions about contemporary culture. Crook asks 'how far dependency has become the typical condition of the "self" in advanced societies, how deeply authoritarian currents run through our superficially pluralistic cultures, and how free our beliefs and opinions are from a pervasive undercurrent of irrationalism' (1994: 28). Further to this Crook draws comparisons between Baudrillard and Adorno, for example the interrelationship of authoritarianism and panic production; the ways in which nostalgia and pastiche reinforce 'cognitive reassurance in the face of a loss of reality' and as a consequence the ways in which shared symbolic meanings simulate a shared symbolic order.

Keith Tester's examination of the 'dialectic of reification' also points to the usefulness of both Benjamin and Adorno for understanding modern social and cultural relations: 'The dialectic of reification implies a process in which social and cultural construction becomes "museal". . . . It describes objects to which the observer no longer has a vital relationship and which are in the process of dying' (Tester, 1995: 49). What we are experiencing is the 'naturalization of culture'. Human fabrications are no longer experienced as constructed but as given, as natural; fabrication is tied to the dialectic of reification and ultimately this means a re-enchantment as second nature, and as 'reification becomes second nature the core of the human condition is re-worked . . . not mute and passive nature but enchanted second nature' (Tester, 1995: 50). Tester's critique of the human condition, the fabrication and reification of the world, our worlds, his critique of all cultural production as kitsch, his notion of the inhuman condition of homelessness and the 'eternal promise, prospect and allure of home' (1995: 134), all show the profound influence of both Adorno and Benjamin. The (in)human condition of the present is not about making but finding; not doing but consuming; not creating but escaping, and at the centre is the concept of reification, the dialectic of reification. Is there any hope? Can we imagine, make, contemplate, create a rehumanized future – realize a *human* condition? For Tester, the human condition can be made human by focusing upon the body. Why? Because the body is ambivalent – it cannot be defined – 'it straddles the milieux of both first and second nature . . . and . . . possesses the ability to undermine social and cultural enterprises' (Tester, 1995: 141). Tester develops a brilliant analysis of Francis Bacon's work with the focus squarely upon our body's being in the world, our thing-ness, our location between human and inhuman conditions. Bacon seeks to communicate the sensuousness of our existence – 'not socially and culturally constructed stories'. This, for Tester, opens up an avenue of rehumanization precisely because Bacon's work makes us uncertain about 'humanity', uncertain about the status of the body, for we are forced to see our location within Deleuze's '*zone of indiscernability*', between man and animal and as 'spirit'. Further to this Tester draws upon Arendt's hope for the world based upon an ethics of care to open up this avenue of rehumanization, through speech, through action, through natality 'in which the faculty of action is ontologically rooted' (Tester, 1995: 141, 143, 147).

The relationships between Tester's work and Adorno's critique of culture and hope for autonomous art is clear. Tester rails against kitsch; Adorno against *Kulturkritik*/mass culture/popular culture. Tester examines the works of Francis Bacon, possibly one of the most 'auratic' of Western painters. Adorno focuses upon great art/autonomous art/auratic art – the works of Schoenberg, Kafka, Klee, Beckett.

For Braidotti, comparing Adorno and the German tradition with Baudrillard and the French tradition is a fruitful exercise (Braidotti, 1994: 63), particularly with respect to explorations around the dis-enchantment and re-enchantment of the world. In this respect Adorno does still matter – for cultural critique needs to ask unsettling questions, needs to grapple with the interrelations of the imaginary and the real, needs to explore relationships between the identical, the non-identical and the potential for the rational identical.

In order to fully understand negative dialectics as *Kulturkritik*, to fully understand the centrality of the ideology/knowledge axis in Adorno's work, and to fully understand why art and criticism are defined as reified cultural heritage, we need to examine Adorno's concept of unintentional truth and its relation to philosophy, and the relationship between popular art and autonomous art.

Unintentional truth and its relation to philosophy

Truth as mimesis makes an appearance in 'autonomous' works of art, not in any static way, but as illusion. Adorno compared artworks to picture puzzles, or to rebuses. 'Specifically artworks are like picture puzzles in that what they hide – like Poe's letter – is visible and is, by being visible, hidden' (Adorno, 1997: 121). What is contained in artworks – in 'Leibnizian terminology' in the form of a monad – is the sedimented content of society: 'The process that transpires in artworks and is brought to a standstill in them, is to be conceived as the same social process in which the artworks are embedded; according to Leibniz's formulation, they represent this process windowlessly'. Art is a social product and 'artistic labour is social labour'. The social forces of production and the social relations of production enter all artworks, and the antagonisms between them ensure the commodity status of artworks: 'Thoroughly nonideological art is indeed probably completely impossible' (Adorno, 1997: 236).

What constitutes truth is that which lies behind appearance. Unintentional truths come from within the artwork, the insignificant becomes significant and contains a whole picture of the bourgeois social structure. Only in that art which is taken to be the unconscious history-writing of society can the truths of society appear. This is because the socio-economic structure is mediated in all cultural production, and expresses itself in cultural objects. Truth does not congeal in the artform as stasis but is explained by Adorno as illusory appearance, as coming and going. Art's contribution to society is

> extremely mediated: It is resistance in which, by virtue of inner-aesthetic development, social development is reproduced without being imitated. At the risk of its self-alienation radical modernity preserves art's immanence by admitting society only in an obscured form, as in the dreams with which artworks have been compared. . . . What is social in art is its immanent movement against society, not its manifest opinions. . . . Insofar as a social function can be predicted for artworks, it is their functionless [*sic*]. (Adorno, 1997: 226–7)

For Adorno, the artwork is the cipher of the social, and via the tension between spirit/mimesis and constructive rationality/instrumental rationality the constructive moment occurs when the mind strives to know it in thought. Truth resides in the form, is activated and reached via interpretive philosophy; every artwork is the product shaped by its own consistent logic and an element in the complex of spirit and society. Philosophy as critical theory can illuminate, explain and interpret artworks. To know the work of art is to grasp the process that renders it spiritual. Philosophy as interpretive criticism recognizes truth content and interprets the spirit of works of art on the basis of the configurations in them. The function of aesthetics is to reveal the unintentional truths of the social world, to uncover the meaning of objects, to preserve independent thinking. Analysis of artworks can be achieved through interpretation, commentary and criticism via immersion, objectification and dissociation. Immersion is the same as getting the feeling of the piece, giving oneself over to the work. Objectification and dissociation are about distancing oneself, witnessing the objective moments of form. The tension between immersion and objectification is similar to that between mimesis and constructive rationality – between sensuousness/playfulness and constructive rationality.

Art is a *product* of society in that it is formed through the objective demands of the material, the historically given techniques and means of production, the subjective experiences and playfulness of the artist as social actor; and at the same time is an *independent* force in society. Hence art's specificity grows out of the subjective freedom of the artist, as well as the historically defined sphere for art in the social world.

Focusing on the concept of 'spirit' more closely, Peter Osborne understands *Aesthetic Theory* as 'a materialist metaphysics of modernity' (Osborne, 1989: 23). Art and philosophy constitute 'a medium for the expression of truth and through its self sufficient positivity, its integral unity "a promise of non-illusion" ' (1989: 30). Osborne shows that the irreconcil-ability of mimesis and rationality, subject and object, concept and object is an ontological, historically specific condition of reified society. The work of Minh-ha, Braidotti, Becker-Schmidt, and the contributors to this volume show this very clearly. The ideal of unity is not realizable in today's conditions. Adorno expresses this in *Negative Dialectics* as follows:

> Living in the rebuke that the thing is not identical with the concept is the concept's longing to become identical with the thing. . . . The untruth of any identity that has been attained is the obverse of truth. The ideas live in the cavities between what things claim to be and what they are. Utopia would be above identity and above contradiction, it would be a togetherness of diversity. (Adorno, 1973: 149–50)

Adorno's aesthetics of modernism does not simply need to be materialist, historical and concrete, it also needs metaphysics, if metaphysics is taken to be the utopian possibility of rational identity – the 'unsayable', the *promesse de bonheur* (Osborne, 1989: 27). Art's *form* is sedimented content. Mimesis and constructive rationality emerge from the unresolved contradictions between the subjective freedom of the artist and the objective demands of the material. Mimesis makes an appearance as illusion. Mimesis is not stasis but a coming and going. Art's opposition to the world, for Adorno, is in its form (see López and Weber Nicholsen in this volume). 'It is through the (*dialectical*) combination of mimesis and rationality that art is produced' (Osborne, 1989: 31). These two moments are irreconcilable: they combine in the production of artworks so that they are realized only through each other (Osborne, 1989: 32).

Once again there are resonances with contemporary feminisms. In one sense the work of Minh-ha and Braidotti, and the work of the contributors to this volume, shows the necessity for 'metaphysics', if by this we mean saying or attempting to say the 'unsayable', the 'unspeakable'. For Weber Nicholsen (1997) the very conjunction of non-discursive rationality and the aesthetic dimension are the key to Adorno's potential usefulness to us. As feminists we are intractably aware of the concrete dimensions to phallocentric culture, experiencing domination and oppression in our lived experiences in concrete ways but also in unseen and unspoken ways. Contemporary feminist thought emerges out of the tension between sub-jective freedom and material, sexual and social inequalities. For Adorno, the pivot of his dialectical thinking is the interrelationship of ideology and knowledge (see Becker-Schmidt and Knapp, Chapters 5 and 6 in this volume). For some contemporary feminisms the pivotal focus is on the body, subjectivity, difference and power, although knowledge and ideology are of course part of our understanding of the social world, but ideology as reification does not have the same central, powerful status as it does in Adorno's work.

The crisis of modernism (ideology as reification) is the increas-ingly affirmative nature of art. Adorno's concept of *Entkunstung* (de-substantialization) of art expresses this most fully. This is the loss of art's capacity to act as a medium for the truth. The two extreme forms of *Entkunstung* are reification (art viewed as a thing amongst things) and psychologism (art viewed as a vehicle for the psychology of the viewer or art as a vehicle for the psychology of the producer), resulting in the commodification of art which sells cheap the mimetic moment. The central concept of dissonance turns into its opposite as affirmative art. For Adorno the enigmatic character of artworks gives them their significance, and the concept of dissonance (modernism) lets in the moment of sensuousness by transfiguring it into its opposite: pain. Spirit is not the cause of art, nor is it created in art's reception, but lies within the product itself. Spirit animates artworks, it is truth and illusion. The crisis of art is its integration into life – *Entkunstung*. The growing power of the social world – constructive rationality – and the retreat of mimesis – sensuousness – is indicative of the loss of aura, the loss of spirit and the take-over of the administered society, of instrumental reason, of reification as ideology.

Auratic art (autonomous or true art) invokes 'tremor' as 'concern', 'thrill' and 'frisson' or 'shudder'. Not all art is auratic: the truth of art is in the form, not the content, and it is critical theory as interpretive philosophy which unlocks this in the reception of artworks. Philosophy does not dictate to art what art ought to be (a criticism Adorno levelled at traditional aesthetics), but art needs aesthetics to illuminate what art is.

The true in art escapes affirmation in the 'new'. The 'new' attempts to escape the tyranny of the affirmative society. The concept of the 'new' is the perfect 'this here'. Against the continuum of history and tradition, against reducing modern art to similarities with what went before, Adorno posits the centrality of the concept of 'the new' (Adorno, 1997: 20–4). 'The new' is necessarily abstract, and encapsulated within the abstract is a quality which Victor Hugo named *frisson nouveau*, a new thrill, thrill being the subjective response to the 'cryptic inaccessibility' of 'the new'. Thrill is understood here as mimetic response: 'Only in the new does mimesis unite with rationality without regression' (Adorno, 1997: 20).

'The new' is a blind spot (reminiscent of Klage's dialectical pictures and Benjamin's dialectical images in the *Trauerspiel*) on the side of mimesis, striking a blow against the increasingly constructive character of art within an increasingly reified society (Roberts, 1982). The problem is that art's opposition is minimal within the context of increasing reification, *Entkunstung* and the de-aestheticization of art (art as manipulation). This is the real crisis of art. The truth content of art has been explained via the dialectic of art – mimesis versus constructive rationality – but there is also always an element of ideology even in those artworks Adorno describes as being autonomous. Within Adorno's conceptualization of society this element of ideology grows with the take-over of the constructive/rational pole in the dialectic of art, and mimesis retreats into abstraction in an attempt to avoid affirmation. In this instance, art survives as cultural heritage, as affirmative pleasure, as business for profit – a far cry from the notion of artworks as rebuses or as picture puzzles pointing to and beyond the existing reality of capitalism.

Culture as redemption becomes its other, culture as manipulation, save for those few autonomous works which still shine forth as spiritual illusion. So, interpretive philosophy for Adorno must engage in the immanent reflection of works of art, and the truth content must not be confused with the philosophical content that the artist or critic projects onto the work. Through the intensive critical examination of works of art using interpretive philosophy, through 'micrology', better knowledge can be gained of 'administered society'. Individual artworks contain sedimented aspects of the social, of the subjective/collective, and in the tension between mimesis and constructive rationality truth unfolds from within the work rather than being posited intentionally on the work by the artist.

> Art negates the categorical determinations stamped on the empirical world and yet harbours what is empirically existing in its own substance. If art opposes the empirical through the element of form – and the mediation of form and content is not to be grasped without their differentiation – the mediation is to be sought in the recognition of aesthetic form as sedimented content. (Adorno, 1997: 5)

Adorno talks of aesthetic experience as involving awareness of the antagonisms between the inside and the outside of art. Every artwork is a product of its own consistent logic and the complex of spirit and society. This is reflected most pertinently in the tension between Kantian and Hegelian themes, in ideas of disinterestedness and sensuous appearance: 'the most powerful aesthetics – Kant's and Hegel's . . . cannot be reduced to a common formulation as their truth; rather their truth is to be sought in their conflict' (Adorno, 1997: 353).

It is only through spirit that art constitutes itself in opposition to empirical reality, moving towards the determinate negation of the status quo. The opposite of spirit is contained in the artworks themselves, in the historically given materials, in the techniques of production, in the construction of artworks. Artworks emerge out of the interplay of the unresolved contradictions between mimesis and constructive rationality. Autonomous works 'crackle' because of the friction between the antagonistic moments they try to hold together, which are straining towards totality.

Art cannot be understood until its social essence is understood. Society is mediated through aesthetic form as content expressed through antagonisms and conflicts, between the mimetic – sensuous and rational – constructive poles. For Adorno, modernism's refusal to communicate is a necessary but not sufficient condition of ideology – free art: art also requires 'the force of expression'. Through expression artworks can 'reveal themselves as the wounds of society'. Picasso's *Guernica* is used as an example which 'precisely by means of inhumane construction, achieves a level of expression that sharpens it to social protest beyond all contemplative misunderstanding'. The socially critical dimensions of artworks are those that hurt 'where in their expression, historically determined, the untruth of the social situation comes to light. It is actually this against which the rage of art reacts' (Adorno, 1997: 237).

Feminisms and culture

As I have shown, in order to better understand Adorno's social theory we need to engage with his aesthetic theory. However, in re-appropriating Adorno's work as an aid to the development of contemporary feminist thought we do need to question his social theory. According to Adorno's dialectical criticism it is the power of reification in the social world that pushes art into a retreat into nominalism and abstractionism, thereby ushering in the crisis and the end of art. If we relocate Adorno's central aesthetic categories, situating concepts of power, subjectivity, difference and a focus on the body in place of his ideology/knowledge axis, then we can call into question the totalizing power of reification in the social world and can instead focus upon reification as one aspect of the centrality of power and difference. This move serves to free that aspect of Adorno's work which drove him (to paraphrase Benjamin) into a one-way street: the totalizing power of reification and the de-substantialization of art. In exploring 'the riddle of femininity' we are forced to loosen the relationship between ideology as reification, and knowledge, in order to examine future possibilities, the longer-term processes of psychic and social structures and practices.

In freeing up the relationship Adorno constructs between popular art and autonomous art we can explore examples of 'popular art' as transformative, as liberating, as transgressive, thus facilitating Adorno's use for us today within cultural studies, interdisciplinary studies and feminist studies. As Chris Rojek points out in his conceptualization of 'Modernity 2', the messiness and untidiness of human relations, the ways in which people act and think contrary to the theorems of positivist and critical sociology, and the ways in which people resist and subvert the culture industry's 'codes of manipulation' point very clearly to everyday acts of rebellion and resistance to administered society (Rojek, 1995). Both Barbara Engh and Hilde Heynen write about the productive use of Adorno's work for remaining non-identical. In resisting and subverting identification feminisms can both: 'jam the theoretical machinery' (Engh); and in the interplay of mimesis, negativity and utopia our dwelling as well as our thinking 'is continually permeated by its opposite – a dwelling in the feminine' (Heynen).

However, is it even necessary to decentre Adorno's use of reification? Perhaps the most useful and salient influence on feminist theorists and feminist-informed theorists is that in his work on music, aesthetics, philosophy and methodology he 'constructed theories out of opposing and contradictory tenets' (Buck-Morss, 1977: 185). On the one hand he illuminates the disintegration of society and on the other he illuminates administered society as totalized and totalizing: 'His was a negative anthropology, and its knowledge was to keep criticism alive' (Buck-Morss, 1977: 186). Ultimately, Adorno never gave up the hope for social transformation, even though this hope could only expressed through art. For Weber Nicholsen in *Exact Imagination/Late Work* the importance of Adorno's use for us today means exploring the connection between his work on the aesthetic dimension and a non-discursive form of truth, which in turn means looking at the role of the subject and of subjective experience (Weber Nicholsen, 1997: 3–4), particularly the imaginary, imagination. The focus on imagination is very pertinent to critical thought in contemporary society. Weber Nicholsen tells us that Adorno's term *exakte Phantasie* marks 'the conjunction of knowledge, experience, and aesthetic form'. An exact imagination is confined by scholarship and science yet goes beyond the material 'by reconfiguring the material at hand'. At the same time, critical of those theorists who see Adorno's work as outmoded by the limited subject–object paradigm, Weber Nicholsen instead focuses upon the dilemma of subjectivity and subjective experience in Adorno – a dilemma 'that is still more advanced in our own time' and the legacy of Benjamin's work, particularly via concepts of mimesis, aura and constellation, for the use of these concepts derives from 'Benjamin's work as Adorno appropriated it'.

The task ahead for us is to explore possibilities for genuine subjectivity – unity in difference – within the context of postmodern times at the close of the twentieth century. As Hullot-Kentor informs us, for Adorno 'subjectivity could only be transcended by subjectivity, and not by its limitation' (Hullot-Kentor, 1997: xiii). This holds true, as does the fact that for Adorno human suffering is at the centre of social/cultural/philosophical reflection.

In using Adorno to access better understandings of the relationships between the body (inside and outside of history), subjectivity, power and both unity and difference we can perhaps go beyond the present, the here and now, through negative anthropology/renewed methodologies in order to develop a rehumanizing of the human condition – morally/analytically. We can use this better understanding as a platform for theoretical/experiential analysis regarding the sensuousness of our experience, of our being in the world – as women and as men. In doing so we will be fulfilling our role as 'interpreters', as cultural critics, through feminist politics as feminist praxis rooted in the need to understand the complexity of our lived experience and lived relations in order to reflect upon, challenge and transform sexual and social inequalities.

Notes

1 See Adorno's essay on 'Commitment' in *Aesthetics and Politics* (1980); see also Adorno's letter to Benjamin, London, 18 March 1936 also in *Aesthetics and Politics* and *The Correspondence of Walter Benjamin* (1994).

2 See Susan Buck-Morss's section on 'Aesthetic experience' and the influence of Schoenberg on Adorno (1977: 122–4).

3 See Chapter 3, 'The lament over reification' in Gillian Rose's *The Melancholy Science* (1978).

References

Adorno, T.W. (1973) *Negative Dialectics*, trans. E.B Ashton. London: Routledge & Kegan Paul.

Adorno, T.W. (1978) *Minima Moralia: Reflections from a Damaged Life*, trans. E.F.N. Jephcott. London and New York: Verso.

Adorno, T.W. (1980) 'Commitment', in *Aesthetics and Politics*, trans. and ed. Ronald Taylor. London and New York: Verso.

Adorno, T.W. (1984) *Aesthetic Theory*, ed. Gretel Adorno and Rolf Tiedemann, trans. Christian Lendhart. London: Routledge.

Adorno, T.W. (1991) *The Culture Industry: Selected Essays on Mass Culture*, ed. and with an introduction by J.M. Bernstein. London: Routledge.

Adorno, T.W. (1995) *Prisms*, trans. Samuel and Shierry Weber. Cambridge, MA: MIT Press.

Adorno, T.W. (1997) *Aesthetic Theory*, ed. Gretel Adorno and Rolf Tiedemann, trans. Robert Hullot-Kentor. Minneapolis, MN: University of Minnesota Press.

Adorno, T. and Horkheimer, M. (1995) *Dialectic of Enlightenment*, trans. John Cumming. London: Verso.

Bauman, Z. (1988) 'Is there a postmodern sociology?' *Theory, Culture & Society*, 5: 217–37.

Beck, U. and Beck-Gernsheim, E. (1995) *The Normal Chaos of Love*. Cambridge: Polity Press.

Benjamin, W. (1992) *Illuminations*, trans. Harry Zohn. London: Fontana.

Benjamin, W. (1994) *The Correspondence of Walter Benjamin 1910–1940*, ed. Gershom Scholem and Theodor Adorno, trans. Manfred Jacobson and Evelyn Jacobson. Chicago and London: University of Chicago Press.

Bloch, E. (1987) *The Utopian Function of Art and Literature: Selected Essays*. Cambridge, MA: MIT Press.

Braidotti, R. (1994) *Nomadic Subjects*. New York: Columbia University Press.

Buck-Morss, S. (1977) *The Origin of Negative Dialectics: Theodor W. Adorno, Walter Benjamin and the Frankfurt Institute*. Brighton: Harvester Press.

Crook, S. (1994) *adorno the stars down to earth and other essays on the irrational in culture*. London: Routledge.

Geulen, E. (1994) 'Gender in the early Benjamin'. Paper presented at the Susan B. Anthony Institute for Women's Studies, 26 April.

Hegel, G.W.F. (1967) *The Phenomenology of Mind*. New York: Harper and Row.

Held, D. (1980) *Introduction to Critical Theory: Horkheimer to Habermas*. Berkeley and Los Angeles: University of California Press.

Heynen, H. (1992) 'Architecture between modernity and dwelling: reflections on Adorno's aesthetic theory', *Assemblage*, 17: 78–91 (Cambridge, MA: MIT Press).

Hullot-Kentor, R. (1997) 'Translator's introduction' to T.W. Adorno, *Aesthetic Theory*. Minneapolis, MN: University of Minnesota Press.

Jameson, F. (1990) *Late Marxism: Adorno, or, The Persistence of the Dialectic*. London and New York: Verso.

Lukács, G. (1971) *History and Class Consciousness*. London: Merlin Press.

Merquoir, J.G. (1986) *Western Marxism*. London: Paladin.

Mies, M. and Shiva, V. (1993) *Ecofeminism*. London: Zed Books.

Minh-ha, Trinh T. (1991) *When the Moon Waxes Red: Representation, Gender and Cultural Politics*. New York and London: Routledge.

O'Neill, J. (1996) *Hegel's Dialectic of Desire and Recognition*. New York: SUNY Press.

Osborne, P. (1989) 'Adorno and the metaphysics of modernism: the problem of a postmodern art', in A. Benjamin (ed.), *The Problems of Modernity: Adorno and Benjamin*. London: Routledge.

Roberts, J. (1982) *Walter Benjamin – Theoretical Traditions in Social Sciences*. London: Macmillan.

Rojek, C. (1995) *Decentring Leisure: Rethinking Leisure Theory*. London, Thousand Oaks and New Delhi: Sage.

Rose, G. (1978) *The Melancholy Science: An Introduction to the Thought of Theodor W. Adorno*. New York and London: Routledge.

Tester, K. (1995) *The Inhuman Condition*. New York and London: Routledge.

Weber Nicholsen, S. (1997) *Exact Imagination/Late Work: On Adorno's Aesthetics*. Cambridge, MA: MIT Press.

2 Adorno, Benjamin and the Aura: An Aesthetics for Photography

Shierry Weber Nicholsen

The aura and its aftermath

> For the first time in world history, mechanical reproduction emancipates the work of art from its parasitical dependence on ritual.
>
> (Walter Benjamin)

Students of the work of Theodor Adorno and Walter Benjamin are well aware that Adorno was highly critical of Benjamin's essay 'The work of art in the age of mechanical reproduction' (1936),[1] in which Benjamin claimed that photography and the associated processes of photomechanical reproduction to which it gave rise had fundamentally altered the nature of art, by destroying the aura of uniqueness and authenticity that had surrounded the original of a work of art. With the capacity for easy production and transport of multiple prints of an image, Benjamin argued, the idea of an original which is more precious than inauthentic copies loses its force. The quality of unique authoritative presence that Benjamin calls the 'aura' and that was associated with the physical presence of the work of art in space and time signalled art's origins in ritual and religion and its location in tradition. With the decreasing importance of the original, the aura withers. Art ceases to have 'cult value' and acquires 'exhibition value' instead: it becomes a commodity and it enters the world of politics.

So runs the argument of Benjamin's Artwork essay, as I will refer to it here. In that text Benjamin gives a positive assessment of the changes wrought by photomechanical reproduction. First of all, photography and its offshoots – film in particular – fit the nature of modern experience; their rapid development and public acceptance attest to this. That experience is characterized both by shock and by mass reproduction, whether of commodities or – in a different sense – in the formation of 'the mass'. The speed, volume and intensity of stimuli in the contemporary urban environment transform the individual's experience into a barrage of shocks that must be coped with at the same time as the individual is absorbed in the larger collective. The nature of perception – which, Benjamin notes, is historically determined – changes accordingly. The kind of slowly digested and savoured experience that Benjamin associates with premodern cultures and the contemplation of works of art, which requires time and solitude on the part of the viewer, is no longer possible. Instead, contemporary artforms are absorbed by a collective in a state of non-distanced, mindless distraction and habit, much as architecture, the most public of the arts, has always been. This movement away from a thoughtful, contemplative stance is a way of coping with the overwhelming, assaultive character of modern experience. Similarly, Benjamin argues that the cutting and editing that characterize photographic technique, and the identification with the camera that it induces, help the individual to cope with fragmentation and with the pervasive penetration of reality by technology.

Benjamin's positive assessment of this transformation becomes more understandable when one sees the political terms in which he frames it. Not only do the techniques of photomechanical reproduction provide ways for the individual to adjust to the specific nature of contemporary urban experience (and of course Benjamin means European experience); they also embody a corresponding critical stance. They are in tune with the modern demand for a 'universal equality of things' and with a critical stance toward tradition and the authority structures embodied in tradition. Identification with the capacity for technological penetration implies an analytic, objective attitude. But in the contemporary situation this critical stance is compatible with, indeed requires, the kind of slow distracted absorption and build-up of habit that we witness in the reception of, for instance, film. 'The public is an examiner, but an absent-minded one' (Benjamin, 1969: 241).

The central thrust of Benjamin's analysis – that photomechanical repro-duction has led to the withering of a cult-based, contemplatively experienced art and to the development instead of a reproducibility-based art that is absorbed collectively and in a state of distraction – is designed to contribute to the struggle against Fascism taking place at that time. Fascism attempted to deny the transformations in art and instead extend the aura to politics by making war a spiritual-aesthetic matter. Benjamin's arguments, in contrast, are designed to preserve a non-auratic art's capacity to contribute to the struggle for political justice.

Adorno first articulated his criticisms of the Artwork essay in one of a series of well-known letters from the 1930s that are his contribution to what has come to be known as the 'Adorno–Benjamin dispute'; and his comments in his posthumous *Aesthetic Theory* (1970a) indicate that his assessment did not change.[2] Adorno's criticisms focus on Benjamin's espousal of mass culture, and film in particular, and on Benjamin's negative assessment of the aura. Benjamin's arguments amount to a conflation of art with politics, Adorno says, a conflation that is damaging to what Adorno calls 'auto-nomous art'. Benjamin's criticism of the aura, that is, 'is easily extended to real modern art, which puts distance between itself and the logic of practical action'.[3] The issue for Adorno is not a defence of the aura *per se* but rather a proper understanding of the aesthetic of modernist art with its critical potential. For Adorno, the aura, like art as such, is dialectical and ambiva-lent. On the one hand, it cannot avoid participating in the dynamics of an oppressive culture and thus can be perverted into the service of domination. But on the other hand it retains the potential for critical distance, and that distance relates it – ambivalently – to the aura. From this point of view, Benjamin's arguments are oversimplified and undialectical, Adorno says, and the simplifications of the Artwork essay, he asserts in *Aesthetic Theory*, have 'contributed in no small way to its obtrusive popularity' (*Aesthetic Theory*: 89–90; 82–3).

Obtrusive popularity indeed: Benjamin's thesis that photomechanical reproduction has destroyed the aura of the original work of art has become a cornerstone of contemporary photocriticism, and there is much in the further evolution of photography that would seem to corroborate his ideas, or at least some of them. Adorno, in contrast, who has little to say directly about photography and whose direct comments tend to be disparaging – as when he refers in *Aesthetic Theory* to photography's 'thing-likeness' and associates it with 'copyrealism' (*Aesthetic Theory*: 89–90; 82–3) – tends not to figure in later discussions of the nature of photography. But in fact the further evolution of photography raises issues for which Benjamin's theses do not prove satisfactory, and in this light we are reminded of Adorno's insistence that the matter of the aura – and by implication the aesthetic status of photography and its relation to modernist art as well – is more complex than Benjamin made it out to be.

Certainly it is the case, as Benjamin's analysis would lead us to expect, that photography (and the visual arts in general) has become the scene of what I will call 'aura wars'. The art establishment is attempting to revitalize the aura and to include photography among the auratic arts. A place has been established for photography in the museum world and, if more tenuously, the gallery world, with the 'vintage print' used as the photographic equivalent of the original work of art. Photography exhibitions are hung on the model of exhibitions of paintings, and a pantheon of major photographers has been established. Postmodernist critics like Douglas Crimp and Victor Burgin, invoking Benjamin, have worked to expose the ideology implicit in the art world's dealings with photography. Like Benjamin, whose analysis emphasized technology and modes of experience rather than the individual artist, and for whom the notion of a 'creator' was an allusion to art's religious origins, these critics attack the whole complex of notions associated with the aura – original, creator, contemplation, museum and so on – and celebrate photography's capacity to subvert the concepts of authority, authenticity and authorship on which the art world's enterprise of re-auratization is based.[4]

The postmodernist critics link their critique of individual authorship in photography with notions of intertextuality and collage. This linkage harks back to Benjamin's comments on the way the cutting and editing intrinsic to photomechanical processes fits the fragmentation of the modern individual, whose consciousness becomes absorbed into the mass. The linkage also demonstrates Benjamin's thesis that it is photomechanical processes that drive the transformations of modern art; collage, so central to modernist art, can be seen as derived from photographic practice. Crimp's analysis of the painting of Robert Rauschenberg, much invaded by photography, for instance, follows these lines. In Rauschenberg's work, he says, 'the fiction of the creating subject gives way to frank confiscation, quotation, excerptation, accumulation and repetition of already existing images' (Crimp, 1983: 53).

It is art historian Rosalind Krauss, herself much influenced by Benjamin, who has in my view most tellingly formulated the characteristic of photography that accounts for its role in these transformations. Like the Surrealists' 'found object' and the collage itself, which incorporates bits of the everyday world, the photograph derives directly from physical reality. Accordingly Krauss calls it an 'index' rather than an 'icon' – it is a direct trace of the real rather than a representation of it, more like a death mask or a fossil than a drawing or a painting (Krauss, 1986). It is important to note that Benjamin did not stress this aspect of photography, although it is linked with the things he did stress – photography's technological aspect, and photomechanical reproduction.

Photography's indexical quality is problematic. It raises a claim to objectivity unaffected by individual subjectivity. But it thereby invites interpretive captioning, as Benjamin pointed out. Both editing processes and this linguistic framing permit images to be socially constructed while claiming empirical objectivity, as the social-constructionist critique of the body of work produced under the aegis of the Farm Security Administration during the Depression has tried to show. Further, photographic images seem to retain an aesthetic appeal despite, or because of, their empirical derivation. Hence photography may by its very nature sabotage its intentional use for social criticism. In fact, in 1934 Benjamin had already noted that photography 'had succeeded in turning abject poverty . . . into an object of enjoyment' (Curtis, 1989). Susan Sontag, who calls Benjamin 'photography's most original and important critic', makes a related argument in her book *On Photography*, which offers a damning assessment of photography's contribution to contemporary culture. The alienation effect that photography produces in both photographers and viewers, she says, contributes not to critical examination but to a sense of unreality and lack of engagement. The 'promiscuous acceptance of the world' that photography and Surrealism both manifest, she says – the indexical quality, in other words – is essentially aestheticizing and thus works against a truly moral, socially critical stance (Sontag, 1977).

Benjamin was certainly right both in raising the issue of aestheticization in connection with photography and in linking photomechanical processes to threats to a reflective individual subjectivity and to the promotion of a habitual, absent-minded absorption of images. Sontag's formulations – debatable though they might be in other respects – make this clear. But they also point up the fact that Benjamin's hopes for a positive critical political impact from photomechanical processes have not been realized. The way in which photomechanical reproduction is involved in shaping our experiences and our opinions without the intervening stages of critical reflection and discussion – in other words, its anti-democratic aspect – is far more evident than the opposite. The increasing importance of the computer and its capacities for digital imaging and the creation of virtual realities brings us to a new stage in the evolution of photography and crystallizes these issues in a way that was not previously possible.

In his book *The Reconfigured Eye: Visual Truth in the Post-Photographic Era*, William J. Mitchell, still referring to Benjamin, explains how digital imaging takes the dissolution of the aura to a stage beyond the one Benjamin had described (Mitchell, 1992). This new stage is characterized by a difference in the relationship between the image and physical reality. Digital imaging, which is electronically based, differs from photographic processes, which are optically and chemically based, in being generated not by traces of the real but by a mathematically based program. Hence the digital image's basic mode of existence is indeed purely virtual – the potential for appearance in the form of an electronic display – in contrast to the still physical existence of each of the potentially multiple photomechanical reproductions of an image. Given its virtual mode of existence, the digital image can be transformed at will through the application of programming without leaving traces of its earlier states. Whereas photomechanical reproduction devalues the original and the experience of its unique presence, then, digital imaging, with its capacities for constructing and transforming images, renders the very notion of an original meaningless at the same time as it abolishes the physical presence of an original. Further, while our awareness that images are socially constructed puts the idea of an 'innocent' or 'truthful' photographic representation into question, digital imaging does away with the criterion of truthfulness or empirical accuracy altogether by dispensing with the image's indexical quality, its connection to physical reality (Ritchin, 1989).

While it would seem that the shift from photomechanical reproduction to digital imaging represents a shift from the issue of authority (the aura) to the issue of truthfulness, I believe it represents a more fundamental shift from threats to individual reflective subjectivity (fragmentation and the impossibility of contemplation in modern experience) to threats to embodied experience as such. The electronically generated virtual reality is an almost dematerialized reality that is not co-ordinated with, and in some sense almost overrides, the embodied self's orientation in space, time and sensory perception. Benjamin conceived of the aura in terms of the original artwork's unique presence in space and time, accessible to the embodied viewer's sensory contemplation. For him, the destruction of the aura meant, in effect, a simultaneous multiplication and fragmentation both of the viewer's subjectivity and of the work of art. Perception changed, but the material world and the embodied state remained the tacit ground for reception of artworks. The virtual image and its electronic display, however, represent a further severance of connection with the viewer's sensory modes of perceiving and with the material world that is in some sense no longer even referred to in the image. The shift is not toward a further fragmentation of subjectivity but rather toward a disconnection, an irrelevance of the physical. The disconnected 'electronic environment' becomes a closed world unto itself. It may be that we will absorb its images still more directly and unreflectively than the pervasive images of the culture of photomechanical reproduction, and that we will find it still more difficult to attain a critical but engaged awareness in the post-photographic era.

In this light, photography's indexical quality, its direct link with physical reality, of which, as Krauss reminds us, it is the trace, seems particularly important. If the aura was inseparable from the work's unique physical presence, then photography's indexical quality now seems somehow auratic itself, perhaps an echo or a transmutation of the aura of the original work of art. Similarly, the collage-like practices associated with photography, which derive from its link with physical reality, now seem to point to the distinctions, multiplicities and crossed boundaries that disappear for ever when the digital image blends the multiplicity of image-material into a seamless virtual image with no trace of its history.

Contemporary thought is responding to the implied threat of disembodiment with an intensification of environmental awareness, an expanded and urgent insistence on our embodied state in a physical environment with which we are both continuous and discontinuous. If photography's indexical quality reopens the question of photography's relationship to the aura in this context, then Adorno's insistence on the dialectical ambivalence of the aura and the critical potential of the aesthetic may prove timely, and may shed light on an aesthetic dimension of photography that Benjamin's political urgency obscured.

Although Adorno wrote very little that focused directly on the subject of photography, his work contains numerous allusions to it. Adorno's aesthetic writings are constructed not of linear or systematic arguments but rather of what he calls 'constellations' or 'configurations' – complexes, that is, of interrelated concepts and images. In his work photography figures prominently in a constellation whose other primary elements include Kafka and Benjamin himself, modernist art, shock, and the dialectic of violence and non-violence. It is by elucidating that constellation that I will attempt to articulate Adorno's contribution to the question of the relationship between photography, the aesthetic and the aura. Reopening this question also affords us the opportunity of re-examining Benjamin's own writings on photography. In addition to the Artwork essay, these include his 'Short history of photography' (1977) and portions of his autobiographical *A Berlin Childhood, circa 1900* (1989). These writings prove to offer a perspective on the

relationship between photography, the aura and the aesthetic that comple-
ments the one we find in Adorno's work.

Two Kafka photographs

> At the age of approximately six the boy is presented in a sort of
> greenhouse setting, wearing a tight, heavily lace-trimmed, almost embar-
> rassing child's suit. Palm branches loom in the background. And as if to
> make these upholstered tropics still more sultry, the model holds in his
> left hand an oversized, wide-brimmed hat of the type worn by Spaniards.
> Immensely sad eyes dominate the landscape prearranged for them, and
> the auricle of a big ear seems to be listening to its sounds.

> (Walter Benjamin)

In December 1934 Adorno wrote Benjamin a highly critical letter about an
essay on Kafka that Benjamin was writing. Benjamin's essay includes a
description of a boyhood photograph of Kafka that Benjamin possessed; a
similar photograph of Benjamin himself, taken in a similar studio, also
figures in Benjamin's writings. Adorno's criticisms closely parallel those he
will make of other works by Benjamin, including the Artwork essay, in the
so-called Adorno–Benjamin dispute, which may be said to open formally
with the famous Hornberger letter of less than a year later. It is not, perhaps,
surprising that Benjamin's essay on Kafka contains a description of a
photograph. But what is surprising is that Adorno's letter on the Kafka essay
begins by emphasizing the common ground between Adorno and Benjamin,
and does so by way of Adorno's own evocation of photography. Adorno has
never before, he says – before reading Benjamin's Kafka essay, that is –
been so aware of his and Benjamin's agreement on central philosophical
issues. And as evidence of this agreement he cites his own earlier attempt to
interpret Kafka's work as a

> photograph of earthly life from the perspective of the redeemed life, nothing of
> the latter appearing in the photograph but a corner of the photographer's black
> cloth, while the horribly distorted optic of the picture is none other than that of the
> obliquely placed camera itself . . . (Letter of 17 December 1934, Adorno, 1970b:
> 103)

This comparison of Kafka's work to a photograph tells us immediately how
important a role photography plays in Adorno's imagination, and how
closely it is connected in his mind with Kafka and Benjamin, two figures
who, for Adorno, are quintessential embodiments of modernism. The details
of Adorno's comparison already show us the essential elements in the
constellation formed around photography in his imagination. Adorno
describes a photograph of the earth seen from somewhere else, in an
unearthly perspective. The photographer's transmundane perspective produces a kind of photographic negative – in the sense that negation produces

the difference between the thing seen in its ordinary light and the thing seen under the extraordinary gaze of the photographer. And it is particularly the earth and the cities on it, rather than its human subjects, that are the objects of this gaze. We find in Adorno's writings references to aerial photographs of bombed-out cities, to photographs of the earth taken by 'fairy aeronauts', and to photographs of the earth from space.[5] Further, although Adorno's comparison of Kafka to a photographer has little in common with the boyhood photograph of Kafka that fascinated Benjamin, it is essentially the photographer's transmundane gaze that Adorno ascribes to Benjamin himself, as we see in his descriptions of Benjamin's intellectual and spiritual (*geistige*) capacities: Benjamin's gaze, Adorno says, 'revealed the ordinary world in the eclipse which is its permanent light'. The world that lies before Benjamin in eclipse is the world 'seen from the perspective of the dead man', but also the world 'as it appears to the redeemed man' – as it really is. This gaze is described in terms of a non-ordinary, transformative energy: everything that 'falls under the scrutiny of Benjamin's words' is transformed, 'as though it had become radioactive', and his intellectual energy 'might well be described as a mental atomic fission'.[6]

Despite his explicitly disparaging comments about it, then, photography clearly stands in Adorno's mind for a vision of the utmost intellectual and aesthetic potency. 'The earth seen from somewhere else' implies not so much a different physical perspective as a vision that both negates and transforms, a vision that is both non-mundane and extra-mundane and that is allied with the dangerous and penetrating processes made possible by science and technology, a vision that can present the world in negative and reveal its inner and its inorganic dimensions. Further, photography is not only the locus of a dispute between Adorno and Benjamin, but also, as Adorno tells us, a locus of their common ground – and given Benjamin's importance for Adorno, and the respect and even awe in which the younger man held the elder, a most energetically charged ground.

Clearly, however, as we see from the contrast in the way Adorno and Benjamin link photography with Kafka, there is a difference in the way photography figures in the two men's imaginations. A comment made by Roland Barthes in *Camera Lucida*, his book on photography, will help us to articulate this difference. Barthes notes that one may consider photographs from the point of view of the operator (the photographer), the spectator (the person looking at the photograph), or the 'target' or spectrum (the person or thing being photographed) (Barthes, 1991). In these terms, as his description of the boyhood photograph of Kafka indicates, Benjamin is concerned primarily with the experience of the 'target' of photography (and how apt is Barthes's word in this instance!), the person being photographed. Indeed, Benjamin is particularly concerned with the fate of the face in photography, that prime object of photography and also the prime seat of the target's sense of self. Adorno, in contrast, as is evident in his comparison of Kafka to a photographer, is interested primarily in the point of view of the photographer. The face does not even appear in the constellation that Adorno associates with photography.

This simple distinction highlights the differences in the two men's analysis of photography and its development and consequences. Benjamin's interest focuses with poignancy on the connection between the destruction of the aura wrought by photography and the impact of modernity on individual subjectivity. Adorno's interest centres on the negative aura (or para-aura, to use the language of 'The moon', a miniature from Benjamin's *Berlin Childhood* that particularly fascinated Adorno) that accompanies photography, as it does modernist art in general, and that photography can make us particularly aware of.[7] The unearthly light that is both the medium and the hallmark of the photographer's transmundane gaze, in other words, the light that makes the photograph a photographic negative, may be conceived as a transformation of the radiance associated with the aura.

Formulating this difference makes the complementarity of Benjamin's and Adorno's analyses more apparent. Benjamin's analysis of the fate of the face in nineteenth-century photography reveals an early and specifically photographic form of the aura which was quickly subverted by a perverted and commodified form of the aura, which did indeed need to be combated. Adorno's analysis gives us a sense of the twentieth-century form that the specifically photographic aura would take, the negative aura that is photography's genuine potential and that would mark its kinship with modernist art rather than with mass culture.

The auratic face and its demise in the commodified interior

> The cult of remembrance of loved ones, absent or dead, offers a last refuge for the cult value of the picture. For the last time the aura emanates from the early photographs in the fleeting expression of a human face.
>
> (Walter Benjamin)

Benjamin's concern with the face as the exemplary 'target' of photography points to something crucial in the relationship of photography to the aura, for it is clear that the face is the original locus of the aura as well as (according to Benjamin) its last refuge. At the same time, the face as representative of the self also stands for the capacity for critical reflection and engaged intersubjectivity that is a crucial political concern for us now, as it was for Benjamin and Adorno earlier in this century.

Psychoanalytic theory can be of use to us in understanding these linkages as a context for Benjamin's discussion of the fate of the face in nineteenth-century photography. We have seen that the positive political potential Benjamin saw in de-auratized art was not realized. When Benjamin's colleagues in the Frankfurt School tried to explain the failure of the German working class to oppose Hitler – an instance of this lack of realization – they turned to psychoanalytic theory, analysing that failure in terms of a dismantling of ego structures in a commodity culture in which the direct authority of society shapes the individual, bypassing the socializing influences of the family structure.[8] In other words, the kinds of ego structures required for democratic social engagement are those in which individuals are capable of mutual recognition in Hegel's sense: 'Love proper exists only between living beings who are alike in power and thus in one another's eyes living beings from every point of view; in no respect is either dead for the other' (Hegel, 1948: 304). The capacity for such intersubjective recognition requires in turn the ability to differentiate between self and other. These capacities are acquired in the course of the development of the self, or ego, which occurs through experiences of being recognized by others.

The initial locus for this development of self or ego – and here we come to the role of the face and its connection with the aura – is the relationship between the infant and the mothering one, a relationship which involves both bonding and differentiation and which is a bodily as well as a psychic experience and a tactile as well as a visual one. The face is central to this experience, which may be symbolized by the infant's gazing at the mother's face while nursing. The mother's face serves as a kind of mirror, thus helping to constitute the baby's self, but it also embodies variable distance – the mother comes and goes – and the distinction between the visual experience of the face and the tactile experience of the breast and the holding. All of this helps the infant to differentiate self and other. In such circumstances (or in later, analogous circumstances), as psychoanalyst Michael Eigen notes in his essay 'The significance of the face', the face may take on a radiance: 'The human face when experienced on the deepest level takes on a glowing quality which seems more than itself. . . . It flashes the sign of presence, however opaque' (Eigen, 1993: 59). In short, the face has the qualities of the aura as Benjamin describes it – a distance without which there can be no presence, a radiant quality, and the element of embodiment. The aura around the face is the signal of the intersubjective mirroring that is essential to the life of the self at the most profound level.

Benjamin, of course, emphasizes the religious rather than the infantile origins of the aura, and the link between the auratic face and the religious and spiritual dimension in which auratic art has its origins can be easily seen. In religious traditions the face has long been linked with the aura, which by another name is the halo. But of particular interest in the context of the role of the mirroring face in the development of the self are the esoteric mystical traditions that celebrate the embodied state. In those traditions – and here I should state that I am basing myself solely on the work of Henry Corbin, the noted scholar of Iranian mystical spirituality – the radiance of the aura indicates the appearance of the divine in corporeal form: a theophany. In the Sufi mysticism deriving from the Manichaean tradition, for instance, we find the notion of the *caro spiritualis*, the spiritual face or countenance, which is perceived as radiantly beautiful and which serves not as an object of fusion or union but as a physical receptacle which acts as a mirror of the sensory and suprasensory capacities of the one who contemplates it. A mirroring face, in other words, which is an ally in the higher development of the person (Corbin, 1978).[9]

These links between the aura, the face, and embodied experience strongly suggest that the aura in some form may retain a positive potential in the contemporary struggle to preserve the capacity for critical reflection and for engaged, embodied caring, and that it may do so – again, in some form – in photography itself. But in Benjamin's narrative of the history of photography it is precisely the face as the bearer of the aura that is obliterated.

It is not in the Artwork essay but in his 'Short history of photography' (Benjamin, 1977) that Benjamin deals with the fate of the face in photography. (Adorno much preferred the 'Short history', precisely because there Benjamin talked about the aura around the first photographs.) The 'Short history' begins with the supplanting of portrait painting by these peculiarly auratic early photographs from photography's first decades, in which the face and the gaze play a special role. It then traces the disappearance of this aura as the face becomes engulfed in the bourgeois interior of the second half of the nineteenth century, followed by the substitution of the empty cityscape for the face in the 'cleansing' of photography initiated by Atget, and then the return of the face in non-auratic form in twentieth-century photography. The 'Short history' thus provides the background for Benjamin's depiction of the anti-auratic and anti-contemplative stance of the twentieth-century politicized masses in the Artwork essay.

In the 'Short history' Benjamin defines the aura as a 'strange web of time and space: the unique appearance of a distance, however close at hand' (Benjamin, 1977: 49), a definition which proves fruitful in analysing the vicissitudes of the photographic aura. In the early, auratic photographs, this 'distance however close' takes the form of a surprising and inextricable link between past and future, that is, between the present moment of the subject in the photograph and the present moment of the viewer looking at the photograph, and thus between life and death. Hence Benjamin on a photograph by David Octavius Hill:

> One encounters something strange and new: in that fishwife from Newhaven who looks at the ground with such relaxed and seductive modesty something remains that does not testify merely to the art of the photographer Hill, something that is not to be silenced, something demanding the name of the person who lived then, who even now is still real and will never entirely perish into art. (Benjamin, 1977: 47)

The individual in the photograph continues to live as a real person in a way that would not have been true in a painted portrait. The change can be attributed precisely to the photograph's fidelity to nature, to the indexical quality Krauss refers to: the empirical reality of that individual is carried into the present by the physical action of the light that touched that person in the past. The early photographs, in other words, have what we might call an 'empirical' aura; the unique presence that characterizes the aura takes the form of the empirical trace of the past. As Benjamin puts it,

> All the artistic preparation of the photographer and all the design in the positioning of his model to the contrary, the viewer feels an irresistible compulsion to seek the tiny spark of accident, the here and now. In such a picture, that spark has, as it were, burned through the person in the image with reality, finding the indiscernible place in the condition of that long past moment where the future is nesting, even today, so eloquently that we looking back can discover it. (Benjamin, 1977: 47)

Despite the fact that the fishwife from Newhaven looks down at the ground, this empirical aura of the early photographs is a version of the reciprocal gazing we see in the mother/nursing baby couple; it attests to the embodied presence of a face. The peculiar form that this reciprocal gaze takes in the early photographs is exemplified in the experience with which Barthes begins his book on photography: 'I am looking at eyes that looked at the Emperor,' he exclaims on viewing an 1852 photograph of Napoleon's brother (Barthes, 1991: 3). Not, again, that the subjects in the early photographs necessarily look directly into the camera; on the contrary. Rather, because of the sensed empirical presence of the living human subject, the early photographs arouse an intense awareness of the potential for a reciprocal gaze of subject and viewer across the gap between past and future. This is particularly striking in the early photographs of faces; hence the almost embarrassing intensity of the photographic encounter and the consequent modesty and reserve of both model and photographer. Benjamin calls attention to this intensity, quoting Dauthendey speaking about the daguerreotype:

> 'At first one does not trust himself,' he reported, 'to look for very long at the first pictures he has made. One shies away from the sharpness of these people, feels that the puny little faces of the people in the picture can see him, so staggering is the effect on everyone of the unaccustomed clarity and the fidelity to nature of the first daguerreo-types.' (Benjamin, 1977: 47–8)

In supplanting portrait painting, then, photography did not in fact obliterate the aura. Rather, it initiated a new form of the aura, in which the auratic function of the face, the reciprocity of gazes, was facilitated precisely by the empirical, indexical quality of the photographic process. The technological character of photographic processes, in other words, is not inherently anti-auratic, or anti-aesthetic. (Indeed, as Adorno pointed out in his critique of the Artwork essay, it is autonomous art rather than mass art that has used and integrated technological developments.)

But the next step in the history of photography as Benjamin presents it in the 'Short history' does indeed detail the destruction of the auratic face in photography. In this phase, which is the phase of photography's flourishing in the mid- to late nineteenth century when retouching became an important photographic practice, the early empirical aura is simulated by an artificial aura of the kind we now characterize by the word 'atmosphere'. This change occurs in conjunction with the development of the 'bourgeois interior' as the setting for 'bourgeois inwardness' (*Innerlichkeit*, implying the cultivation of individual subjectivity). The generation after the first photographs, Benjamin notes, 'withdrew . . . into its living space' (Benjamin, 1977: 50). In Benjamin's interpretation, the development of the interior and its correlate, interiority or inwardness, is an ideological reflection of the new dominance of commodity fetishism.[10] While the aura originally signalled the authenticity of the unique original work of art, and in the early photographs signalled the uniqueness of the empirical individual, in this new phase of the interior the individual's uniqueness disappears. It is replaced by the commodified living space in which the face figures as another standardized commodity. In Kierkegaard's pointed formulation, quoted by Susan Sontag: 'With the daguerreotype everyone will be able to have their portrait taken – formerly it was only the prominent, and at the same time everything is being done to make us all look exactly the same – so that we shall need only one portrait' (Sontag, 1977: 208).

The artificial aura created by the photographers of this period replicates that of the bourgeois interior. It is in a very precise sense a perversion of earlier forms of the aura. The aura as Benjamin defined it in the 'Short history' is a kind of container or casing, an exterior or husk with an interior; this is what makes for the sense of distance despite the closeness of physical proximity. These same elements – a container, with an exterior and an interior, a mix of space and time, distance and closeness – also define the bourgeois interior. In contrast to the artwork or the early photographs, however, the bourgeois interior as commodified living space is a container containing nothing, in which the surface negates time and space and the distinction between difference and closeness. The indiscriminate, commodity-based use of exotic elements from all over the world and from all periods of cultural history – what we would now call historicism and Orientalism – that prevailed in the furnishings of the bourgeois interior provides only an illusion of distance in time and space, like the picture postcards of colonial cities decorating his grandmother's apartment that Benjamin describes in the *Berlin Childhood*. In Marxist terms, the exchange value of these furnishings has been separated from their use value, or their embeddedness in historical and cultural context, so that difference is obliterated in the sameness of exchange and, in Adorno's words, 'the self is overwhelmed in its own domain by commodities' (Adorno, 1989: 44).[11]

In contrast to an empirical aura that links past and present, death and life in such a startling way, this perverse aura represents an ideological fusion of closeness and distance that is death-like. 'Living in the interior rooms of that era,' as Benjamin puts it, 'was having woven, spun oneself tightly into a spider web in which world events hung all around like the bodies of insects whose insides had been sucked out' (Benjamin, 1982: 286). And for Benjamin, the photographer's studio of the period, which he describes as a cross between a throne room and a torture chamber, is the exemplary place in which the self is assimilated into the bourgeois interior. Both the boyhood photograph of Kafka we saw before, which makes an appearance in the 'Short history', and the photographs of Benjamin as a boy described in the *Berlin Childhood* witness the child's difficulty in retaining a sense of self in the studio, where the screens, cushions and pedestals of the décor thirst for the child's image 'the way the shades in Hades thirst for the blood of the sacrificial animal' (Benjamin, 1955: 607).

In the further evolution of photography, this phase of the bourgeois interior with its perverted aura (and its correlate, the atmospheric haze of colonial cities in tourist postcards) is followed by a period of what Benjamin characterizes as 'cleansing'. Atget, photographer of empty streets and small neglected details, 'disinfected the sticky atmosphere spread by conventional portrait photography in that age of decline'. His pictures 'turn reality against the exotic, romantic show-offish resonance of the city name: they suck the aura from reality like water from a sinking ship' (Benjamin, 1977: 49). The empty city thus becomes a more truthful image than the (apparently) full bourgeois interior with its standardized face. The city supplants the face as the exemplary object of photography and, at least for Benjamin, the aura disappears from the forward movement of photography. When the face reappears in twentieth-century photography and film, it is in its scientific or political aspect, as with the masses in Russian film or in August Sanders's comparative anatomy of social classes, rather than in its individual and aesthetic aspect.

Shock, violence and the mute gesture: photography as the figure of modernist art

> Eternalized gestures in Kafka are the momentaneous brought to a standstill. The shock is like a surrealistic arrangement of that which old photographs convey to the viewer.
>
> (Theodor Adorno)

If Benjamin considers the aura to have been eliminated from photography once the cleansing initiated by Atget begins, Adorno's work in contrast presents us with another stage in the relationship between photography and the aura, a stage that begins at about that time. In this stage, photography, like the modernist art for which it stands in Adorno's mind, is characterized by a weak aura closely associated with the phenomenon of shock that Benjamin describes in the Artwork essay. I have spoken of this aura as a 'negative' or 'para'-aura. Surrealism is a good place to begin to understand the constellation associated with this negative aura in Adorno's work.

Benjamin's 'Short history of photography' skips quickly over Surrealism, and neither he nor Adorno discusses the very considerable role that photography played in that movement.[12] But many of Adorno's figurative allusions to photography refer to Surrealism, which for him often stands for modernist art as such. Adorno's essay on Surrealism, 'Looking back on surrealism', collected in *Notes to Literature* (1991a) revolves around Surrealist shocks. The link between photography and shock, with its moments of violence and instantaneousness, is, already evident in the English term 'snapshot' and its German equivalent, *Momentaufnahme*.

Adorno's essay on Surrealism is intent on setting Surrealist shocks in a socio-historical as opposed to a psychologistic context. Surrealist images are not, he says, dream images or symbols of the unconscious. Rather, they look both backward in time to the fetishized commodities of the nineteenth century and forward in time to the explosive destruction of cities to come: 'After the European catastrophe the Surrealist shocks lost their force. It is as though they had saved Paris by preparing it for fear: the destruction of the city was their center' (Adorno, 1991a: 87). If the Surrealist portrayal of the city is not simply a 'cleansing' but a reference to social violence, the Surrealist images, created through montage technique, are also references to the reification which has already taken place in the fetishized commodity objects of the nineteenth-century bourgeois interior.

Surrealist images, which link reification and violence, aim to awaken critical consciousness precisely through shock. Hence when Adorno compares Surrealist works to photographs, as he does at several points, he is invoking not only photography's capacity to record historical violence or simulate a fetishized commodity, but also and especially the role of the negative in the photographic process, which becomes a figure for critical consciousness. Adorno's interpretation of Surrealist shocks as awakening rather than dreaming, and consciousness of denial rather than symbolism of the unconscious, is captured in the notions of photography as snapshot and negative, and he ends his essay on Surrealism with that analogy:

> As a freezing of the moment of awakening, Surrealism is akin to photography. Surrealism's booty is images, to be sure, but not the invariant, ahistorical images of the unconscious subject to which the conventional view would like to neutralize them; rather, they are historical images in which the subject's inner-most core becomes aware that it is something external, an imitation of something social and historical. . . . If Surrealism now seems obsolete, it is because human beings are now denying themselves the consciousness of denial that was captured in the photographic negative that was Surrealism. (Adorno, 1991a: 89–90)

Whereas earlier the aura represented the reciprocity of gazes that constitutes intersubjective recognition, now that possibility is blocked by reification. Instead, Adorno shows us the aura in the shock of recognition in which the subject sees the fetishized object it has become. In the capacity for this shock of recognition lies the remaining hope for critical consciousness and thus for subjectivity itself.

The linkages Adorno makes here between shock, violence and reification, and awareness and denial, testify to photography's involvement in the dialectics of modern experience and modern art as Adorno conceives them.

In order to further elaborate these linkages I will return to the letter from Adorno to Benjamin in which we first saw Adorno making a positive connection between himself and Benjamin and between Kafka and photography. In that letter Adorno makes a number of points critical of Benjamin's interpretation of Kafka, and they will serve to elucidate, via Kafka, Adorno's conception of photography's weak modernist aura.[13]

First of all, it is important to be clear that for Adorno, as for Benjamin, there is no question either in photography or in modernist art of a serene, contemplative relationship to a work of art such as arguably characterized the relationship to the auratic work of art in the past. Shock and violence are too central to the dynamics of modernist art. In the Artwork essay Benjamin refers to Dadaist art, for instance, as 'an instrument of ballistics' that 'hit the spectator like a bullet' (1969: 238), and Adorno speaks similarly about the shocks in Kafka's work. The demand for interpretation exerted by Kafka's Surrealist images, he says, is a kind of 'aggressive physical proximity' that destroys the contemplative relationship between text and reader by collapsing the distance between them, agitating the reader's feelings to the point where 'he fears that the narrative will shoot toward him like a locomotive in a three-dimensional film' (Adorno, 1983: 246).

It is particularly obvious that film can disrupt the 'web of time and space' that constitutes the aura, for its shifting focus renders the relationship of viewer to work unstable. Hence Benjamin locates the shock effect of film in its rapid shifting of place, such that the viewer cannot project himself into what he sees: 'The distracting element of film is . . . based on changes of place and focus which periodically assault the spectator. . . . No sooner has his eye grasped a scene than it is already changed. It cannot be arrested' (1969: 238). But Adorno, by evoking a photograph to discuss Kafka's work, makes it clear that Kafka's modernist text has the same destabilizing effect. In the essay 'Titles', Adorno introduces a photograph from his edition of 'The Stoker', the early fragment of what later became Kafka's novel *America*: 'This work has as much to do with America as the prehistoric photograph "In New York Harbor" that is included in my edition of the Stoker fragment of 1913. The novel takes place in an America that moved while the picture was being taken, the same and yet not the same America on which the emigrant seeks to rest his eye after a long, barren crossing' (Adorno, 1992b: 7).[14] While we might trace the effect of 'an America that moved' to the motion of the boat from which the photograph was taken (and to the impact of America on the viewer), we may also attribute the incapacity to 'rest one's eye' to the destruction of the possibility of stable contemplation. The contrast between Benjamin's point about film and Adorno's complex metaphorical portrayal of Kafka's work is instructive. In both cases the crux is the relationship between modern experience and the formal characteristics of the artwork in question, but in Benjamin's case the linkage is to the technical aspects of the medium, whereas in Adorno's it is to the substance of the work, with the medium of photography serving only to highlight features of that substance.

For Benjamin in the Artwork essay, the shock nature of modern experience means that contemplation is replaced by distraction and auratic art by the non-auratic media of photomechanical reproduction. Adorno has a more complex case to make. For him shock is associated not with distraction but with critical consciousness, and not only with photographic processes but also with other forms of modernist art. The reader of Kafka's texts may experience the narrative barrelling down on him like a locomotive, but if the train wipes the reader out the shock will not result in critical consciousness. In other words, modernist art must walk the fine line between beautifying what is intolerable and arousing denial as a defence against an unbearable reality.

Adorno's interpretation of Kafka, which is interwoven throughout with references to photography, attempts to articulate the nature of that fine line. First of all, the shocking snapshot of violence both freezes and contains the unbearable. It adds a moment of indirection to what would otherwise be a frontal assault. Kafka himself, comparing his stories to photography, describes them in this way, if we are to believe the anecdote from Janouch's *Conversations with Kafka*: ' "The necessary condition for an image is sight," Janouch told Kafka; and Kafka smiled and replied: "We photograph things in order to drive them out of our minds. My stories are a way of shutting my eyes" ' (cited in Barthes, 1991: 53). Adorno's description of a passage in Kafka's *Castle* demonstrates the way Kafka's work freezes the moment with a violent motion equivalent to the shock of a snapshot: 'Josef K. opens the lumber-room, in which his warders had been beaten a day earlier, to find the scene faithfully repeated, including the appeal to himself. "At once K. slammed the door shut and then beat on it with his fists, as if that would shut it still more securely." This is the gesture of Kafka's own work, which . . . turns away from the most extreme scenes as though no eye could survive the sight' (Adorno, 1983: 253).

The oblique perspective that figures in Adorno's comparison of Kafka to an unearthly photographer ('the horribly distorted optic of the picture is none other than that of the obliquely placed camera itself') is simply another metaphor for this indirect approach to a reality too monstrous to be looked at directly. This is another reason we see no faces in Adorno's references to photography – or indeed in his figurative depictions of modernist art: something that cannot be confronted has in effect no mirroring face. Conversely, we might say, following the Benjamin of the 'Short history', that people no longer have faces when the face itself becomes a fetishized commodity.

If photography for Adorno is a way of both shutting one's eyes and seeing, of combining denial with recognition, what is captured when the snapshot freezes the moment is not a face but a gesture. And if the photograph-like work is a literary text, as in the case of Kafka, then language, the counterpart of the mirroring face, will be compromised. Hence, while Benjamin associated gesture in Kafka with archaic Chinese theatre, for Adorno it is quintessentially modern: 'If one were to look for the basis of gesture,' he says in the letter to Benjamin cited earlier, 'it might be less to be found in Chinese theater than, it seems to me, in modernity, that is, in the withering away of language. In Kafka's gestures the creature whose words have been taken away finds release' (1970b: 108).

Just as photography combines the regressive and the transcendent, residing in an intermediate zone between fetishized commodity and shock-induced critical consciousness, so gesture resides in the intermediate zone between meaningfulness and regression to meaninglessness. Like modernist art, and like photomechanical processes with their indexical tie to empirical reality, gesture is inherently ambiguous and enigmatic. Adorno links these ideas by asserting that Kafka's novels are not theatrical but rather 'the last, vanishing captions for silent film' (1970b: 109). 'The ambiguity of gesture,' Adorno continues, 'is that between sinking into muteness (with the destruction of language) and rising out of it into music'. Thus for Adorno, gesture, which links the theme of shock and violence with that of transcendence, takes the place of the face as the locus of the aura, but its aura is the weak and enigmatic negative aura that characterizes both modernist art and photography.

The peculiar quality of this aura around gesture is highlighted in the constellation of gesture, animals and music in Kafka's work. In his letter to Benjamin, Adorno draws Benjamin's attention to this constellation, and specifically to 'the depiction of dogs silently making music in "Investigations of a Dog" ' (1970b: 109). That passage in Kafka's work shows us a striking instance of the modernist aura as a negative version of the 'web of space and time'. Here is the core of Kafka's depiction:

> Seven dogs stepped into the light. . . . They did not speak, they did not sing, they remained, all of them, silent, almost determinedly silent; but from the empty air they conjured music. . . . The music gradually got the upper hand, literally knocked the breath out of me and swept me far away from those actual little dogs, and quite against my will, while I howled as if some pain were being inflicted upon me, my mind could attend to nothing but this blast of music which seemed to come from all sides . . . seizing the listener by the middle, overwhelming him, crushing him, and over his swooning body still blowing fanfares so near that they seemed far away and almost inaudible. (Franz Kafka, 'Investigations of a Dog', in Kafka, 1952: 206–8)

'Fanfares so near that they seemed far away and almost inaudible': this is a distance in closeness, but one whose closeness is violent and whose distance borders on vanishing.

As a further instance of this peculiar intermediate zone in Kafka's work, let me follow Adorno in citing Odradek, the 'creature' in Kafka's obliquely titled story 'The Cares of a Family Man' (1948: 161).[15] Odradek exists in an intermediate zone between the organic and the inorganic that is as shocking to our sensibilities as Kafka has shown the intermediate zone between music and muteness to be. Such monstrousness, which Adorno, as we have seen, considers to have forced Kafka to adopt an oblique optic, reflects the dialectic of modernist art, which becomes increasingly inorganic while retaining a refracted mimetic relation to nature and thus a negative, dialectical relation to the early aura, and which retains a note of transcendence and hope within that dialectical negative relationship. 'Certainly Odradek as the reverse side of the world of things is a sign of distortion', Adorno says, ' – but as such precisely a motif of transcendence, namely of the removal of the boundary and reconciliation of the organic and the inorganic or the *Aufhebung* of death: Odradek "survives." To put it another way, only to life that is inverted in an object-like way is escape from the context of nature promised' (Adorno, 1970b: 106). And of course photography itself, the Odradek of art, a fossilized form of shock, exists in this intermediate zone, in some sense a mere inorganic trace of empirical reality and in another sense a negative auratic survival of past life in the present moment, an emblem of hope.

The final element in this constellation of shock, violence and enigmatic gesture is that of epic. Again in opposition to Benjamin's association of Kafka with theatre, Adorno links Kafka's work with epic, theatre's antithesis. For Adorno, epic plays a crucial role in the dialectic of violence and non-violence in modernist art. Like the gestural element, the epic element in Kafka testifies not only to the role of shock and violence in modern experience but also to the non-violent strategies through which the modernist aesthetic transcends and survives domination.

For Adorno, art as such, like the aura, is two-faced. It participates in the context of social domination both through its material and through its tendency to a logic-like formal order, but at the same time it struggles to transcend both the violence it must contain and the violence that its own form can impose. It struggles, in fact, toward non-integration; Beethoven's late music, following the heroics of his middle period, is for Adorno the paradigmatic case of allowing non-integration. The turn to non-integration means that nothingness – in the form of the trifling, the insignificant, the amorphous – enters the work and becomes the agent or, better said, the medium of coherence: 'In great music the so-called primal elements unearthed by analysis are often trifling. It is only insofar as these elements approach nothingness asymptotically that they fuse into a whole as pure becoming' (*Aesthetic Theory*, 154; 148).

For Adorno, the epic element in art, as opposed to the dramatic, stands for this tendency to allow the trifling, the insignificant and the non-identical – that which cannot be subsumed under pre-given categories and the laws of logic – into art. It represents a renunciation of pre-given pattern or design and an abandonment to a logic of form that proceeds from individual figures. In these terms, of course, the epic element is not confined to literary works; in fact, Adorno uses Mahler, whom he repeatedly compares to Kafka, to exemplify it. The ultimate instance of the epic element in Mahler's music is to be found in certain notes in which the music comes to a halt or is suspended. These notes 'do not represent any build-up of power', says Adorno. 'Nor are they simply a pause in which the movement temporarily comes to rest, but something different again: they are the seal of permanence, of the music's inability to fight free of itself.' These notes represent the overcoming of dramatic violence by epic non-violence. In them, 'the epic sense of form of Mahler's symphonies has penetrated right down into the motivic cell and there resists non-violently the essentially dramatic thrust of the symphony'.[16]

Such notes may be the musical equivalent of Kafka's uninterpretable gestures, the means by which the immediacy of experience can be retained in a work of language. This is why it is so important – as Adorno and Benjamin both emphasize – to take Kafka's gestures not symbolically but literally, as uninterpretable allegories. One might say more generally that it is the presence of an unassimilable and in that sense alien material element in any medium – the unintegrated note in a work of music, the gesture in a written work, the empirical trace in a photograph – that constitutes for Adorno the movement of non-violence. In a situation where the forces of violent reification make full subjecthood impossible, such non-violence is a cunning form of resistance, designed to preserve a little of the subject in an inconspicuous and uninterpretable form of survival. Like Odradek, the uninterpretable gesture is both monstrous and a motif of hope and transcendence.

Photography as index, carrying with it the mark of the original object through the actual light that struck it at a specific instant, brings the traces of alien and uninterpretable matter into the realm of illusion and image. And like the faded photograph in Kafka's *Castle* to which Adorno draws our attention ('Only with difficulty can K. recognize anything on it': Adorno, 1983: 253), the individual photographic print, exemplar of reproducibility, is as subject to fading and oblivion as the refuse of which Kafka, as Adorno says, makes his art. The negative aura produced by the unearthly light of the perspective of redemption is as inconspicuous and pale as moonlight, barely perceptible or perceptible only to the weak remnants of critical subjectivity which it mirrors, like photography's transformations by negation, taking place in the red light of the darkroom.

The non-violent resistance which is both a note of hope and an acceptance of the alien, the mute and, by extension, matter, the inorganic and death, is nowhere shown more vividly than in Adorno's depiction of Mahler's death mask. That mask seems to have preserved a smile on Mahler's face in death, Adorno says, a smile that is more than a mere illusion caused by some muscular reflex:

> In Mahler's face, which seems both imperious and full of a tender suffering, there is a hint of cunning triumph, as if it wished to say: I have fooled you after all. Fooled us how? If we were to speculate we might conclude that the unfathomable sorrow of his last works had undercut all hope in order to avoid succumbing to illusion, rather as if hope were not unlike the superstitious idea of tempting fate, so that by hoping for something you prevent it from coming true. Could we not

think of the path of disillusionment described by the development of Mahler's music as by no other as an example of the cunning not of reason but of hope? (Adorno, 1992a: 110)

Photography as index, a trace of the real and material, is more like a death mask than a work of art, as Rosalind Krauss pointed out. And for Adorno, the various images of photographs of the earth from space, whether he uses them in connection with Mahler, with Kafka or with Benjamin, are emblems of hope in hopelessness. 'Kafka, the land-surveyor', says Adorno, 'photographs the earth's surface just as it must have appeared to those Jewish victims hung head down during the endless hours of their dying. It is for nothing less than such unmitigated torture that the perspective of redemption presents itself to him' (Adorno, 1983: 269).

Compassion and the contemporary photographic aura

> In the love stirred by Photography (by certain photographs), another music is heard, its name oddly old-fashioned: Pity.
>
> (Roland Barthes)

In a weak sense, the association between the face and the aura that Benjamin noted in the early photographs can be said to characterize the peculiarly photographic aura today. We have seen that in Barthes's terms, Benjamin was concerned with the experience of the subject of photography and Adorno with the perspective of the photographer. Barthes himself wrote *Camera Lucida* from the perspective of the viewer of photography. There he describes how he discovered what for him was the essential nature of photography through his search for the one photograph of his recently deceased mother that would most piercingly remind him of her reality – that she had once lived. But, Barthes concludes, it is not so much the literal face of the literal beloved in photographs that is crucial; rather, through certain details which (perhaps without the photographer's having intended it) have the power to pierce us in this way, photographs can bring us into contact with 'intractable reality' and arouse our love and compassion for it. This same compassion for reality in its otherness, he says, is what the society of images we live in attempts to tame and inhibit.

Barthes's comments suggest that photography has the capacity to extend the aura, now understood as the sign, however mute and uninterpretable, of a love-based intersubjective recognition, beyond the sphere of intimate human relationships to 'reality' in the sense of the larger physical, embodied environment in its various forms – social, material, natural. This does not mean extending the range of victims rendered beautiful through photography. Adorno has shown us that the realm of beauty opens only in negative, through the flash in which the violence is done it is momentarily visible. Instead, the weak photographic aura of our time, made possible by the transmundane perspective Adorno described, emanates to the viewer not from the 'original' of the vintage print but rather from the photograph itself as embodied object – from the individual, still physical photographic reproduction in whose presence the viewer stands and which the viewer may, at least potentially, hold in her hand and meet with her gaze, the same gaze that also turns away from it. Like Odradek, the actual print is a 'creature', containing the traces of intractable reality, functioning as a minimally surviving subject and arousing our compassion. In some sense the print both stands in for embodied reality as such and also reflects the viewer back to herself. In this way the photograph may be a contemporary form of the mirroring face that aids our development to a broader, more compassionate and more acute consciousness. It is just that in this case what we develop is compassion for the mirror, which in showing us a quick and oblique glimpse of intractable reality arouses our capacity to value and respect the larger physical world, which is mute, immediate and fragile.

FIGURE 2.1 *Photograph by Shierry Weber Nicholsen*

FIGURE 2.2   *Photograph by Shierry Weber Nicholsen*

Notes

Translations from the German have sometimes been altered. Where not otherwise indicated, translations of works by Adorno and Benjamin are my own.

Earlier versions of some of the material in this chapter appear in the *Antioch Community Record*, 12 February 1993; and in the author's *Exact Imagination/Late Work: On Adorno's Aesthetics* (1997).

1 Walter Benjamin, 'The work of art in the age of mechanical reproduction', in his *Illuminations* (Benjamin, 1969).

2 The letters that make up Adorno's contribution to the dispute are collected in Adorno, *Über Walter Benjamin* (1970b). For a synopsis and discussion of the 'Adorno–Benjamin dispute', see Wolin (1994: Chapter 6).

3 See Adorno (1970a), English translation Adorno (1984). Hereafter cited in the text as *Aesthetic Theory* in my own translations, with page numbers given first to the German original and then to Lenhardt's English translation.

4 See, for instance, Crimp (1983) and Burgin (1982).

5 See, for instance, Adorno's '*Nachwort*' to Benjamin's *Berliner Kindheit um 1900* (Adorno, 1987), as well as this paradigmatic instance from Adorno's discussion of the *Abschied* (farewell) section of Mahler's *Das Lied von der Erde*: 'For *Das Lied von der Erde* the earth is not the universe, the totality, but rather something that the experience of those flying at high altitudes fifty years later could recoup – a star. To the gaze of the music that is in the process of leaving it, the earth becomes rounded to a sphere which one can see the whole of, just as it has now been photographed from space, not the center of creation but something tiny and ephemeral' (Adorno, 1992a: 154).

6 See, respectively, 'Introduction to Benjamin's *Schriften*', in *Notes to Literature* (Adorno, 1992b: 228); '*Zu Benjamins Gedächtnis*,' in Adorno, 1970b: 10; 'A portrait of Walter Benjamin' in Adorno, 1983: 230; and 'Introduction to Benjamin's *Schriften*', 228.

7 Benjamin's miniature opens as follows: 'The light that streams down from the moon is not intended for the scene of our everyday existence. The sphere it illuminates in such a confusing manner seems to belong to a counter-world, a para-earth. It is no longer the earth of which the moon is a satellite but rather the earth itself transformed into a satellite of the moon' (Benjamin, 1989: 426–7). For a discussion of the connection between mimesis, the aura and a dreamworld of resemblances in Benjamin's and Adorno's thought, see my essay '*Aesthetic Theory*'s mimesis of Walter Benjamin', in Nicholsen (1997).

8 Cf. for instance Max Horkheimer (1987).

9 Cf. Corbin (1978). The aesthetics of this tradition highlight the same link between the suprasensory (or transmundane) and the inorganic which we have seen in the constellation around photography in Adorno's work. Specifically, in Man-ichaeanism this connection between radiance and personal development was linked with the form of painting we call the Persian miniature. Radiance is a quality of light, and the mirror works by reflecting light. Mani, the founder of Manichaeanism, was considered the originator of painting, the purpose of which was to lead vision beyond the sensory, to light. In Persian miniature paintings, light was represented by the precious metals used, notably in the 'light of glory' or *xvarnah* around certain figures – the aura. We might, accordingly, see this artform less as an early version of painting than as a precursor of photography, which is also based on the interaction of light and precious metals. Cf. Corbin (1978: 137–8).

10 Benjamin and Adorno are in close agreement in their analysis of the bourgeois interior and its relation to commodity fetishism. Adorno articulated his analysis in his *Kierkegaard: Construction of the Aesthetic* (1989), and Benjamin relied heavily on it, copying out passages from Adorno's book on Kierkegaard for his own projected work on nineteenth-century Paris.

11 Cf. the miniature 'Blumeshof 11', in Benjamin's *Berlin Childhood*: 'Madonna di Campiglio and Brindisi, Westerland and Athens and wherever else (my grand-mother) sent picture postcards from on her journeys – all of them were filled with the air of Blumeshof. And the large, comfortable handwriting that played around the bottom of the pictures or formed clouds in their skies showed them to be so completely inhabited by my grandmother that they became colonies of Blumeshof' (1989: 411).

12 On the Surrealists' use of photography, see Rosalind Krauss (1985).

13 Adorno claims Kafka for Surrealism, and interprets his work along similar lines, describing it explicitly as a critique of Kierkegaardian inwardness. As in Surrealism, 'the crucial moment . . . toward which everything . . . is directed is that in which men become aware that they are not themselves – that they are things' (1983: 255).

14 Theodor Adorno (1992) 'Titles,' in Adorno (1992b: 7).

15 Franz Kafka, *The Cares of a Family Man*, in Kafka (1948: 161). Odradek's laughter too occupies an intermediate zone, between voice and noise; it is 'the kind that has no lungs behind it. It sounds rather like the rustling of fallen leaves.'

16 Theodor Adorno, 'Mahler', in *Quasi una fantasia* (1991b: 104–5).

References

Adorno, T.W. (1970a) *Aesthetische Theorie: Gesammelte Schriften* vol. 7, ed. Rolf Tiedemann and Gretel Adorno. Frankfurt-on-Main: Suhrkamp.

Adorno, T.W. (1970b) *Über Walter Benjamin*. Frankfurt-on-Main: Suhrkamp.
Adorno, T.W. (1983) *Prisms*, trans. Samuel and Shierry Weber. Cambridge, MA: MIT Press.
Adorno, T.W. (1984) *Aesthetic Theory*, trans. Christian Lenhardt. London: Routledge & Kegan Paul.
Adorno, T.W. (1987) '*Nachwort*', in Walter Benjamin, *Berliner Kindheit um neunzehnhundert*. Frankfurt-on-Main: Suhrkamp.
Adorno, T.W. (1989) *Kierkegaard: Construction of the Aesthetic*, trans. Robert Hullot-Kentor. Minneapolis, MN: University of Minnesota Press.
Adorno, T.W. (1991a) *Notes to Literature*, vol. 1, trans. Shierry Weber Nicholsen. New York: Columbia University Press.
Adorno, T.W. (1991b) *Quasi una fantasia: Essays on Modern Music*, trans. Rodney Livingstone. London and New York: Verso.
Adorno, T.W. (1992a) *Mahler: A Musical Physiognomy*, trans. Edmund Jephcott. Chicago: University of Chicago Press.
Adorno, T.W. (1992b) *Notes to Literature*, vol. 2, trans. Shierry Weber Nicholsen. New York: Columbia University Press.
Barthes, R. (1991) *Camera Lucida*. New York: Hill and Wang.
Benjamin, W. (1955) *Schriften*, vol. 1, ed. Theodor and Gretel Adorno. Frankfurt-on-Main: Suhrkamp.
Benjamin, W. (1969) *Illuminations*, trans. Harry Zohn. New York: Schocken.
Benjamin, W. (1977) 'A short history of photography', trans. Phil Patton, *ArtForum*, 15 (6 February): 46–51.
Benjamin, W. (1982) *Das Passagen-werk*, vol. 1, ed. Rolf Tiedemann. Frankfurt-on-Main: Suhrkamp.
Benjamin, W. (1989) *Berliner Kindheit um 1900: Gesammelte Schriften*, vol. 7: 1, ed. Rolf Tiedemann and Herman Schweppenhauser. Frankfurt-on-Main: Suhrkamp.
Burgin, Victor (ed.) (1982) *Thinking Photography*. London: Macmillan.
Corbin, H. (1978) *The Man of Light in Iranian Sufism*. Boulder, CO: Shambhala.
Crimp, D. (1983) 'On the museum's ruins', in Hal Foster (ed.), *The Anti-Aesthetic*. Port Townsend, WA: Bay Press.
Curtis, J. (1989) *Mind's Eye/Mind's Truth*. Philadelphia: Temple University Press.
Eigen, M. (1993) 'The significance of the face', in *The Electrified Tightrope*. Northvale, NJ: Jason Aronson.
Hegel, G.W.F (1948) 'Love' in T.M Knox and R. Kroner (eds), *On Christianity*. Chicago: University of Chicago Press.
Horkheimer, M. (1987) *Studien über Autorität und Familie*. Lüneburg: Zu Klampen.
Kafka, F. (1948) *The Penal Colony*, trans. Willa and Edwin Muir. New York: Schocken.
Kafka, F. (1952) *Selected Stories of Franz Kafka*, trans. Willa and Edwin Muir. New York: Modern Library.
Krauss, R. (1985) *L'Amour fou: Photography and Surrealism*. New York: Abbeville Press.
Krauss, R. (1986) *The Originality of the Avant-Garde and Other Modernist Myths*. Cambridge, MA: MIT Press.
Mitchell, W.J. (1992) *The Reconfigured Eye: Visual Truth in the Post-Photographic Era*. Cambridge, MA: MIT Press.
Nicholsen, S.W. (1997) *Exact Imagination/Late Work: On Adorno's Aesthetics*. Cambridge, MA: MIT Press.
Ritchin, F. (1989) *In Our Own Image*. New York: Aperture.
Sontag, S. (1977) *On Photography*. New York: Farrar, Straus & Giroux.
Wolin, R. (1994) *Walter Benjamin: An Aesthetic of Redemption*, revised edn. Berkeley and Los Angeles: University of California Press.

3 The Encoding of History: Thinking Art in Constellations

Silvia L. López

There is a strange aura that surrounds Adorno's *Aesthetic Theory*. It is the aura of the mute object that refuses to deliver. In its insistence on the primacy of the object, the text itself achieves a second degree of reflection, inviting us to listen to how it speaks itself. This is not a minor methodological observation. In the introductory draft to the text, Adorno emphasizes the crucial relationship between epistemology and aesthetics: 'The problematic of theories of knowledge returns directly in aesthetics, because how aesthetics interprets its objects depends on the concept of the object held by the theory of knowledge' (1996: 332).[1] It is precisely this object of knowledge that Adorno exposes through his construction of art as a form of knowledge that implodes the very category of knowledge through the mimetic impulse. Each encounter with what this object could be is rapidly diffused and postponed, as if it were a moving syndrome confronting the fallacy of constitutive subjectivity in the current epistemological order. It is for this precise reason that Adorno maintains that art refuses definition and its location is in a 'historically changing constellation of elements' (1996: 2).

Art as a cipher of history can be appreciated momentarily when the dialectic comes to a standstill and the constellation of its elements makes a figure, as if in a kaleidoscope. The materiality of that figuration can only become objective by passing through the subject (the hand that turns the kaleidoscope), which will imprint the historical moment that determines the actual figure (through what Adorno would call *métier*). What is stored up in these figures is 'the unconscious writing of history, anamnesis of the vanquished, of the repressed, and perhaps of what is possible' (1996: 259). At stake is not a theory of art but an *ars memoriae* that mimics the very character of art as cipher but insists on a philosophical mediation of its traces. Aesthetics is for Adorno not the bankrupt philosophical subfield of bourgeois philosophy but the philosophical modality that deals with the dialectic of mimesis and rationality that artworks encode. This modality is always social:

> The objectivation of art, which is what society from its external perspective takes to be art's fetishism, is itself social in that it is the product of the division of

labour. That is why the relation of art to society is not to be sought primarily in the sphere of reception. This relation is anterior to reception, in production. (1996: 228)

Adorno's exclusion of the problem of reception when it comes to artworks results from his suspicion of the constitutive character of bourgeois subjectivity that is always already determined by the history of its own perception. The increased rationalization of life as consequence of the advanced processes of technology and production encroaches upon the field of subjective experience in unimagined and unexplored ways (1996: 34).[2] The power of the subject must be understood as not residing in its self-proclamation but rather in 'its methexis in the universal' (1996: 201).

Subjectivity, experience and the politics of catharsis

This objectification of art is a product of the social division of labour in a system of reified social relations. In this context, it is the primacy of the commodity fetish that makes the communal context of communicable experience impossible. It is for this reason that Adorno maintains that to determine the nature of the relation between art and society, and therefore the nature of aesthetic experience in its social context, one must look not at the sphere of reception but rather at the basic sphere of production:

> Since time immemorial, human reactions to artworks have been mediated to their utmost and do not refer immediately to the object; indeed they are now mediated by society as a whole. The study of social effects neither comes close to understanding what is social in art nor is it in any position to dictate norms for art, as it is inclined to do by positivist spirit. (1996: 228)

The work of art must be able to incorporate into its own constitution the social contradictions under which it is produced. In order to exist in a reified world the work of art must absorb reification into itself, even if its formal laws can never fully digest it. As if in an attempt at immunization the work of art survives by taking in a dosage of the deathly principle. By locating the possibility of resistance in the object rather than in the subject of experience, Adorno denies the relativity of truth implied by the many subjects of understanding and locates the realm of truth in the very contradictions embodied in the object of art. In this move toward the object he follows Hegel's critique of Kant: 'Beauty that is to be more than symmetrically trimmed shrubbery is no mere formula reducible to subjective functions of intuition: rather, beauty's fundament is to be sought in the object' (1996: 352). He defends firmly the idea that the particular character of the object can never be subsumed under the domination of the universal, parting ways here with Hegel and the belief in the ultimate sublation of subject and object. Works of art are monads that lead to the universal by virtue of their principle of particularization; universality and particularity are unconscious in them.

In other words 'the universal determinations of art are not simply an exigency of their conceptual reflection, rather they testify to the boundaries of the principle of individuation, which is no more to be ontologized than its opposite' (1996: 181). Aesthetics in dialectical fashion brings that unconscious relationship of universal and particular to consciousness.

The distrust of an aesthetic experience not mediated by concepts is founded upon Adorno's understanding of the status of culture in contemporary society. The intervention of technology in the massification of culture through the commodity form makes Adorno suspicious of any understanding of experience that does not question its own relationship to those very forms of artistic expression. After all, those commodity forms that circulate as part of the culture industry develop modes of responses on the part of audiences that reduce them to mere consumers of commodities. Adorno's suspicion of the subjective makes him declare the need to rescue the dimension of thought from experience and the need for philosophy to come to the aid of the elucidation of the artwork: 'Every artwork, if it is to be fully experienced, requires thought and therefore stands in need of philosophy, which is nothing but the thought that refuses all restrictions' (1996: 262). This must be understood not as a privileging of philosophy as discipline but as a belief in the power of the critique of reason and its mediation.

The experience of the artworks is always mediated through what is only possible through what Adorno understands as objective *Verstehen* (understanding). In this sense 'Art is knowledge, though not knowledge of objects' (1996: 262). Any association of feelings with aesthetic experience must be suspected of playing into the hands of the repressive order of the day. Pleasure cannot escape an ideological component that makes it a substitute gratification associated with the repression of instincts. He goes so far as to maintain that 'the doctrine of catharsis imputes to art the principle that ultimately culture industry appropriates and administers' (1996: 238). Aristotelian poetics are only an instrument of domination in an era that maintains that the self and its needs dictate understanding:

> The purging of affects in Aristotle's *Poetics* no longer makes equally frank admission of its devotion to ruling interests, yet it supports them all the same in that his ideal of sublimation entrusts art with the task of providing aesthetic semblance as a substitute for the bodily satisfaction of the public's interests and needs: Catharsis is a purging action directed against the affects and an ally of repression. (1996: 238)

The proper aesthetic response is not based on feeling (*Gefühl*) but on a sense of concern (*Betroffenheit*). Concern is not some repressed emotion that is brought to the surface of the receiver via aesthetic presentation; rather it 'is the moment in which recipients forget themselves and disappear into the work; it is the moment of being shaken' (1996: 244). The recipients lose their ground and at this moment the possibility of truth, embodied in the aesthetic image, becomes graspable. That shudder in which subjectivity stirs without yet being subjectivity is the act of being touched by the other.

Aesthetic comportment assimilates itself to that other rather than subordinating it. The importance of shudder is that it is not an experience of feeling and that it is radically opposed to a traditional idea of experience (*Erlebnis*). Shudder does not provide a satisfaction to the ego and is removed from desire: 'Rather, it is a memento of the liquidation of the I, which, shaken, perceives its own limitedness and finitude. This experience (*Erfahrung*) is contrary to the weakening of the I that the culture industry manipulates' (1996: 245). The sense of immediacy experienced in relation to the artwork is a function of mediation and 'of penetrating and encompassing experience (*Erfahrung*); it takes shape in the fraction of an instant, and for this the whole of consciousness is required, of isolated responses' (1996: 244). Consciousness without shudder is reified consciousness. Adorno's disdain for lived experience (*Erlebnis*) must be understood as pointing stubbornly to the darkest moments of culture, moments where precisely through recourse to sensual experience and the aestheticization of culture millions were murdered. It is perhaps in this light that he justifies suffering as not only the central expression of art but as that which gives substance to its form and grants its enigmatic quality to the shudder 'not in its presence but as recollection', in other words, art as Mnemosyne (1996: 197). Lived experience (*Erlebnis*) suppresses 'the interplay of the constructive and the mimetically expressive elements in art. The equivalence I posits is not an equivalence at all: rather, one particular aspect is abstracted' (1996: 244).

The distinctions drawn by Adorno between the two types of experience – lived experience (*Erlebnis*) and mediated historical experience (*Erfahrung*) – deserves some attention. His understanding of the crisis of experience in the modern world and of the artwork as index of it is heavily influenced by Benjamin's work on Baudelaire.[3] For those aware of the theoretical exchange between them regarding Benjamin's work, it may seem both somewhat paradoxical and ironic. Paradoxical given the serious criticism Adorno levelled against the Baudelaire manuscript for lacking 'mediation' and for being 'at the crossroads of magic and positivism',[4] ironic since that very criticism has been levelled against the *Aesthetic Theory* itself.[5] Nonetheless, it is worth noting how almost thirty years after the exchange Benjamin's methodological problems became sedimented material for Adorno's work. Fundamental to the *Aesthetic Theory* is Benjamin's inversion of the question of how to read modernist poetry in light of a general theory of modernity into how does Baudelaire's poetry bring out the modern? This is a radical shift in the understanding of the work of art in modernity. It no longer exemplifies something given to us by social theory but it does reveal something about the very notions that try to apprehend it. The resonances between Benjamin's idea of the modernity of art and Adorno's theoretical protocol are unmistakable. The modernity of art consists, according to Adorno, in 'the capacity to absorb the results of industrialization under capitalist relations of production, while following its own experiential mode and at the same time giving expression to the crisis of experience' (1996: 34).

Two Benjaminian discussions are taken up by Adorno: the one concerning the modes of experience and the one concerning memory. The experience of the everyday in modernity is the experience of lived moments (*Erlebnis*) that can't be transmitted as historical experience (*Erfahrung*). The historical predicament of their intervention, however, leads them to part company with regard to the future of *Erfahrung*. While Benjamin believes that *Erfahrung* could still be passed on through storytelling and grants the storyteller the gift of counsel,[6] Adorno does not think this to be possible except as a historical encoding in the artwork. Artworks are windowless monads that bear witness to *Erfahrung* rather than vehicles of change and transformation. The big gap between them resides in their respective notions of subjectivity:

> when art works have no external referent to hold on to any more, the missing thing, i.e. meaning, cannot be supplied by an act of will on the part of the subject. Meaning was canceled by the trend to subjectification, which is no accident of the history of ideas but reflects the contemporary state of truth. (1996: 220)

The decades that separate their reflections weigh heavily, in particular if we consider their differing opinions regarding the problem of aura which Adorno thinks Benjamin discarded too quickly and undialectically:

> The simple antithesis between the auratic and the mass-reproduced work, which for the sake of simplicity neglected the dialectic of the two types, became the booty of a view of art that takes photography as its model and is no less barbaric than the view of the artist as creator. . . . The failure of Benjamin's grandly conceived theory of reproduction remains that its bipolar categories make it impossible to distinguish between a conception of art free of ideology to its core and the misuse of aesthetic rationality for mass exploitation and mass domination, a possibility he hardly touches upon. (1996: 56)

Adorno criticizes Benjamin for not seeing how the cultic element can have an ideological valence that is critical. The negation of aura leads to the negation of modern art which distances itself from 'the logic of familiar things'. The exhibition value of the mechanically reproduced art is an 'imago of the exchange process' (1996: 45); realist expression is ruled by the capitalist logic of exchange. The critique here applies to socialist realism as well for its categories can very well be adjusted to the culture industry. What he is after is the undialectical idea of representation that is implicit in the liberation of the artwork from its aura.

At stake is the problem of truth. Art in its mimetic comportment is the only medium of truth and to some degree the contemporary loss of experience coincides 'with the bitter repression of mimesis that takes the place of its metamorphosis' (1996: 331).[7]

Mimesis: art as the other of society

In the *Dialectic of Enlightenment* (1988) Adorno and Horkheimer described how the Enlightenment brought with it a secular, sceptical and abstract thought that intended to overcome superstitious and magical thinking.[8] It claimed to have overcome those overtly mimetic forms but what it did was to repress mimesis through the ban on graven images (*Bildverbot*) while abstracting the mimetic process even further. It is with this understanding that the articulation of Enlightenment as myth becomes possible. Artworks remain witnesses to this process by being 'the objectivation of images, objectivation of mimesis, schemata of experience that assimilate to themselves the subject that is experiencing' (1996: 287). Traditional aesthetics has failed in Adorno's view precisely because it has not accounted for the dialectic of rationality and mimesis:

> The sentimentality and debility of almost the whole tradition of aesthetic thought is that it has suppressed the dialectic of rationality and mimesis immanent to art. This persists in the astonishment over the technical work of art as if it had fallen from heaven. (1996: 54)

It is mimetic comportment which differentiates art from conceptual knowledge or from the drive of instrumental rationality:

> The Aristotelian dictum that only like can know like, which progressive rationality has reduced to a marginal value, divides the knowledge that is art from conceptual knowledge: What is essentially mimetic awaits mimetic comportment. If artworks do not make themselves like something else but only like themselves, then only those who imitate them understand them. (1996: 125)

In a world of an alienated reality art is a refuge for mimetic comportment (1996: 56) and its modernity resides precisely in its mimetic relation to that petrified reality (1996: 21). This mimetic mode is a response to the irrationality in the rational world and acts as resistant witness of the overadministration of the lifeworld. The paradoxical space occupied by the artwork consists of the rationality of its organizing elements. This is why artists are obsessed with the formal manipulation of their material. The same rationality that governs the external world governs art while at the same time not reflecting that rationality's categorizing order. Rationalization is the source of all of art's means and methods of production yet it mobilizes it in an opposite direction than does domination. Art is then 'rationality criticizing itself without being able to overcome itself' (1996: 55). Adorno is careful not to ascribe to art the old place of magic, maintaining that art cannot be irrational or pre-rational given the interdependence of all human activities in society. Art is part of Enlightenment as myth and therefore disavows magic:

> Artworks as such remain semblance, the conflict between semblance – form in the broadest sense – and expression remains unresolved and fluctuates historically.

> Mimetic comportment – an attitude toward reality distinct from the fixated antithesis of subject and object – is seized in art – the organ of mimesis since the mimetic taboo – by semblance and, as the complement to the autonomy of form, becomes its bearer. (1996: 110)

Mimesis is an articulating comportment and concept. It is 'the ideal of art, not its practical procedure it is an attitude towards expressive values' (1996: 112). The way in which the artist contributes to expression is precisely through the power of mimicry which in him releases the expressed. What is expressed must be more than 'the tangible content (*Inhalt*) of the artist's soul' because if that is all the artwork expresses the work becomes nothing more than 'a blurred photograph' (1996: 112). Mimesis and expression are drawn together in the world of form 'what is formed, the content (*Inhalt*) does not amount to objects external to form; rather, the content is mimetic impulses that are drawn into the world of images that is form' (1996: 142). Art is mimesis of the world of imagery and simultaneously it is enlightenment through form. This is the basic dialectic of mimesis and rationality that defines the new aesthetics proposed by Adorno. The political character of this aesthetics and its relation to the mimetic impulse is stated by Adorno quite clearly:

> Among the human rights of those who foot the bill of culture is one that is polemically directed against the affirmative, ideological totality: That the stigmas of degradation be dedicated to Mnemosyne in the form of an image. (1996: 48)

Aesthetics as *ars memoriae* preserves the relationship to the other. In the preservation of historical experience through mimetic comportment art becomes the antithetical other of society. Art creates the possibility of recording the traces of the totalizing process by its ability to incorporate formally all those things that are excluded by bourgeois culture. Fantasy

> shifts whatever artworks absorb of the existing constellations through which they become the other of existing, if only through its determinate negation . . . fantasy may be redefined as the differential of freedom in the midst of determination. (1996: 174)

Adorno's positing of this realm of historical figuration and of memorial potential, however, is not mystical or irrational in character: 'the survival of mimesis, the conceptual affinity of the subjectively produced with its unposited other, defines art as a form of knowledge and to that extent as "rational" ' (1996: 54). For the reader of the *Aesthetic Theory* the text itself becomes a cipher of figures that can be discerned at times through the constellation of some concepts like the other, experience, mimesis and shudder, among others. They encode what Fredric Jameson has called 'the persistence of the dialectic'.[9] The figures are not arbitrary nor are the memorial sites they encode. In this sense the *Aesthetic Theory* is radical for its times. While decrying the rationalization brought about by late capitalism, it rescues the rational capacity of the fragile subject to engage with its other in a dialectical fashion to encounter the truth of barbarism and the potential of freedom buried in the contradiction of objects that bear the mimetic comportment. Quite radical indeed, at a moment when the logic of capitalism has incorporated all other forms of thought into itself.

The contribution of Adorno's *Aesthetic Theory* to the theorization of artistic production in late capitalism, the critique of subjective experience, and the uncompromising exploration of form and history has yet to find an audience. This is not coincidental. Its difficult style stands as philosophical challenge to a reinvention of reading in constellations and to the impossibility of the theoretical soundbite, leaving one to the dialectical process between particular and universal in constant motion. This relentless undermining of the reader in her encounter with the object stands, perhaps, as the most important methodological tribute to critique in an age when the venues for reflection have all been recuperated. While trapped in its drive the world acquiesces and for an instant we seize the present in a writing that was clearly meant for posterity. It is in this light that the idea that Adorno's *Aesthetic Theory* may have something to offer to feminism seems less preposterous than once thought.

Notes

1 I'd like to thank Dr Hullot-Kentor for his help in making the manuscript of the *Aesthetic Theory* available to me before it had been published by the University of Minnesota Press.
2 For a concrete example of this process consult Barbara Engh's 'Adorno and the Sirens: tele-phono-graphic-bodies', in Leslie A. Dunn and Nancy A. Jones (eds), *Embodied Voices: Representing Female Vocality in Western Culture*. Cambridge: Cambridge University Press, 1994.
3 Cf. Benjamin's *Charles Baudelaire* (1983).
4 Cf. Benjamin (1944: 579).
5 Cf. *Materialen zur Aesthetischen Theorie Th. W. Adornos Konstruktion der Moderne*, ed. Burkhart Lindner and Martin Lüdke. Frankfurt-on-Main: Suhrkamp, 1980.
6 Cf. Benjamin's 'The storyteller' (1968).
7 I am indebted to John Mowitt for stimulating further thoughts on the crisis of experience through his seminar on the emergence of everyday life, especially his lucid lecture on memory and perception held at the University of Minnesota in the spring of 1994.
8 Cf. Adorno and Horkheimer's *Dialectic of Enlightenment* (1988), especially Chapter 1 on the concept of Enlightenment.
9 Cf. Fredric Jameson's *Late Marxism* (1990).

References

Adorno, Theodor W. (1996) *Aesthetic Theory*, ed. Gretel Adorno and Rolf Tiedemann, trans. Robert Hullot-Kentor. Minneapolis, MN: University of Minnesota Press.
Adorno, Theodor W. and Horkheimer, Max (1988) *Dialectic of Enlightenment*, trans. John Cumming. New York: Continuum.

Benjamin, Walter (1968) 'The storyteller', in *Illuminations*, trans. Harry Zohn. New York: Schocken Books.

Benjamin, Walter (1983) *Charles Baudelaire: A Lyric Poet in the Era of High Capitalism*, trans. Harry Zohn. London: Verso.

Benjamin, Walter (1994) *The Correspondence of Walter Benjamin 1910–1940*, ed. Gershom Scholem and Theodor W. Adorno, trans. Manfred R. Jacobson and Evelyn M. Jacobson. Chicago: University of Chicago Press.

Jameson, Fredric (1990) *Late Marxism: Adorno, or, the Persistence of the Dialectic*. London: Verso.

4 *Fremdwörter* as 'The Jews of Language' and Adorno's Politics of Exile

Sinkwan Cheng

In 'Heine the Wound' (*'Die Wunde Heine'*), Adorno observes that 'today, the fate Heine suffered has literally become the common fate: homelessness has been inflicted on everyone. All in *language and being*, have been damaged as the *exile* himself was' (1991a: 85/100; added emphasis).[1] The damaging impact of exile on language and being is even more concretely and vividly captured in *Minima Moralia*, where they come together in a chilling constellation: 'Foreign words are the Jews of language' (Adorno, 1974: 110/123; translation modified).[2] Adorno's anguish as an 'intellectual in emigration' is superimposed here upon his agony as a half-Jew caught between nationalism in Germany on the one hand, and the conformism of America's administered world on the other.[3]

The frequent presence of foreign words throughout Adorno's writings is more than a passive reflection of the conditions of alienation and displacement experienced by the author as part of an age of anxiety and estrangement.[4] Foreign words assume for Adorno an active moral dimension, such as when he insists that 'it is part of morality not to be at home in one's home' (Adorno, 1974: 39). Even more important is the hope Adorno places in the critical or what he calls the 'explosive' force of foreign words. Surprisingly, while Adorno valorizes most foreign words for their supposedly critical function of negation, he uses English expressions (in his German writings) to stage the 'absurdity' of American culture. Thomas Levin, a sympathetic reader of Adorno's *Fremdwörter*, uses Adorno's *oeuvre* to construct a catalogue of English words which reads like a 'paratactic social symptomatology'. The examples he gives include 'teamwork', 'hit parade', 'conditioned reflexes', 'corny', 'crooner', 'jitterbugs', 'sampling', and 'name bands', as well as the following whose foreignness is not even signalled by quotation marks or italics: streamlining, tough guy, underdog, lowbrow, discriminatory power, and best-seller (Levin, 1985: 115–16).[5] Levin himself refers to this list of *Fremdwörter* as a 'hilarious catalogue of cultural stereotypes' more revealing of 'Adorno's perception of America' than the German thinker's explicit accounts of his stay in the United States such as 'Scientific Experiences of a European Scholar in America' (Levin, 1985: 115–16). Without realizing it, Levin calls attention to a contradiction between Adorno's theory and the practical applications he derives from it:

Adorno himself commits the same habitual stereotyping for which he faults the anti-Semites and the nationalist fanatics.[6] These lapses seriously compromise Adorno's role as a spokesman against totalitarianism and its persecution of otherness. More disturbingly, Adorno's rejection and subsequent exclusion of American culture as irredeemably 'foreign' is matched by an uncanny return in some of his later writings to an unacknowledged linguistic and cultural nationalism. Despite his opposition to German nationalism and its campaign for linguistic purity, Adorno eventually returns home to the German language.[7] His account of the way foreign words create *discontinuities* that disrupt myths of organic unity is undermined by his longing for his German home(-land) and by his need to 'reestablish a sense of *continuity*' with the point of his 'origin' (quoted from Löwenthal, 1989: 70; added emphasis). His radical subversion of the mythical 'homeland' into 'the state of *having escaped*' (Adorno, 1972: 78; added emphasis) thus reverts to the state of *having escaped back to the mythical homeland*. In a way, Adorno repeats the trajectory of Odysseus whom he criticizes in *Dialectic of Enlightenment*: the writer, no less than the Homeric figure he criticizes, 'wrenches [himself] free from the mythical homeland only to return to it in another form'.[8]

What, then, explains this inconsistency between Adorno's theory and praxis? Given Adorno's identification in *die Wunde Heine* of the Jewishness pervading *both* language and being, what 'perversion' allows Adorno to find a home for his Jewish being in the German language? These are the questions I seek to address in this chapter, especially from the perspectives of Lacanian psychoanalysis and deconstruction.

Fremdwörter and Adorno's campaign against the myth of organic unity

Adorno's deep mistrust of social and political metaphors of organic unity leads him to be highly critical of the myth of a pure Ur-idiom and the associated ideology of an internally coherent and organic nature of language. The concept of the nation as an organic unity depoliticizes fundamental inequalities and injustices – be they injustices directed against race or inequalities established among classes. The non-identical must, Adorno insists, be made apparent in the form and the content of a work. By doing so, the non-identical poses a threat to the status quo. Both nationalists and the bourgeoisie find foreign words offensive because, by remaining the absolutely other in language, these words prevent an unreflected affirmation of society. As Adorno puts it, foreign words take on an 'alien' posture in language:

> They [foreign words] are residues of the operation of the social contradiction between cultured and uncultured strata, a contradiction that no longer permits either the unreflective 'folk-etymological' development of language or a thoroughgoing construction of language, because free use of the forces of language is

reserved for the cultured stratum, which is alienated from itself as well as from the others. (Adorno, 1991b: 289)

Ironically, it is in their alienation from the organic whole of language that *Fremdwörter* open a space for freedom. As concrete embodiments of the non-identical, *Fremdwörter* erode consistency within a system, thereby disrupting the ontology of language and shattering the stifling grip of homogeneity:

> Foreign words demonstrate *the impossibility of an ontology of language*: they confront even concepts that try to pass themselves off as origin itself with their mediatedness, their moment of being subjectively constructed, their arbitrariness. (Adorno, 1991c: 189; added emphasis)[9]

Foreign terms cut through the mythical web of natural organicity and open a space for the experience of freedom:[10]

> foreign words are the points at which a knowing consciousness and an illuminated truth break into the undifferentiated growth of the aspect of language that is mere nature: the incursion of freedom. (Adorno, 1991b: 289)

Adorno does not confine the critical, disruptive function of *Fremdwörter* to a realm of 'mere language' abstracted from politics. The incorporation of foreign terms into a language helps realize Adorno's vision of *writing as a political act* – that is, as a series of analytic interventions into any closed system of thought and politics, whether Hegelian idealism or orthodox Marxism, German Fascism or American capitalism. The militant role of Adorno's *Fremdwörter* is evident from his two essays 'Alien Words' (*'Wörter aus der Fremde'*) and 'On the Use of Foreign Words' (*'Über den Gebrauch von Fremdwörtern'*).[11] Here Adorno explores the 'negative, dangerous, and yet assuredly promised power' of *Fremdwörter* (1991b: 291). For him, 'a determined defense of the use of foreign words' has a very specific goal:

> its task is not so much to demonstrate the harmlessness of foreign words as to release their explosive force: not to deny what is foreign in them but to use it. (1991a: 286)

This 'explosive' power comes precisely from the way the *Fremdwort* functions as an outlaw in the land of linguistic purity and organicity – as an outlaw which nonetheless promises to be the founder of a new law in the world 'to come':

> A worthy task for folklore would be to examine how foreign words operate beneath the sphere of culture but without fusing with the body of language – at the deepest level of language, in political jargon, in the slang of love, and in an everyday way of speaking that from the standpoint of organic language and linguistic purity would have to be called corrupt, but in which we may see the

contours of a language to come that cannot be understood either in terms of the idea of the organic or in terms of education. (1991b: 290)

It is with this 'utopia of language, a language without earth, [and] without subjection to the spell of historical existence' (Adorno, 1991c: 192) that Adorno seeks to blast open the prisonhouses of nationalism on the one hand and capitalism on the other.

A *language in exile and the exile's language: the disruption of the national order of things*

Paradoxically, it is the proliferation of myths of an organic homeland which is responsible for the creation of exile as a generalized condition in the twentieth century. Expelled outward, victims of exclusion return to haunt the ideology of nationalism – in the figure of the Jew – both in language and in being. Forbidden to 'exist', *die Wunde Juden* nonetheless insists.[12] Prevented from rooting themselves legally and socially, the exiles refuse to root themselves linguistically. Adorno himself exemplifies this by insisting on being 'a [writer] unhoused and a wanderer across language'.[13] This refusal of confinement within one national language is one of Adorno's most important forms of socio-political resistance around which different kinds of political protest – for example, protest against nationalism – can be structured. In 'Alien Words' Adorno recounts how, as a child, he delighted in using foreign words to offend his 'indispensable patriots' along with their close ally, the educational institution: 'Foreign words constituted little cells of resistance to the nationalism of World War I' (1991c: 186).

It is no surprise that the Nazis should systematically eliminate *Fremdwörter* from their literature and pedagogy.[14] Given the significant role played by language in the construction of national and cultural identity, the threat posed by foreign words to the national order of things cannot be easily ignored. From the onset of the ideology of nationalism, language as much as human beings has been subjected to inclusion/exclusion based on categories of 'citizenship'; thus the status of the *Fremdwort* has always been debated within the framework of linguistic nationality. Adorno calls *Fremdwörter* 'the Jews of language'. Like Georg Simmel's 'stranger', neither foreign words nor the Jews are '*organically* connected, through established ties of kinship, locality, and occupation, with any single one' of the community in which they uneasily reside (Simmel, 1950: 404; added emphasis). As much as 'people without a homeland' are looked upon as 'matter out of place', a 'homeless language' is discriminated against for its symbolic danger. To the extent that people without citizenship are deemed to be devoid of personal, social and political responsibilities (see, for example, Cirtautas, 1957: 70, 73), words that move across national linguistic borders are also suspect because they float free of language rules and clearly defined meanings. In other words, the exile – be it a linguistic form or a human being – is an anomaly existing outside the national order of things. It is the unwanted 'infiltrator' who threatens the purity of the nation as well as the prerogative of the state to define its citizenry.

Adorno does not limit himself to exploring the fear of otherness as the sole basis for nationalism's exclusion of the racial and linguistic other. He points out in addition how the purists' fear is a fear of facing their own truth – that is, the fear of confronting existing reality in its disjunctions and 'suffering'. Citing Benjamin's 'silver rib of the foreign word', Adorno demonstrates the way *Fremdwörter* return to linguistic purism its own truth in inverted form.[15] This operation allows Adorno to underscore the bad faith of the Nazis' violent attempt to impose a false unity upon a Germany saturated with social contradictions:

> Benjamin spoke of the author inserting the silver rib of the foreign word in to the body of language. *What seems inorganic here is in actuality only historical evidence, evidence of the failure of that unification.* Such disparateness means not only suffering in language, and what Hebbel called the 'schism of creation', but suffering in reality as well. From this perspective Nazism may be regarded as a . . . deadly attempt to force a bourgeois integration of Germany that had not taken place. (Adorno, 1991c: 187–8; added emphasis)

Pushing this logic, Adorno is able to detect, long before the development of post-colonial scholarship, the relationship between imperialism and organic language:[16]

> No language . . . is organic and natural[17] . . . but every victory of the advanced, civilizatory linguistic element contains as a precipitate something of the injustice in something like the way British imperialism dealt politically with its subject peoples. (1991c: 188)[18]

Nationalism is not only a set of explicit political propaganda. The idea of nation is also a deeply metaphysical construct. By revealing the heterogeneous nature of existing reality, foreign words can prevent an unreflected affirmation of society and dismantle the metaphysics of authenticity used for its legitimation:

> Every foreign word contains the explosive material of enlightenment, contains in its controlled use the knowledge that what is immediate cannot be said in unmediated form but only expressed in and through reflection and mediation. Nowhere do foreign words in German prove their worth more than in contrast to jargon of authenticity, terms like *Auftrag, Begegnung, Aussage, Anliegen* [mission, encounter, message, concern], and the like. (1991c: 190)

By debunking the ideology of immediacy, foreign words mount a robust challenge to cultural and nationalist metaphysics that naturalize scholarly and popular quests for 'authenticity'. The myth of immediacy or authenticity, it should be noted, is partly a product of the 'rootedness' of culture. The culture of national essentialism is always 'rooted in place'. In contrast to this rootedness, Adorno emphasizes cultivating a 'state of awareness' modelled upon the rootless and restless character of the exile. This critical awareness renders Adorno an adversary not only to nationalism but also to the administered world.

Jewishness in language and being: a threat to the administered world (Verwaltete Welt)

The perniciousness of the myth of the home(-land) makes it a moral obligation for the exile to refuse the temptation of settling down in a new 'home' in place of the old. Adorno confirms this principle by following his flight from Germany with a no less strong desire also to flee the American 'burden of conformism' (1971: 103). That Adorno should find America to be as damaging to his 'language and being' as Nazi Germany is not surprising, given Adorno's conviction that capitalist America is an equally 'totalitarian' system that has managed and processed all differences out of existence. Like fascism, the exchange economy of capitalism operates according to a logic of identity that strives to suppress all contradictions and differences.[19] Both systems are 'revolted by the sight of otherness, of that which threatens to escape its own closed system' (Eagleton, 1991: 126). Whereas Fascism responds to otherness by eliminating it, capitalism 'violently reduces it [otherness] to its own image and likeness' (Eagleton, 1991: 126).[20]

The other which refuses to be totally silenced, returning to haunt the system's will-to-closure, is well captured by the image of the Jew. As Martin Jay puts it, the Jews become for the first generation Frankfurt School thinkers 'the metaphoric equivalent of that remnant of society preserving negation and the non-identical':

> The Jews, in other words and in their very refusal to be assimilated, represent an obstacle to the total integration of the 'administered world' or 'one-dimensional society', as Marcuse was to call it. (1980: 148)[21]

In a similar spirit, Adorno pays homage to foreign words – the 'Jews of language' – for effecting 'a beneficial interruption of the conformist moment of language' (1991c: 189) and for validating individual experience against the objectifying force of reified consciousness:

> When language confronts the language-forming subject as something objective, the subject forces its own impulses through, in opposition to language, in words that are not subject to language, words it mobilizes in opposition to linguistic convention, however rigidly conventional those words may be when one meets them in everyday language. *Foreign words become the bearers of subjective contents*: of the nuances. The meanings in one's own language may well correspond to the meanings of the foreign word in every case; but they cannot be arbitrarily replaced by them because the expression of subjectivity cannot simply be dissolved in meaning. (1991b: 287; added emphasis)

Not unlike Lacan's idea of the Real which cannot be contained by the symbolic order, foreign words as Adorno conceives them explode the reification and ontologization of language by disrupting conventions of language and meaning. The decompletion of the big Other opens a space for the 'expression of subjectivity' and for the preservation of 'the social force of liberation' in face of 'the totalitarian unison, with which the eradication of difference is proclaimed as a purpose in itself' (Adorno, 1974: 18).[22]

While the subject finds a refuge in foreign words, those who fall victim to the ideology of linguistic purity are no longer subjects but 'objects of manipulation':

> A critique of foreign words that mistakenly considers itself progressive serves a communicative ideal that is in actuality an ideal of manipulation; today the word that is designed to be understood becomes, precisely through this process of calculation, a means to degrade those to whom it is addressed to mere objects of manipulation and to harness them for purposes that are not their own, not objectively binding. (1991c: 191)[23]

Adorno's insistence on preserving the individual's 'integrity' along with his/her claim to a 'rational indissolubility in language' and in society (1991b: 287) is no doubt closely connected to his negative dialectics which uphold non-identity as a process of concrete negation, and propose 'the preservation of the enclaves of negation' as 'the best to be hoped for in the present world' (Jay, 1980: 149). Foreign words, modern art and the Jews are all symbols of non-identity resisting the exchange process, bureaucracy and the culture industry. Much Like Horkheimer's understanding of Critical Theory as 'the Jew' of the administered society, Adorno's dictum that 'Foreign words are the Jews of language' affirms the critical function of the non-identical.

Fremdwörter *and the exile's refusal to assimilate*

By remaining untranslated and untranslatable, Adorno's *Fremdwörter* constitute a politics of refusal – that is, a refusal to conform and assimilate. Contrary to common sense, Adorno does not think that German nationalists and the German immigrants eager to assimilate into American culture are in opposition to each other. Rather, nationalists easily become immigrants ready to adapt themselves to a new nation when circumstances require, since both of them subscribe to the logic of conformity:

> People who conform, who generally feel comfortable with the given environment and its power relations, always adapt more easily in the new country. Here a nationalist, there a nationalist. Anyone who, as a matter of principle, is never completely in agreement with the state of things and not predisposed to playing along also remains oppositional in the new country. (Adorno, 1985: 126)

In a similar spirit, Adorno's reading of 'Aldous Huxley and utopia' (1967: 85–118) criticizes the intellectual *émigrés* for their obsequious drive for successful adjustment. Their 'interests of self-preservation', he says, are 'stronger than those of preserving the self' (1967: 97). For Adorno, 'the True and the Better in every people is much more likely that which does *not* adapt itself to the collective subject but, wherever possible, even resists it' (1985: 121). Adorno's preoccupation with *Fremdwörter* can be understood in the light of Said's description of the exile who 'clutch[es] difference like a weapon to be used with stiffened will', thereby 'jealously insist[ing] on his or her right to refuse to belong' (Said, 1990: 363).[24]

For Adorno, objections to *Fremdwörter* raised by both the purists in Germany and the immigrants who have assimilated themselves to American culture can be traced primarily to 'a defense against ideas, which are imputed to the words'. To prove his point, Adorno cites his experience in the United States delivering a lecture in which all foreign words had been carefully deleted; despite this precaution, he was still criticized for sounding foreign (1991c: 185). According to Adorno's logic, complaints made by Americans against the linguistically alien betray the hypocrisy of the 'spokesmen of unitary tolerance' who are 'always ready to turn intolerantly on any group that remains refractory' (1974: 103). Indeed, Adorno does not hesitate to call the editorial policy of a psychoanalytic journal in San Francisco a 'machine' to whose 'universal technique of adaptation' those without power will 'have to submit'.[25]

Adorno's criticism of the ideology of adjustment no doubt goes hand in hand with his aversion to the 'reified, bureaucratized, administered world of advanced capitalism' (Eagleton, 1991: 127) – a world that 'adjusts' all distinct phenomena to the homogenizing exchange principle. In a rather strange way, however, Adorno seems to consider the 'nature' of commodity as intrinsic to the English language itself. In a piece called 'English Spoken' from *Minima Moralia*, Adorno describes his childhood reaction to the English picture books given him by some elderly British ladies. Even though he had no understanding of English at the time, he immediately linked the language to blatant commercialism:

> The peculiar inaccessibility of the books, with their glaring pictures, titles and vignettes, and their indecipherable text, filled me with the belief that objects of this kind were not books at all, but *advertisements* . . . (Adorno, 1974: 47; added emphasis)

Adorno even congratulates himself on having the 'truth' of his intuition confirmed later by his experience living in English-speaking cultures: 'Since I came to live in Anglo-Saxon countries and to understand English, this awareness has not been dispelled but strengthened' (ibid.).

By contrast, Adorno never associates commercialism with the German language. To appropriate Eagleton's expression, if advanced capitalism is guilty of 'transmut[ing] the uniqueness and plurality of things into a mere simulacrum of itself', Adorno can be taken to task for expelling his American other 'beyond [his] own borders in a panic-stricken act of exclusion' (Eagleton, 1991: 126).

'Das Eigene' is already 'das Fremde', and 'das Fremde' reverts to 'Das Eigene': the restricted economy of Adorno's politics of exile[26]

Two kinds of Fremdwörter, *or two faces of the other: the sacred and the profane*

Even though *Fremdwörter* have often been idealized by Adorno, in practice one can detect in his writings two varieties of foreign words treated by the author respectively with veneration and contempt.

In 'Alien Words' Adorno points out that foreign terms '[illuminate] something true of all words: that language imprisons those who speak it, that as a medium of their own it has essentially failed' (1991b: 189). However, if most foreign expressions are employed by Adorno to highlight the limits and inadequacy of the (German) national idiom, English words are, by contrast, often used as vivid tableaux that stage the peculiar 'absurdity' of Anglo-American culture – a phenomenon for which one can find 'no possible German equivalent'. The Anglicisms and Americanisms in Adorno's works make up a striking list of cultural stereotypes.[27] Terms like 'teamwork', 'best-seller', 'healthy sex life' and 'likes and dislikes' are consistently left in the original in Adorno's texts, drawing attention to the alien character of such concepts and expressions to the German culture. In so doing, *Adorno's own practice ironically turns English words into 'the Jews of language' – or, to expropriate his expression elsewhere – it is Adorno who makes English terms into 'language's scapegoat'* (1991c: 189; added emphasis).

The 'profane' English language finds its 'sacred' counterpart in other foreign words used by Adorno – primarily French, Latin, Italian and Greek. However, even the latter group of *Fremdwörter* are not unproblematic. As much as Adorno talks about the non-identical, critical function of foreign words, he does not always choose them to obstruct unreflected affirmation or to prohibit premature positivity. At times, Adorno's fascination with foreign expressions resembles a superficial longing for exotic women:

> since language is erotically charged in its words, at least for the kind of person who is capable of expression, love drives us to foreign words. In reality, it is that love that sets off the indignation over their use. The early craving for foreign words is like the craving for foreign and if possible exotic girls; what lures us is a kind of exogamy of language, which would like to escape from the sphere of what is always the same, the spell of what one is and knows anyway. (1991c: 187)

The sexist and racist overtones of this passage become even more disturbing when read alongside Adorno's '*On parle français*', (1974: 27) where he describes the *im*-mediate, instinctive feel foreign language allows for understanding pornography. Here, Adorno's eroticization of foreign language by attributing to it a mysterious power which grants immediate access to meaning contradicts and undermines his usual valorization of foreign words for their resistance to the ideology of immediacy:

> How intimately sex and language are intertwined can be seen by reading pornography in a foreign language. When de Sade is read in the original no dictionary is needed. The most recondite expressions for the indecent, knowledge of which no school, no parental home, no literary experience transmits, are understood with the instinctive feel of a sleepwalker [*nachtwandelnd*], just as in childhood the most tangential utterances and observations concerning the sexual crystallize into a true representation. (1974: 48/53; translation modified)

In other words, Adorno himself has made a fetish of foreign words.[28]

Ironically, despite Adorno's glamorization of foreign words, it is ultimately German that turns out for him to be the 'most sacred' of all languages – that is, the language with an undefined, almost mystical character that allows it to 'express something about phenomena that does not exhaust itself in their mere this-ness, their positivity and given-ness' and as such best captures the 'speculative element' of philosophy (1985: 129). And it is to this language that Adorno must return after his exile. *Fremdwörter*, be they sacred or profane, in the end amount to being merely two faces of 'the other'. It is the *self-presencing* of the German language, rather than 'the other', that calls Adorno back to his 'home(-land)'.

The 'special character' of the German language

Adorno opens his 1965 Hessische Rundfunk lecture 'On the Question: "What is German?"' by rejecting the 'reified consciousness' of 'national collectivities' (1985: 121). At the same time, however, he mentions language as an 'objective factor' compelling his return to Germany:

> The decision to return to Germany. . . . There was an *objective* factor. It is *the language. . . . [T]he German language seems to have a special elective affinity for philosophy* and especially for its speculative element [*Moment*] which is so easily distrusted in the West as dangerously unclear – and not entirely without justification. Historically, in a process which has yet to be seriously analyzed, the German language has acquired the capacity to express something about phenomena which does not exhaust itself in their mere this-ness, their positivity and given-ness. (1985: 129; added emphasis)

Despite his cautions against an uncritical hypostatization of the 'speculative element' in German language and metaphysics, Adorno's belief in the 'special elective affinity' between the German language and philosophy makes him an ally, at least on this issue, of his enemies Hegel and, above all, Heidegger. Adorno is just as enthusiastic about the uniqueness of the German language as the other two great ontologizers of the German language:

> German is not merely the signification of fixed meanings; rather it has retained more of the power of expression, in any case, than would be attributed to Western

languages by someone who did not grow up in them, for whom they are not second nature. But whoever is convinced that . . . what is essential to philosophy is the mode of presentation . . . will gravitate to the German language. . . . [T]he impossibility of non-violently transposing into another language not only highly developed speculative thoughts but even particular and quite precise concepts such as those of spirit [*Geist*], the element [*Moment*], and experience [*Erfahrung*], with all the connotations with which they resonate in German – this impossibility suggests that there is a specific, objective quality of the German language. (1985: 129–30)

It is the untranslatability of certain German concepts and idioms that confirms the special character of the German national idiom, and compels Adorno to return to Germany. Returning to the 'homeland' of the German language, Adorno claims, is necessary in order to 'spare' himself an uncomprehending audience and the violent editing of his writing by American publishers.[29] Adorno the committed defender of *Fremdwörter* – of those 'heterogeneous fragments that slip through the conceptual net' (Jay, 1984: 178) – ends up reinscribing himself within an idealist economy that privileges identity over non-identity as he espouses the ideologies of expressive self-presencing and unproblematic intersubjective communication associated with the 'native tongue':

In one's own language, however, were one only to say something as exactly and as uncompromisingly as possible, one might also hope through such relentless effort to become understandable as well. In the domain of one's own language, it is this very language which stands in for one's fellow human beings. (Adorno, 1985: 130)

In spite of his concern for 'preserving the subject' (1967: 97), Adorno also becomes implicated in the 'national collectivities' (1985: 121) the moment he believes that his 'own' language can allow him to fully articulate his thoughts as well as to unproblematically 'share the world' with those speaking his own tongue. In Lacanian terms, if immigrants who too readily give up their subjectivity to their host culture are alienated in the undivided big Other, Adorno's subjectivity suffers a similar fate at the precise moment he believes his 'native' tongue grants him the happy coincidence of thought and expression.[30]

Adorno's inability to separate himself from the big Other is not without political ramifications. He deliberately avoids a traditional ontological approach to the question 'What is German?' and addresses instead the subject matter obliquely, via a detour through the 'nature' of the German language. Nonetheless, his talk still ends up as a mere recasting of the question of nationality as an issue of language. The reason is, in order to trace the contours of the German language, one must establish the 'foreign' against which the 'character' and 'identity' of a national idiom can be defined. In the same way, one cannot map out the boundaries of a nation except by delineating it against other countries. Adorno cannot avoid duplicating the structure of a national territory in his tracing of a linguistic territory. In fact, the history of Adorno's exile and return is telling evidence of the impossibility of separating linguistic nationality from political geography and the boundaries of the nation-state. Despite his misgivings about nationalism, Adorno finds it impossible to return to the German language without returning to Germany the nation. The *home-land* of his language is also the country where he feels 'at *home*' with himself. The non-conforming Adorno, who insists that he is at home in neither the old world nor the new, ultimately re-cognizes Germany to be a 'home' for both his 'language and being'.[31]

The dialectic between 'das Fremde' and 'das Eigene': Adorno's return to his linguistic homeland

Upon a first reading of 'On the question: "What is German?" ', it would be easy to dismiss Adorno's neglect of the intimate relationship between language, culture and nationalism as his blindspot or a gesture of bad faith. It would be tempting, for example, to fault Adorno for failing to understand that nationalism can never be reduced to self-consciously held political ideologies. Or, to borrow Benedict Anderson's expression, one could say that Adorno has avoided confronting the alignment between nationalism and 'the large cultural systems that preceded it, out of which – as well as against which – it came into being' (Anderson, 1983: 19; see also Bhabha, 1990: 1ff.). However, what makes Adorno's case so puzzling is precisely his apparent sensitivity on other occasions to the danger of fetishizing one's own language and culture – a sensitivity evident in his relentless attacks on jargons of authenticity and on ideas of 'German *property*' and 'cultural *property*' (1985: 122; added emphasis).

Why, then, given his critical awareness, should Adorno still insist on the unique 'property' of the German language which inevitably evokes ideas not only of cultural but also of national boundaries and boundedness? In arguing for the 'fundamentals' of the German language, isn't Adorno guilty of – to borrow David Morley and Kevin Robins's expression – protecting 'exclusive, and therefore, excluding, identities against those who are seen as aliens and "foreigners" ' (1990: 5)? To further complicate the case, in the same essay where Adorno discusses the 'elective affinity for philosophy' of the German language (1985: 126), he begins by speaking, in a spirit very similar to Morley and Robins's, against a narrow-minded glorification of 'one's own group' and its correlative exclusion of the alien:

> The fabrication of stereotypes . . . promotes collective narcissism. Those qualities with which one identifies oneself – the essence of one's own group – imperceptibly become the Good; the foreign group, the others, Bad. (1985: 121)

Considering Adorno's passionate criticism of exclusionism, and his enthusiastic defence of foreign words, what could possibly explain his vehement repudiation of the other – as he does with his long-standing rejection of American culture as incomprehensible to the European mind? Instead of hastily brushing aside the various inconsistencies in Adorno's theory and practice as mere naivety or a want of philosophical rigour, I would prefer to examine the ways Adorno contradicts himself *in spite of*, and perhaps even *because of*, his sophisticated critical theory and cultural criticism. Specifically, I will examine the uncanny way Adorno seems to get caught up in the same dialectic that, according to his argument elsewhere, binds myth and enlightenment into a vicious cycle. He escapes through his critical vigilance the ideology of 'home(-land)' only to be entrapped by it anew because, to expropriate Adorno's own expression, his valorization of foreign words 'already contains the seed of [its] reversal' (1972: xiii). Which is to say, '*das Eigene*' is already '*das Fremde*', and '*das Fremde*' reverts to '*das Eigene*'.

'Breaching the limit' ('*Franchir la limite*') versus 'crossing the border': 'the step beyond' and the politics of exile from exile[32]

'*Internal limit*' versus '*external boundary*'

In 'On the question: "What is German?" ', Adorno ascribes his decision to return to a sense of 'continuity and loyalty to one's own past'. In his account, he '*simply* wanted to go back to where I had spent my childhood, to where whatever was most specifically mine was mediated to the core' (1985: 126; added emphasis). In other words, he postulates an unproblematic past to which he can 'simply' return, and a point of origin with which he can re-establish his 'continuity'.[33] Interestingly enough, even his idea of 'mediation' is itself unmediated, as he assumes uncritically that in his 'homeland' 'whatever was most specifically [his]' was necessarily 'mediated to the core'.

Against the very specific contours of 'that which is specifically mine' ('*das Eigene*') we find the no less fetishized concept of '*das Fremde*' in Adorno's writings. Adorno refers to the explosive force of *Fremdwörter* (1991a: 286), as if there were a generic *Fremdwort* that challenged the 'ontology of language' (1991c: 189) and prevented unreflected affirmation of society (1991b: 289). Even as Adorno insists on opposing ideology with the differential and non-identical, he himself hastily collapses particularities into a general category.

As a result, Adorno has a rather positivized and self-contained notion of *Fremdwörter* on the one hand, and of the German language on the other. Adorno's critical thinking thus lapses into ideology, as his emphasis on foreign words as the embodiments of heterogeneity is undermined by his inability to see how difference also 'differ[s] from itself' (Derrida, 1973: 129). To deny this difference internal to the different – or the foreignness internal to the foreign – is to revert to thinking in terms of identity. The problem is that difference without self-distancing implies the possibility of becoming identical with – or, in Derrida's terms, 'fully present to' – itself.

Because of his obliviousness to the difference within the different, or the foreignness within the foreign, Adorno stops short of taking into account the ways '*das Fremde*' is always already inhabited by '*das Eigene*', and vice versa, since the two fields cannot be defined except with reference to one another. What is missing from Adorno's theory is the fact that heterogeneity is not merely a matter of defining the other *externally* to the self, nor simply an assertion of the foreign as that which exists outside the boundaries of the German language. Rather, there is a *limit* or an otherness internal to language *per se* – that is, an opposition internal to both foreign words and words of one's native tongue – by which language turns against its own fulfilment. 'Foreignness' is by no means a private property of *Fremdwörter*. Rather, *language is always already in exile from itself*. Derrida's comment in *Aporias* on the ambiguity of the word *hôte* helps dislodge language from itself by pointing out the mutually dependent relations between the self and the other, the host and the guest:[34]

> Babelization does not therefore wait for the multiplicity of languages. The identity of a language can only affirm itself as identical to itself by opening itself to the hospitality of a difference from itself or of a difference with itself. Condition of the self, such a difference *from* and *with* itself would then be its very thing, the *pragma* of its pragmatics: the stranger at home,[35] the invited or the one who is called. The *at home* [*chez-soi*] as the host's gift recalls a being at home [*chez-soi*] (*being at home, homely, heimisch, heimlich*) that is given by a hospitality more ancient than the inhabitant himself. As though the inhabitant himself were always staying in the inhabitant's home, the one who invites and receives truly begins by receiving hospitality from the guest to whom he thinks he is giving hospitality. (Derrida, 1993: 10)

Derrida's discussion deconstructs the 'autonomy' of both '*das Eigene*' and '*das Fremde*'. The identity of any language – be it foreign or native -'can only affirm itself by opening itself to the hospitality of a difference from itself or of a difference with itself'. That is to say, one must move beyond an idea of '*das Fremde*' which is identical to itself to a politics of the foreign which is itself inhabited by a foreignness that prevents it from being positivized into an objective entity called 'the foreign'.

The 'Other' versus the 'other': a challenge to Adorno's nostalgic negative dialectics

Other post-structuralist perspectives can also help elucidate problems in Adorno's thought. Jean-François Lyotard, for example, points out that nostalgia for a lost totality permeates even a negative dialectics. In addition to Adorno's explicit association of foreign words with a lost plenitude,[36] there is another more subtle nostalgia supporting the straight distinctions he makes between '*das Fremde*' and '*das Eigene*'. Lurking behind his self-enclosed categories of '*das Eigene*' and '*das Fremde*' is a yearning for, and even a belief in, some originary coherence and unity capable of binding distinct speech phenomena into clearly separated language groups.[37] What Adorno does not realize is that this originary plenitude or, in Lacanian terms, the 'good object' (whether in the form of a non-lacking self or a complete other), is 'impossible' because it is always already lost. Failure to recognize the void opened by the lost object results in Adorno's inability to register what Lacan would refer to as the heterogeneous structure of desire or guilt. Lacan discusses desire in terms of 'the desire of the Other'.[38] In the language of Samuel Weber, desire is 'constitutively involved in a debt that can never be entirely effaced' (1993: 140). Adorno misses the critical possibilities opened up by such a radical heterogeneity when he dwells on the external oppositions between languages rather than pursuing 'the foreign' always already inhabiting any/all language.

To acknowledge the foreign as the truly foreign entails appreciating an Other within the other – a third term that exceeds the dual economy governing the self and the other. Adorno's *Fremdwort* occasionally lapses into an exotic other – sometimes sacred, sometimes profane – because, failing to acknowledge a third term which is radically other to both 'the native' and 'the other', his schema is locked into an imaginary binary opposition between '*das Fremde*' and '*das Eigene*'. To resolve this impasse, it would be instructive to look at Lacan's critical revision of Kojève. Like Kojève, Adorno does not distinguish between the 'other' and the 'Other'. Lacan disrupts an intersubjective (or binary) notion of desire by 'unleashing' a new level of difference at the moment when he seems to be repeating Kojève's formulation 'man's desire is the desire of the other'. As Charles Shepherdson points out, Lacan's rewriting of Kojève's formulation into 'man's desire is the desire of the *O*ther' (with a capital 'O') 'takes the entire analysis out of the domain of intersubjective rivalry and places it in a triangulated structure, governed by the logic of the symbolic order (the Other)' (1999: 9). The 'Other' cannot be understood in intersubjective terms, since, according to Lacan, the Other's presence 'can only be understood at a *second degree of otherness*, which situates him from the very start in the position of *mediating between me and the double of myself*' (1977: 172/524; Shepherdson's translation and italics).

It is the absence of this second degree of otherness that allows Adorno's '*das Fremde*' and '*das Eigene*' to remain self-contained categories. Lacanian desire, by contrast, can never have such a calm presence. As Lacan tells us in 'Subversion of the Subject and Dialectic of Desire in the Freudian Unconscious', 'it is precisely because desire is articulated that it is not articulable' (1977: 302/804).[39] As such, desire can never be recuperated into the economy of the selfsame. Seen in the light of the heterogeneous structure of desire, neither 'the foreign' nor 'the native' tongue can be traced back to an originary plenitude. In 'The Direction of the Treatment', Lacan explicitly points out that desire is both 'produced in the beyond of demand' and 'hollowed within the demand' (1977: 265 and 629). As the 'essentially unspeakable, the "unsaid" or the half-said (*le mit-dit*)' haunting the discourse of the ego (Shepherdson, 1999: 10), the Lacanian concept of desire opens a space for thinking of a foreignness that continues to evade the regimentation of any symbolic category.[40]

When theorizing about '*das Fremde*', Adorno does not demonstrate a sensitivity toward the radically foreign. He remains unaware of 'the relation of the symbolic to the real'. Which is to say, he is unmindful of the 'symbolic "containment" of lack' (Shepherdson, 1999: 19).[41] By opposing 'the foreign' *externally* to 'the German', Adorno domesticates 'the awareness of the Other' into an 'awareness of others'.[42] This is why, despite the special role the *Fremdwort* assumes in Adorno's writings as a concrete embodiment of mediation, it occasionally lapses into a mere fetish of immediacy, or else becomes a mysterious, alien object from the realm of the sacred or the profane. Adorno has failed, in other words, to take the step *beyond* a mere crossing of boundaries or borders to 'breaching the limit'[43] – a '*franchissement*' that would reverse without return the identity of the other into the Other of identity. Only by embracing the Real within the symbolic can one preserve the perpetual otherness of the other. And only then will it be possible for foreign words to 'stick out' (Adorno, 1991c: 187) and to remain 'unassimilated' (1991c: 187) as Adorno wants foreign words to be.[44]

'Antagonism' versus 'contradiction'

In fact, despite Adorno's hypostatization of *Fremdwörter*, there are also occasions when he senses the radically foreign dimension of foreign words – a new level of difference that would enable them to resist absolutely the purists' sophisticated programme of integration. Take, for example, the special attention Adorno pays to the artificiality of foreign words. By asserting their artificiality, foreign words interrupt the easy flow of 'meaning' and resist being neutralized by the machinery that collapses difference into the organic history of language:

> the hard, artificial, unyielding foreign words whose life intersects the sphere of nuance for only a moment; the words that do not yield, do not even carry the expression of their own past . . . (1991b: 288)

Like Lacan's 'Thing', foreign words as Adorno envisions them here cannot be so easily made transparent.[45] There is a 'little piece' of subjectivity subsisting in *Fremdwörter* which cannot be glossed over by the 'organic flow' of one's native tongue, nor can it be exchanged for meaning.[46] *Fremdwörter* operating in this manner can be as unyielding as the Lacanian Real to the exchange economy:

> The meanings in one's own language may well correspond to the meanings of the foreign words in every case; but they cannot be arbitrarily replaced by them because the expression of subjectivity cannot simply be dissolved in meaning. (1991b: 287)

This way, *Fremdwörter* 'insist' as 'foreign bodies assailing the body of language' (1991b: 288).[47] In Lacanese, the *Fremdwort* in its radical otherness is a 'perpetually alien element' that cannot be assimilated into the host language. Like the unconscious, the foreign word remains as 'the "unspeakable" dimension of desire, the "symbolic debris" that disrupts the narrative of the ego' (Shepherdson, 1999: 10).

The resemblance between Adorno and Lacan, nonetheless, turns out to be superficial. Take, for example, Adorno's discussion of foreign words as an indicator of suffering in both language and reality (1991c: 187–8). Suffering is also a condition pertaining to the Lacanian structure of desire – the lack barring both the Subject and the Other, for instance. However, it is important to bear in mind that for Lacan the split is constitutive of the human subject and as such can never be erased.[48] Adorno, by contrast, believes that suffering is a historical product and can be alleviated along with improved social conditions. In 'Alien Words', for example, Adorno alludes to the disparity between the foreign word and 'the body of language' as merely the 'historical evidence . . . of the failure of that unification'. This leads him to trivialize Nazism as an attempt to 'force a bourgeois integration of Germany that had not taken place':

> Benjamin spoke of the author inserting the silver rib of the foreign word into the body of language. *What seems inorganic here is in actuality only historical evidence, evidence of the failure of that unification.* Such disparateness means not only suffering in language, and what Hebbel called the 'Schism of creation,' but suffering in reality as well. From this perspective Nazism may be regarded as a . . . deadly attempt to force a bourgeois integration of Germany that had not taken place. (1991c: 187–8; added emphasis)

Here, one can begin to grasp why Adorno's foreign words can be recuperated into the economy of the selfsame, and why his advocacy of critical heterogeneity reverts to an ideology of identity. Adorno dreams of a better society where 'the two spheres of language' can be reconciled. In other words, Adorno grants the possibility of a state of society wherein tension between the foreign and the native can be 'done away with':

> The isolated position of foreign words could not be *done away with* through the restitution of an integral language but only *by society*, which names itself along with things. But then it is not the foreign word, the dead-tired messenger from the future kingdom of language, that is replaced by the quasi-natural and historically inappropriate word; instead, the tension between the two spheres of language in which we exist today can prove productive, and the two spheres can move closer to one another in the use of a ready, serviceable terminology. (1991b: 290; added emphasis)

Adorno thus neutralizes the Other by turning it into a product of social contradiction when antagonism is, in fact, ineliminable.[49] While the Other is always already beside itself, in and of itself, Adorno would recognize the foreignness of foreign words as merely contingent, externally caused by deficient social conditions.[50]

In order to break through such a circumscribed notion of the 'foreign'[51] Adorno would need to exceed the restricted economy of *exile versus home(-land)* and instantiate a politics of *exile from exile*. Such a politics would move him away from determination to overdetermination, from positivized notions of '*das Fremde*' and '*das Eigene*' to an uncontainable, non-phenomenal 'Other' and a radical Alterity that would remain in perpetual flight before any kind of formalization.[52]

'Breaching the limit' versus 'crossing the border': beyond Adorno's politics of exile

What is at stake in the leap from a politics of *exile* to a politics of *exile from exile* is a struggle to go beyond *an exile with the possibility of returning* to *an exile without return*.[53] This is the leap which marks, in the language of Levinas, a radical reversal of the possibility of impossibility into the impossibility of possibility. While the exile without return 'breaches the limit', the exile which contains the possibility of an (imaginary) return merely 'crosses the borders'. Return in the latter case is possible because the border is, as Derrida puts it, an 'indivisible line'. The line institutes an (imaginary) origin from which one has been exiled and to which one, under favourable circumstances, can return:

> The crossing of borders always announces itself according to the movement of a certain step [*pas*] – and of the step that crosses a line. An indivisible line. And one always assumes the institution of such an indivisibility. Customs, police, visa or passport, passenger identification – all of that is established upon this institution of the indivisible, the institution therefore of the step that is related to it, whether the step crosses it or not. (Derrida, 1993: 11)

'Breaching the limit', on the other hand, is a 'crossing' that originates in a violation of crossing. Such an act, in the words of Samuel Weber, would be performed upon 'a limit whose origin is a delimitation' (1993: 146). This would be the moment when the 'indivisible line' described by Derrida 'divides the relation to itself of the border and therefore divides the being-one-self of anything' (Derrida, 1993: 11). As such, the exile from exile can be compared to the Sadean 'second death'. The Sadean 'death beyond death' is a crime against nature which subverts the 'natural' opposition of, and even the distinction between, death and life.[54] Likewise, the exile from exile unequivocally disrupts the facile opposition between '*das Fremde*' and '*das Eigene*'. What emerges from such an exile-of-excess is, in Lacanian terms, a movement of 'outrage' that breaches all limits.[55]

This way, the exile from exile, like Žižek's 'sacrifice of sacrifice', brings us to 'the "zero point" of the symbolic suicide' (Žižek, 1990: 33). The exile from exile assumes a particular significance for ethics and politics since, as Žižek tells us, 'the *act* in the Lacanian sense is nothing but this withdrawal by means of which we *renounce renunciation itself* (1990: 33). Exile in its restricted economy still has a 'homeland' as its point of reference and as its addressee even in its renunciation of home.[56] The exile-of-excess, on the other hand, abandons beyond retrieval 'home' as the 'master of signification'[57] – that is, the abandonment of the Master whose very presence assures that any kind of exile and digression will ultimately obtain meaning and consistency by imposing a retroactive temporal schema.[58] The exile-without-reserve hence facilitates a separation (in the Lacanian sense) of the subject not only from the Master-Other but also from itself whose identity is guaranteed by the undivided Other.

In the politics of exile from exile, or the abandonment of abandonment, the Master-Other or the home(-land) which is being abandoned is discovered to be totally null in itself and hence already in exile. The exile-of-excess thus decentres and puts into exile not only the subject, but also the big Other. It displaces the relationship between the two in such a way as to put the imaginary-originary 'homeland' in motion, giving it a movement which is a movement of disintegration, of fragmentation, and of permanent exile with no return. This way, 'homeland', or that which is supposedly one's own, emerges as the bottomless depths of displacement and alienation. In other words, the exile-without-reserve dispossesses and undoes the idea of homeland in a way that reveals homeland to be always already dispossessed. It reveals how exile – seemingly a deviance from one's 'original habitat' – itself reveals a more primary deviance and a more deep-seated dispossession always already there at 'home'.[59] In so doing, the exile from exile brings about a dis-membrance of membership in linguistic nationality, and a defamiliarization of the 'family' of people supposedly 'belonging' to the same national language.

In sum, what is at stake in this chapter is a 'limit' upon which Adorno's politics of writing as an act of exile and a crossing of frontiers calls for critical re-examination. One can of course challenge Adorno's binary opposition of '*das Fremde*' and '*das Eigene*' from a perspective parallel to the one held, for example, by Guy Scarpetta, for whom 'every language is a foreign one, for which *the* language doesn't exist' (1981: 183). However, a position such as Kafka's seems to come even closer to the uttermost 'limit' – as when Kafka abandons explicitly expressions of 'possibility' and transforms instead the writing of the dispossessed into marks of 'impossibility'.[60] Deleuze and Guattari succinctly observe that 'Kafka marks the impasse that bars access to writing for the Jews of Prague and turns their literature into something impossible, the impossibility of not writing, the impossibility of writing in German, the impossibility of writing otherwise' (1986: 16). Deleuze and Guattari also discern in Kafka the ways in which the impossibility of writing for the dispossessed in turn 'deterritorializes' the German population and dispossesses the Master-Other. Kafka's writings, in other words, are an example of how to 'camp on the limit' or 'camp out on the breach', from which one can begin to displace Adorno's nostalgia with a love that is outside the limits of the law.[61]

Notes

1 Throughout this paper, the first page number refers to the translation, the second page number to the original. For this particular passage, I have chosen to adopt Martin Jay's translation provided in his essay 'Adorno in America' (1984: 182). Adorno's observation that 'homelessness has been inflicted on everyone' finds a sympathetic echo in Said's remark in 'Zionism from the Standpoint of its Victims' (1979) about the 'generalized condition of homelessness' in the twentieth century. Interestingly enough, Adorno's comment that 'All in language and being, have been damaged as the exile himself was', also predates contemporary anthropology and ethnography's move beyond examining exile as physical movements of people to exploring the cultural displacements of people, things and cultural products. See, for example, James Clifford's *The Predicament of Culture* (1988).

2 The original goes as follows: '*Fremdwörter sind die Juden der Sprache.*'

3 For a substantial period of time, Adorno and Horkheimer regarded fascism as the perverted truth of capitalism. See, for example, the *Dialectic of Enlightenment*, where they claim that 'anyone who subscribes to the destruction of the trade unions and the crusade against Bolshevism . . . automatically subscribes also to the destruction of the Jews' (1972: 201). The equation of fascism with liberal/capitalist regimes was actually common to the majority of the early members of the Frankfurt School. Leo Löwenthal, for instance, makes the following observation:

> modern anti-Semitism and the culture industry were in the final analysis part and parcel of the same social configuration, even if they may occasionally serve different political functions. What they have in common is the blockage of genuine experience that was paradigmatically apparent for us in the encounter with art. (1991: 180)

4 Adorno's writings are filled at various times with Italian, French, English, Latin, Greek and German expressions. The titles of the aphorisms in *Minima Moralia*, for instance, are indicative of the frequency and variety of foreign words in Adorno's works.

See 'On the Use of Foreign Words', where Adorno explains the pertinence of foreign words as 'an expression of alienation':

> The more alienated human beings have become from their things in society, the more strange are the words that will have to represent them if they are to reach them and to indicate allegorically that the things have been brought home. The more deeply society is cleft by the contradiction between its quasi-natural and its rational character the more isolated will foreign words necessarily remain in the arena of language, *incomprehensible* to one group of human beings and *threatening* to the other; and yet they have their legitimacy as an *expression of alienation itself*, and also as the transparent crystals that may at some future time *explode human beings' dreary imprisonment in preconceived language.* (1991b: 289; added emphasis)

5 Levin further adds to his list H. Stuart Hughes's findings of Anglicisms and Americanisms in Adorno's sociological writings (1985: 116, n.6).

6 See especially his *Authoritarian Personality* and his essay, 'On the Question: "What is German?" ' In the latter, Adorno even draws attention to critical theory's mission to fight stereotypes:

The fabrication of national collectivities . . . common practice in the abominable jargon of war which speaks of the Russian, the American, and certainly also of the German – is the mark of a *reified consciousness* hardly capable of experience [*Erfahrung*]. Such fabrication remains within precisely those *stereotypes which it is the task of thinking to dissolve.* (1985: 121; added emphasis)

7 See especially his 'Scientific Experiences of a European Scholar in America' (1968).

8 This expression is appropriated from Habermas's 'Entwinement of Myth and Enlightenment' (1982).

9 Thomas Levin comments that 'foreign terms [serve] as jarring reminders that no language [is] a self-contained system, nor, moreover, should it be' (1985).

10 Adorno shares Benjamin's apprehensions about myths of organic unity. The following passage taken from 'On the Use of Foreign Words' is, in both language and content, very much reminiscent of Benjamin's works on the subject. See, for example, 'Goethe's *Elective Affinities*', 'Critique of Violence' (in Benjamin, 1978) and 'The Task of the Translator' (1955).

11 I modify Shierry Weber's translation to 'Alien Words' in order to better preserve the idea of '*das/die Fremde*' in the original title. In observance of English linguistic conventions, I have, however, chosen to use the term 'foreign words' rather than 'alien words' in my own discourse.

12 The expression *die Wunde Juden* is coined after Adorno's '*Die Wunde Heine*'. The terms 'exist' and 'insist' are derived from Lacan's *Encore Seminar* (1998).

13 This is a saying by George Steiner (quoted from Said, 1990: 357).

14 As early as May 1933, Wilhelm Frick, Minister of the Interior, proposed a programme of 'New Education' at a conference of ministers of state governments:

Our mother tongue, whose harmony, power and flexibility we can be proud of, belongs to the noblest of values, whose preservation lies close to our hearts. Unfortunately, its purity is not always cared for as much as is desirable. Even government offices employ superfluous *Fremdwörter*, which plainly endanger the comprehension of language among wide sections of the people. The school has in this respect important tasks to fulfil so that we can hand down the precious treasure of the German language pure and unadulterated. (Noakes and Pridham, 1974: 352; Michaelis, 1956–79: 445–6)

15 The way in which the other returns to the subject the truth of the latter's message in its inverted form is examined at length in the four graphs put forward by Lacan in his 'Subversion of the Subject and the Dialectic of Desire in the Freudian Unconscious' (in Lacan, 1977).

16 It is no surprise that Edward Said, the 'grandfather' of post-colonial studies, is a great admirer of Adorno.

17 'No language . . . is organic and natural': this idea is explored in depth by Benjamin in 'Task of the translator' (1955: 69–82).

18 It is very likely that in this extract Adorno is echoing Benjamin's famous dictum in 'Thesis on the Philosophy of History': 'There is no document of civilization which is not at the same time a document of barbarism' (1955: 258).

19 As if to pre-empt possible objections to his equation of fascism with capitalism, Adorno makes the following argument:

There is no need to deny the difference between a so-called culture of the spirit and a technological culture in order to rise nonetheless above a mindless juxtaposition of the two. A utilitarian lifestyle which is insensitive to the relentlessly increasing contradictions and believes that everything is for the best just as long as it functions, is just as myopic as the belief in a culture of spirit [*Geist*] which, due to its ideal of self-sufficient purity, renounces the realization of its content and abandons reality to power and its blindness. (1985: 127)

20 Jamie Owen Daniel describes Adorno's plight as follows:

paradoxically, Adorno's German-Jewish identity, his particular type of 'European selfhood,' was as endangered by the seductive ideology of *inclusion* in the American melting pot as it had been in Germany by the ideology of *exclusion*. (1992: 31)

21 'That remnant of society' representing 'an obstacle to the total integration of the "administered world" ' can be read in the light of Lacan's traumatic Real which cannot be integrated into the symbolic order. I will elaborate on this subject on pp. 88–92.

22 Note, however, that the 'convergence' of Adorno and Lacan's thoughts is merely contingent. The differences between their understanding of the Subject is a case in point. For Lacan, what emerges along with the splitting of the big Other is a Subject divided by desire. Adorno's subject, by contrast, seems to belong more to the realm of the imaginary than that of the Real. The contrast between Adorno and Lacan will be spelled out in detail on pp. 90–3, where I challenge Adorno's politics of 'crossing the border' with Lacan's politics of 'breaching the limit'.

23 'The word that is designed to be understood' is comparable to cheap art produced for easy consumption. Adorno's defence of foreign words can be compared to his 'stubborn defence of a free "spirit" unwilling to succumb to the fetishism of culture' (Piccone, 1993: 3). The faith Adorno puts in modern art or 'genuine' culture in general, for example, can equally well describe the hope he places in foreign words:

what may rightly be called cultural is solely what realizes itself by virtue of the integrity of its own spiritual form, intercedes only via this integrity, reacts to society but not in direct conformity with its laws. (1993: 38)

24 Said's further elaboration on this subject is also pertinent to understanding Adorno's attitude toward America:

This [the exile's refusal to belong] usually translates into an intransigence that is not easily ignored. Wilfulness, exaggeration, overstatement: these are characteristic styles of being an exile, methods for compelling the world to accept your vision – which you make more unacceptable because you are in fact unwilling to have it accepted. (1990: 363)

25 Adorno recounts the incident as follows:

I had presented a lecture at the Psychoanalytic Society in San Francisco and had given it to their professional journal for publication. In proofreading the galleys, I discovered that they had not been content simply to correct the stylistic flaws of an emigrant writer. The entire text had been disfigured beyond recognition, the basic intentions no longer recoverable. In response to my polite protestation I received a less polite and sympathetic explanation that the journal owed its reputation precisely to its practice of subjecting all contributions to such *editing*

[*Reduction*]. This editorial policy accounted for the journal's *homogeneity* [my italics], they said; I would be standing in my own way if I passed up its advantages. I passed it up nevertheless: today this essay can be found under the title '*Die revidierte Psychoanalyse*' ('Psychoanalysis Revisited') in the volume *Soziologica II* in a quite faithful German translation. It could be used to check whether the text really had to be filtered through a machine according to that almost universal technique of *adaptation* [added emphasis], reworking and arranging to which authors without clout have to submit in America. (1985: 128)

26 '"Das Eigene" is already . . .': I am alluding to Horkheimer and Adorno's famous formulation: 'myth is already enlightenment; and enlightenment reverts to mythology' (1972: xvi).
The 'restricted economy': compare this to Wim Wenders:

The idea is that, not being at home [my heroes] are nevertheless at home with themselves. In other words, not being at home means being more at home than anywhere else. . . . Maybe the idea of being more oneself when one's away is a very personal idea. . . . Identity means not having to have a home. Awareness, for me, has something to do with not being at home. Awareness of anything. (Quoted in Elasasser, 1985: 48)

27 For a quick reference, see the list provided by H. Stuart Hughes of the Anglo-American idioms in Adorno's sociological writings: healthy sex life, some fun, go-getters, social research, team, middle range theory, trial and error, administrative research, common sense, fact finding, statement of fact, case studies, facts and figures, nose counting, likes and dislikes (1975: 166, n. 50). See also Levin's 'Nationalities of language' (1985: 115–16).
28 Paul F. Lazarsfeld, director of the Princeton Radio Research Project and long-time supporter of Adorno, is annoyed by another fetishistic use of *Fremdwörter* in Adorno's works. He makes no effort to hide his irritation when he tells his friend and colleague the following in a letter:

Don't you think it is a perfect fetishism the way you use Latin words all through your text? There is no doubt that the words 'necessary condition' express everything which the corresponding Latin words express, but you evidently feel magically more secure if you use words which symbolize your education. (quoted in Morrison, 1978: 336)

29 See the account given by Adorno in 'On the Question: "What is German?" ' (1985: 127–9).
30 The fact that Adorno is always already alienated in the myth of the plenitude of (the German) language is further complicated by the fact that German is never really his 'native tongue', given his half-Jewish identity. If Adorno's fellow intellectual *émigrés* are 'more American than the born Americans', Adorno is no more capable of sustaining his Jewish 'self' in the German context. In a way, Adorno is even more mystified by the big Other than his fellow immigrants, since he does not even recognize the German tongue as already the tongue of the other, and as such (following his own logic) would never be fully present to his half-Jewish 'self'.
31 In ' "What is German?" ', Adorno claims that his decision to return to Germany 'was hardly motivated simply by a subjective need, by home-sickness [*Heimweh*], as little as I would deny having had such sentiment' (1985: 129). While

denying homesickness as the main reason prompting his return to Germany, it is worth noting that he does use the word *Heim*weh to describe his relationship to Germany.

32 I borrow the expression 'franchir la limite' from Lacan's Antigone chapters in the *Ethics Seminar* (1992).

Note that the word 'versus' throughout this section is used in an overdetermined manner: terms joined by it in the present chapter by no means form a binary opposition.

33 Needless to say, the reference to his childhood presupposes a metaphysics of the self.

34 Prior to Derrida, J. Hillis Miller had already pointed out in his essay 'The Critic as Host' (1991) the equivocal and 'inter-parasitic' relations between the host and the guest (see especially *Theory*, 1991: 146).

35 The 'stranger' in German modernity is perhaps even more pertinent to a critique of Adorno. Contrast, for example, Simmel's stranger as an internally split figure with Adorno's rather self-enclosed notion of '*das Fremde*': 'distance means that he [the stranger], who is close by, is far, and strangeness means that he, who also is far, is actually near' (Simmel, 1950: 402).

36 Note that the utopian thrust Adorno grants to foreign words is very much a product of the 'lost plenitude' he attributes to them:

> Like Greeks in Imperial Rome, foreign words, used correctly and responsibly, should lend support to the lost cause of a flexibility, elegance, and refinement of formulation that has been lost and that people do not want to be reminded of. . . . In this way foreign words could preserve something of the utopia of language. (1991c: 192)

37 Adorno's linguistic nostalgia is matched by his *Heimweh* for the land of his childhood and his wish to re-establish continuity with that 'originary' home. His indulgence in the memory of the 'protected beautiful life' of his childhood (see Löwenthal, 1989: 63–4) might, at least partly, have prevented him from realizing that the idea of 'originary plenitude' in both 'language and being' is a mere fiction.

38 Note that the Other associated with desire and radical Alterity is a big Other for Lacan. I will soon turn to address the significance of this capitalization.

39 Recall also Lacan's famous slogan in 'Agency of the Letter in the Unconscious': 'the unconscious is the discourse of the Other' (1977: 172/524). Shepherdson clarifies the radically heterogeneous structure of desire by pointing out that the unconscious is a *perpetually* alien element in its 'appearance' in speech within the 'articulations' of demand (1999: 11).

40 This is how desire preserves the other in its *radical singularity*.

41 In other words, Adorno has overlooked the 'loss of the object' – the 'small part of the subject that detaches itself' (see Shepherdson, 1999: 19).

42 Lacan points out in 'The Agency of the Letter in the Unconscious' that, as far as the Other is concerned, 'the problems are of an order the heteronomy of which is completely misconstrued if reduced to an "awareness of others," or whatever we choose to call it' (1977: 173/525).

43 Žižek's creative explanation of the differences between boundary and limit sheds important light on the role of the 'limit' in Lacanian psychoanalysis as well as in some other post-structuralist thinkers (Žižek's disagreement with 'post-structuralism' notwithstanding):

> *boundary* is the external limitation of an object, its qualitative confines which confer upon it its identity (an object is 'itself' only within these confines, in so far

as it fulfils a set of qualitative conditions); whereas *limit* results from a 'reflection-into-itself' of the boundary: it emerges when the determinatedness which defines the identity of an object is reflected into this object itself and assumes the shape of its own unattainable limit, of what the object can never fully become, of what it can only approach into (bad) infinity. (1991: 109–10)

'Reverse without return': see pp. 92–3 of this chapter for an explanation of the politics of an exile without return, or, to appropriate Derrida's expression, a politics of 'expenditure without reserve' – that is, an 'irreversible usage of energy' (1982: 19).

My idea of the reversal of 'the identity of the other into the Other of identity' is inspired by Levinas's reversal of Heidegger's possibility of impossibility into the impossibility of possibility.

Note that the reversal of the identity of the other into the Other of identity would entail that the boundaries circumscribing '*das Eigene*' and '*das Fremde*' each be folded back into itself, thereby revealing their internal splits or lacks.

44 It is interesting to compare Adorno's vision to Lacan's little piece of the Real which also 'sticks out' from the symbolic order.

45 The 'hard, artificial, unyielding' quality of foreign words can also be compared to Benjamin's '*Wörtlichkeit*'. There is a certain materiality to the words themselves which is destructive of sense – a destruction which de Man in his interpretation of Benjamin refers to as 'disarticulation' (1986: 84). Foreign words '[should] not mean, but be'. Which is to say, foreign words as the radically Other do not perform for sense; rather, to appropriate a Benjaminian expression again, they are performative of the 'interruption' of sense.

It is also interesting to note the compatibility between Lacanian and Benjaminian thought: they can be jointly used here to radicalize Adorno's politics of foreign words. Lacan's theory of '*Das Ding*' and Benjamin's notion of '*Wörtlichkeit*' are remarkably close in spirit. Both thinkers recommend a 'word for word' translation. For Lacan, such a practice is 'madly instructive' of the 'insistence' of the signifier; for Benjamin, it illuminates the 'destructive', non-sensical character of words. Benjamin explicitly invokes Hölderlin on this point (1955: 78, 81–2). It is possible that Lacan has in mind the same 'mad poet' when he suggests an interlinear translation of Sophocles's text.

46 By ' "little piece" of subjectivity' I am alluding to the 'little piece of the Real' in Lacanian psychoanalysis.

47 'Insist' is a term used by Lacan in his discussion of the 'female logic' in the *Encore Seminar* (1998).

48 Lacan even states at the end of the *Ethics Seminar* (1992) that the only thing one can be truly guilty of is to have '*cédé sur son désir*'.

49 Theorists of radical democracy such as Ernesto Laclau and Chantal Mouffe have proposed *dis*-placing contradiction (external) with antagonism (internal), determination with overdetermination. Other scholars who share this political stance include Renata Salecl, Slavoj Žižek, Joan Copjec, and Juliet Flower MacCannell (all influenced by Lacanian psychoanalysis).

50 Even though Adorno refers to Benjamin to make his point about suffering 'in language' and 'in reality', Benjamin's ideas are very much domesticated by Adorno in the course of the latter's appropriation. For Benjamin, 'suffering' is by no means a product of social conditions only. In 'The Task of the Translator', Benjamin talks about '*die Wehen des Eigenen*' – the suffering of what one thinks as one's own – that is, the suffering of the original language. Foreignness, disparateness and disjunction are not confined to the 'foreign' language. Rather, our 'own' language is always already alienated from us and from itself. De Man is right in his interpretation of Benjamin: 'What the translation reveals is that this alienation is at its strongest in our

relation to our own original language, that the original language within which we are engaged is disarticulated in a way which imposes upon us a particular suffering' (1986: 84). Unlike Adorno, who sees foreignness as a reflection of social contradictions awaiting resolution, Benjamin aims at 'letting the language be violently overtaken by the foreign' (Benjamin, 1955: 81/1972: 20; translation modified).

51 Adorno's yearning for the 'resurrection' of foreign words 'in a better order of things' (1991b: 192) reminds one of Derrida's description of restricted economy – namely, the economic detour which, 'in the element of the same, always aims at coming back to the pleasure or the presence that have been differed by (conscious or unconscious) calculation' (1982: 19).

52 This is to say, in order to live up to his aspirations of 'untiring vigilance' (1985: 130), Adorno would need to rethink '*das Fremde*' and '*das Eigene*' in such a manner that, to use Derrida's language, they would 'no longer [be] identical to themselves, hence no longer simply identifiable and to that extent no longer determinable' (Derrida, 1993: 7).

53 And of course, Adorno does return to his 'home(-land)' after a long period of exile.

54 The Sadean excess, as Lacan points out, also overlaps structurally with the Kantian unconditional obligation 'to which it is impossible to give determinate, hence recognizable, form' (Weber, 1993: 144).

55 The 'exile from exile' is also referred to in the present chapter as the 'exile-of-excess' or 'exile-without-reserve'.

As Lacan points out, the term 'outrage' 'bears within it the structure of the crossing of some invisible line' (1992: 143).

56 In other words, the politics of exile still reveres 'homeland' as its big Other.

57 'The master of signification' is appropriated from one of Lacan's formulations in the 1950s.

58 See Lacan's 'Subversion of the Subject and Dialectic of Desire' in *Écrits* (1977).

59 This experience is translated by Žižek into Hegelian language as 'the loss of loss'. This takes place when the subject 'becomes aware that what a moment ago she was so afraid to lose is now totally null, i.e., is already in itself a kind of a loss' (1990: 33).

60 The terms 'possibility' and 'impossibility' are modelled after Levinas's usage.

61 I borrow the expressions 'camp on the limit' and 'camp out on the breach' from Samuel Weber in his discussion of Antigone as interpreted by Lacan (Weber, 1993: 152).

The statement 'Love outside the limits of the law' is appropriated from Lacan, *Seminar XI* (1978: 276); see also Juliet Flower MacCannell's highly creative use of Lacan's idea in her article of the same title (1994).

References

Adorno, Theodor W. (1967) *Prisms*, trans. Samuel and Shierry Weber (Studies in Contemporary German Social Thought). London: Neville Spearman.

Adorno, Theodor W. (1968) 'Scientific Experiences of a European Scholar in America', trans. Donald Fleming, in Donald Fleming and Bernard Bailyn (eds), *The Intellectual Migration: Europe and America, 1930–1960*. Cambridge, MA: Belknap Press of the Harvard University Press. pp. 338–70.

Adorno, Theodor W. (1969) 'Erziehung nach Auschwitz', in *Stichworte: Kritische Modelle II*. Frankfurt-on-Main: Suhrkamp. pp. 85–101.

Adorno, Theodor W. (1971) 'Der wunderliche Realist', in *Noten zur Literatur*, vol. 3 (Bibliothek Suhrkamp 146). Frankfurt-on-Main: Suhrkamp.

Adorno, Theodor W. (1972) *Dialectic of Enlightenment*, trans. John Cumming. New York: Continuum. (Originally published as *Philosophische Fragmente*. Frankfurt-on-Main: S. Fischer, 1969.)

Adorno, Theodor W. (1974) *Minima Moralia: Reflections from a Damaged Life*, trans. E.F.N. Jephcott. London: Verso. (Originally published as *Minima Moralia: Reflexionen aus dem beschädigten Leben. Gesammelte Schriften*, vol. 4. Frankfurt-on-Main: Suhrkamp, 1951.)

Adorno, Theodor W. (1975) 'Culture Industry Reconsidered', trans. Anson G. Rabinbach, *New German Critique*, 6: 12–19.

Adorno, Theodor W. (1980) *Gesammelte Schriften*. Frankfurt-on-Main: Suhrkamp.

Adorno, Theodor W. (1985) 'On the question: "What is German?" ', trans. Thomas Y. Levin, *New German Critique*, 36: 121–31.

Adorno, Theodor W. (1991a) 'Heine the Wound', in Rolf Tiedemann (ed.), *Notes to Literature*, trans. Shierry Weber Nicholsen. (European Perspectives) Vol. 2. New York: Columbia University Press. pp. 80–5. (Originally published as 'Die Wunde Heine', in *Noten zur Literatur*, vol. 1 (Bibliothek Suhrkamp 47). Frankfurt-on-Main: Suhrkamp, 1958.)

Adorno, Theodor W. (1991b) 'On the Use of Foreign Words', in Rolf Tiedemann (ed.), *Notes to Literature*, 2 vols, trans. Shierry Weber Nicholsen. (European Perspectives) Vol. 2. New York: Columbia University Press. pp. 286–91. (Originally published as '*Über den Gebrauch von Fremdwörten*', in *Gesammelte Schriften*, vol. 2, ed. Rolf Tiedemann. Frankfurt-on-Main: Suhrkamp, 1974.)

Adorno, Theodor W. (1991c) 'Words from abroad [I translate this title as 'Alien Words' throughout my chapter]', in Rolf Tiedemann (ed.), *Notes to Literature*, 2 vols, trans. Shierry Weber Nicholsen. (European Perspectives) Vol. 1. New York: Columbia University Press. pp. 185–99. (Originally published as *Gesammelte Schriften*, vol. 2, ed. Rolf Tiedemann. Frankfurt-on-Main: Suhrkamp, 1974. Reprinted from *Akzente*, 2 (1959): 176 ff.)

Adorno, Theodor W. (1993) 'Theory of Pseudo-Culture', *Telos*, 95: 15–38.

Anderson, Benedict (1983) *Imagined Communities: Reflections on the Origin and Spread of Nationalism*. London: Verso.

Benjamin, Walter (1955) 'The Task of the Translator', in *Illuminations*. New York: Harcourt. pp. 69–82.

Benjamin, Walter (1972) *Gesammelte Schriften*. Frankfurt-on-Main: Suhrkamp.

Benjamin, Walter (1978) 'Critique of Violence', in *Reflections*. New York: Schocken. pp. 277–300

Bhabha, Homi K. (1990) 'Introduction: Narrating the Nation', in Homi K. Bhabha (ed.), *Nation and Narration*. New York: Routledge.

Cirtautas, Claudius Kazys (1957) *The Refugee: A Psychological Study*. Boston: Meador.

Clifford, James (1988) *The Predicament of Culture: Twentieth-Century Ethnography, Literature, and Art*. Cambridge, MA: Harvard University Press.

Daniel, Jamie Owen (1992) 'Temporary Shelter: Adorno's Exile and the Language of Home', *New Formations*, 17: 26–35.

Deleuze, Gilles and Guattari, Félix (1986) *Kafka: Toward a Minor Literature*, trans. Dana Polan (Theory and History of Literature 30). Minneapolis, MN: University of Minnesota Press.

de Man, Paul (1986) 'Conclusions: Walter Benjamin's "The Task of the Translator" ', in *The Resistance to Theory* (Theory and History of Literature 33). Minneapolis, MN: University of Minnesota Press. pp. 73–105.

Derrida, Jacques (1973) *Speech and Phenomena and Other Essays on Husserl's Theory of Signs*, trans. David B. Allison (Northwestern University Studies in Phenomenology and Existential Philosophy). Evanston: Northwestern University

Press. (Originally published as *La voix et le phénomène: introduction au problème du signe dans la phénoménologie de Husserl*. Paris: Presses Universitaires de France, 1976.)

Derrida, Jacques (1982) *Margins of Philosophy*, trans. Alan Bass. Chicago: University of Chicago Press.

Derrida, Jacques (1993) *Aporias*, trans. Thomas Dutoit. (Crossing Aesthetics) Stanford, CA: Stanford University Press. (Originally published as 'Apories: Mourir-s'attendre aux limites de la vérité', in *Le Passage des frontières: autour du travail de Jacques Derrida*. Editions Galilée, 1993.)

Eagleton, Terry (1991) *Ideology: An Introduction*. London: Verso.

Elasasser, Thomas (1985) 'Germany's Imaginary America: Wim Wenders and Peter Handke', in Susan Hayward (ed.), *European Cinema*. Aston University, Modern Languages Department.

Habermas, Jürgen (1982) 'The Entwinement of Myth and Enlightenment: Rereading *Dialectic of Enlightenment*', *New German Critique*, 26: 13–30.

Hughes, H. Stuart (1975) *The Sea Change: The Migration of Social Thought 1930–1965*. New York: Harper & Row.

Jay, Martin (1980) 'The Jews and the Frankfurt School: Critical Theory's Analysis of Anti-Semitism', *New German Critique*, 19: 137–49. Reprinted in Jay, *Permanent Exiles: Essays on the Intellectual Migration from Germany to America*. New York: Columbia University Press, 1985. pp. 90–100.

Jay, Martin (1984) 'Adorno in America', *New German Critique*, 31: 157–82. Reprinted in Jay, *Permanent Exiles: Essays on the Intellectual Migration from Germany to America*. New York: Columbia University Press, 1985. pp. 120–37.

Lacan, Jacques (1977) *Écrits*. New York: Norton. (Originally published as *Écrits*. Paris: Éditions de Seuil, 1966.)

Lacan, Jacques (1978) *The Four Fundamental Concepts of Psychoanalysis* (also known as *Seminar XI*). New York: Norton.

Lacan, Jacques (1992) *The Ethics of Psychoanalysis, 1959–1960*, trans. Dennis Porter. New York: Norton.

Lacan, Jacques (1998) *On Feminine Sexuality: The Limits of Love and Knowledge* (also known as *Encore, 1972–73*), trans. Bruce Fink. New York: Norton.

Levin, Thomas Y. (1985) 'Nationalities of language: Adorno's *Fremdwörter*: An Introduction to "On the Question: What is German?" ', *New German Critique*, 36: 11–19.

Löwenthal, Leo (1989) *Critical Theory and Frankfurt Theorists: Lectures-Correspondence-Conversations*. New Brunswick, NJ: Transaction Publishers. pp. 63–4.

Löwenthal, Leo (1991) 'Address upon Accepting the Theodor W. Adorno Prize on 1 October 1989', *New German Critique*, 54: 179–89.

MacCannell, Juliet Flower (1994) 'Love outside the Limits of the Law', *New Formations*, 23: 25–42.

Michaelis, Herbert et al. (eds) (1956–79) *Ursachen und Folgen: Vom deutschen Zusammenbruch 1918 und 1945 bis zur staatlichen Neuordnung Deutschlands in der Gegenwart*. Berlin: Dokumenten-Verlag.

Miller, J. Hillis (1991) 'The Critic as Host', in *Theory Now and Then*. New York: Harvester Wheatsheaf. pp. 143–70.

Miller, J. Hillis (1995) 'Border Crossings, Translating Theory: Ruth', in *Topographies*. (Crossing Aesthetics) Stanford, CA: Stanford University Press. pp. 316–37.

Morley, David and Robins, Kevin (1990) 'No Place like *Heimat*: Images of Home(land) in European Culture', *New Formations*, 12 (Winter): 1–23.

Morrison, David E. (1978) '*Kultur* and Culture: The Case of Theodor W. Adorno and Paul F. Lazarsfeld', *Social Research*, 45(2): 347–8.

Noakes, Jeremy and Pridham, Geoffrey (eds) (1974) *Documents on Nazism 1919–1945*. New York: Viking. (Originally published as *Ursachen und Folgen: Vom deutschen Zusammenbruch 1918 und 1945 bis zur staatlichen Neuordnung Deutschlands in der Gegenwart*, ed. H. Michaelis et al. Berlin: 1956–79, vol. 9.)

Piccone, Paul (1993) 'Beyond Pseudo-Culture? Reconstituting Fundamental Political concepts', *Telos*, 95: 3–14.

Said, Edward (1979) 'Zionism from the Standpoint of its Victims', *Social Text*, 1: 7–58.

Said, Edward (1990) 'Reflections on exile', in Russell Ferguson, Martha Gever, Trinh T. Minh-ha and Cornell West (eds), *Out There: Marginalization and Contemporary Cultures*. New York: New Museum of Contemporary Art; Cambridge: MIT Press. pp. 357–66.

Scarpetta, Guy (1981) *Eloge du cosmopolitisme*. Paris: B. Grasset.

Shepherdson, Charles (1999) 'The Epoch of the Body: Need, Demand, and the Drive in Kojève and Lacan', in Honi Haber and Gail Weiss (eds), *Perspectives on Embodiment: The Intersections of Nature and Culture*. New York: Routledge.

Simmel, Georg (1950) 'The Stranger', in *The Sociology of Georg Simmel*, trans. and ed. Kurt H. Wolf. London: Free Press. pp. 402–8.

Weber, Samuel (1993) 'Breaching the Gap: On Lacan's *Ethics of Psychoanalysis*', in Mark Poster (ed.), *Politics, Theory, and Contemporary Culture*. New York: Columbia University Press. pp. 131–58.

Žižek, Slavoj (1990) 'Rosellini: Woman as Symptom of Man', *October*, 54: 19–44.

Žižek, Slavoj (1991) *For They Know Not What They Do: Enjoyment as a Political Factor*. (Phronesis) London: Verso.

Part II

FEMINISM, CULTURE AND SOCIETY: THE RELEVANCE OF CRITICAL THEORY FOR CONTEMPORARY FEMINISMS

---

5   Critical Theory as a Critique of Society: Theodor W. Adorno's Significance for a Feminist Sociology

Regina Becker-Schmidt

Reference to Theodor W. Adorno is seldom made in present-day German sociology. Scarcely anyone from the subsequent generation has taken up his approaches to a theory of society, analysed them, corrected them in light of recently won insight, or developed them further. The diagnostic potential over time of his critique of society, which was oriented towards complexity and contradictoriness within historical transformations, has not been taken up by mainstream sociology. Adorno attempted to relate societal transformations to restructurings of psychical energies on a collective scale. This interdisciplinary project has not been continued. His epistemological premises, which provide fundamental instructions on self-reflection in the social sciences, threaten to be forgotten. At most, it has been feminists who have productively analysed Adorno: his radical questioning of instrumental reason has found its way into concepts of androcentrism. But even here, his sociological work has been given little notice – and justifiably so: in spite of his vehement condemnation of patriarchal violence against women, Adorno's image of femininity is more conformist than progressive. In addition, in his analyses of dominance he neglects gender orders (see Becker-Schmidt, 1991, 1992). Thus, it does not appear that a feminist sociology could directly profit from Adorno's theory.

In order to discover theoretical and methodological impulses within Adorno's work for the development of a feminist sociology, we are forced to make a detour. His ideas must first be transferred into a feminist perspective. I would like to attempt to make such a transfer in the following by devoting myself to two theoretical problems which are central to women's studies, but which have not been adequately dealt with. In both cases, their insufficient clarification has consequences for the political articulation of women's emancipatory strategies. The first question is related to the determinations of equality and difference in theories of gender relations. The second is related to gender orders and the ways that difference in power relations supports social domination above and beyond gender relations.

Since the beginning of the women's movement, there have been sociological positions which emphasize the difference between gender groups in order to grant the social group 'woman' a voice for asserting her own interests. We come across concepts in the social sciences which postulate 'equality' as an absolute demand as well. Why do both of these approaches conceptualize 'equality' and 'difference' as sheer opposites, and not as mediated positions? What effect does this have on the formulation of women's policies?

These questions may be clarified with the aid of methodological instructions developed by Adorno. I am referring to his critique of identitarian logic. Adorno comes out against notions of society that sever relevant aspects of these definitions. Such abstractions constitute biases and tear apart things that belong together. Analyses according to principles of logical identity are derived from non-contradictory hypotheses. Their universal validity is postulated, even if inconsistencies arise in the topics being analysed. That which can be reduced to a common denominator is identified as belonging to the subject; that which is non-commensurable is considered minor and is not taken into account in the definition. The one-sided feminist definitions of difference and equality, which disregard that which is similar in the other and that which is divergent in the same, can be viewed as constructions of identitarian logic. The correction of these methodological biases leads to an altered understanding of gender orders.

It would have seemed reasonable to carry out this exercise on current feminist controversies over the topic of 'equality' and 'difference' – for example the discussions surrounding the concept of difference being led by Italian feminists such as Adriana Cavarero, a comparison of concepts developed by Nancy Fraser and Iris M. Young, or the views held by Andrea Maihofer and Ute Gerhard. But this would have made my contribution unnecessarily long. It cannot be assumed that everyone is acquainted with the literature I have in mind, and I would have had to go into lengthy detail. As I am concerned here with a methodological transfer from critical theory to women's studies, I have drawn on familiar material: the radical feminist approaches to difference and the liberal feminist concepts of equality from the American women's movement of the 1970s and 1980s. I am assuming that the results of a critique of patterns of thought arising out of identitarian logic can be transferred to more recent discourses with similar biases.

Not only do Adorno's methodological insights stimulate self-reflection within feminism, his theory of society can also be productively applied to feminist concepts. His structural analyses of the formation of modern, complex societies can be expanded if we broaden the horizon of research to include gender relations. Adorno emphasized the heteronomy in the functional interrelation of the different social spheres based on the division of labour. Above and beyond this, we can ask the question: in what manner do principles which organize society as a whole influence the hierarchies in gender orders, and vice versa; in what way does the difference in the power of women and men support social domination above and beyond gender relations? This is the focus of the second theoretical transfer.

Adorno demonstrated a series of traps in which sociological ways of thinking can become caught: failure to differentiate between the process of investigating phenomena on the one side, and their socio-historical genesis on the other; improper generalization either by means of abstract negation or abstract positivization; making unambiguous polyvalent or contradictory contexts by ignoring mediations and controversial correlations; linearization of historical developments by neglecting discontinuities, qualitative leaps and non-synchronicities.

In the following I would like to show that these are the problematic points of those feminist theories which are one-sided and which abbreviate the history of women's subordination. We will see that 'equality' and 'difference' are not simple opposites in gender relations, but rather that – in their opposition – they stand in reference to each other.

The theorists who have most decidedly emphasized gender difference are members of the radical feminist movement, a trend in the women's movement in the USA. As a political theory for the liberation of women, radical feminism has been acknowledged and criticized in detail. (In this respect see in particular Jaggar, 1983: 89–122; Rosaldo, 1989.) For this reason I am going to limit myself to two aspects: the implications – when applying identitarian logic – of these approaches from a subject- and social-theoretical perspective; and the fundamental aporia in which radical feminism has become methodologically entangled. By taking the example of liberal feminism as viewed by the American women's movement, which has as its goal the equal status of the genders, I intend to identify the consequences of abstracting from 'difference'. This position also allows a demonstration of the necessity of viewing 'difference' and 'equality' as a dialectical context of reference. (This approach has also been thoroughly analysed by Jaggar [1983: 174–206], so here I will restrict myself to only a few comments.) Both the radical and liberal feminist approaches lack a theory of gender order. In the final section I will outline how such a theory might be formulated along the lines of Adorno's theory.

Before I turn to the radical feminists, I would like to briefly name the different contexts within which 'gender difference' is situated. For me this serves as an aid in tracking the narrowness of identitarian logic, and it offers me the possibility of making my own views transparent, views which in their methodological orientation have been essentially influenced by my teacher, Adorno.

Contextualization of the notion of 'difference'

Differences between the genders are situated at various social-scientific levels. If 'differences' have to do with the social organization of sexuality, I will look for diverging images of the body, for gender-specific developments of object choices, for male and female forms of desire and their social acceptance. If polarized clichés of femininity and masculinity are under discussion, it seems reasonable to make the symbolic order my analytical point of reference. If we come across differences which point towards social inequality between women and men, we will have to concern ourselves with the structures of gender relations.

Feminist theories often do not distinguish between these varied levels of the discourse of difference. The Mailand group of Italian feminists, for example, who orient themselves towards Luce Irigaray, deal with all social differences between the genders without changing the frame of reference: first there are sexual differences, then legal, then differences of social status. Andrea Maihofer speaks of a 'fundamental difference' between women and men which should be taken into consideration in the law, without, however, defining this difference from a historical or social-theoretical point of view – thus 'fundamentality' almost appears to be something ontological. Radical feminists act as though all other forms of gender inequality could be spun out of sexual difference, without considering different sources of power. Such lacks of conceptual clarity go hand in hand with theoretical arbitrariness. What is not taken into consideration is that the ways of choosing points of reference must be appropriate to the object domain being investigated: implementing a subject-theoretical approach I record something different than when applying an approach based on a theory of society; interdisciplinarity has a different scope than a mono-scientific view. The attempt at a contextualized explanation of concepts therefore serves to clarify, in advance, the subsequent critiques, which then examine a decided position of difference under the aspect of implications based on a principle of logical identity.

In the context of sexuality, 'difference' appears in various forms: as a biological characteristic that seems to distinguish men and women; as a gender-specific, intrapsychic phantasm that ignites itself on erotically charged regions of the body and their associated sexual sensations; as a phallocratic impulse to penetrate and seize; as a social construction, that is to say as an imperative which guides behaviour, and which results from a social organization of sexuality. In our society, this implies a norm of heterosexuality geared towards male desire. Gender membership resides along the continuum of a polar system of dual sexuality.

When investigating whether girls and boys develop their sexuality in different ways, one cannot disregard physical differences (females have a clitoris and a vagina, breasts, a mensus, invisible sexual organs inside the body, child-bearing abilities; males have a penis, other visible sexual organs, can ejaculate and fertilize). This is not to be understood in a biologically deterministic light. Physical morphologies are linking-up points of a free-floating phantasy formation, which takes effect in the driving dynamics of desire. But one cathects that which one has oneself differently than that which one attributes to another. Sexuality unfolds as both autoerotic and object-related in interactions between people of the same or different genders. This occurrence cannot be removed from a social framework. Convention moulds what is to be regarded as female or as male sexuality. In this justification, sexual difference is something biographically constituted and socially constructed. Ideas about female and male sexuality are conveyed by society. The assignment to one of the two genders according to the male standard (presence or absence of a penis) is a social occurrence which overlooks the sexual self-determination of many people, which doesn't follow the social norms.

The differences made between female and male gender types are to be found on another conceptual level. Here – at the intersection of individuation and social integration – it is a matter of the analysis of gender-specific patterns of socialization, within which subject potentials are activated and rewarded in different ways. In a way it makes sense to postulate gender types in societies in which women and men are generally ascribed different competencies and assigned different social responsibilities. In the long term, this cannot remain without consequences for the psycho-social structuring of subjective potentials. However, if gender boundaries are open, then it is problematical to stylize gender groups after models of femininity and masculinity. Just as different individuals cannot be seen merely as female or male identities – they assimilate traits belonging to persons they relate to of both the same and different gender, and they integrate experiences made in fields of practice with both female and male connotations – so are gender groups units of identical and not-identical. The societal obligation – for objective reasons, by all means still in force – to behave as 'feminine' or 'masculine', to be obliged to move in fields of action dominated by the other gender, is not congruent with subjective desires to cross boundaries. This is more strongly realized by women than by men.

Social differences between men and women can refer to the way in which they are represented in the symbolic order (the cultural system of significations), or they can refer to their socio-economic and political position in gender orders. The symbolic order and the socio-economic system are interdependent, but they are not the same.

If 'gender' is thought of as a principle of social organization and therefore as a structure category which indicates social inequality, this suggests that members of both genders be understood as social groups. But as the social position of women and men does not depend solely on their gender membership, but also on their ethnic and class-specific situation, gender groups cannot be homogeneous. Thus differences exist not only between, but also within the groups. This has two methodological consequences. First:

if we want to ascertain the social differences between the genders, then we must compare men and women living in comparable social circumstances. Secondly: the forms of discrimination against women can vary according to class and ethnic membership; the focal point in which the oppression of women manifests itself most strongly can change along with their social situation. Differences between women result from the way in which gender, class and ethnic membership work together as stratification criteria in feminine life contexts.

Premises of identitarian logic in the radical feminist construction of difference

In radical feminism, 'difference' refers to the gap between the genders, torn open by male hegemony. The power of male society is based on sexual violence towards women and on social control over their bodies. The succession of historical epochs is characterized by the continual reproduction of one patriarchy (Koedt et al., 1973: 370). This ahistorical view of social developments is not shared by all radical feminists and not all of them draw the same political conclusions from an emphasis on the omnipresence of male sexism (women's renunciation of heterosexual contacts, de(con)-struction of the system of dual sexuality, battle against men).[1] The majority, however, hold on to the organization of society – as a matter of priority – along an impenetrable line of 'gender' separation: men belong to the ruling, women to the oppressed class. All other forms of inequality are secondary (Ti-Grace Atkinson, Kate Millet, Shulamith Firestone, Adrienne Rich and Monique Wittig, amongst others).

Because the world of men is seen as a self-contained, anti-women front (in Mary Daly's words a 'planetary Men's Association') the emancipatory strategies of radical feminists culminate in separation. Demands for more freedom for women (womanspace), where they can periodically escape male influence, be together with their own kind, and develop their own self-images, glide over into aspirations of creating a female counterculture (womanculture) – permanent, exclusively female, insulated against male interference – with its own set of values, an air of sisterly solidarity, and all the possibilities for free expression of personality.

If one follows Adorno's line of thought, this theory of two worlds may be characterized as a construct designed according to principles of identitarian logic.

In the radical feminist analysis of the phenomenon of the 'oppression of women', the return of the ever-same (*Wiederkehr des lmmergleichen*: Adorno) is postulated under the premise of universal patriarchal structures. This is only possible because the construction of the conceptual apparatus, which is meant to serve the search for clues to the source – as well as the handing down – of gender inequality, equivocally appears as a reconstruction of the authentic courses of history, the authentic developments of maleness and femaleness and of forms of domination. The claim of wanting to retrace historical processes back to their origins with the aim of finding the unambiguous truth methodologically leads to a linearization and straightening of the courses of history, which are marked by progress as well as retrogression. That which appears to have survived is recorded; that which changes remains underexposed. For example, in these concepts feudal patriarchy changes into capitalist structures without a break, that is to say without considering its transformations. In spite of the emergence of social systems during the course of industrialization, which produced new forms of social inequality in addition to the gender hierarchy and other patriarchal dependencies, the analysis of social relations remains limited to that of gender orders. The interrelations between the formation of society as a whole and the social organization of gender relations do not come into view; radical epochal changes, which restructure these interrelations, are levelled off into transitions with gradual changes.

Phallic sexuality, masculinity, phallocratic violence, male dominance, oppression of women, the male–female system, patriarchy, womanculture: in this chain there is only one logical principle which accounts for the gender order: male predominance, to which female counter-force reacts. We are confronted with units which are in themselves identical on both sides of the separating line of 'gender'.[2] Men from different classes and ethnic groups, women with different skin colours and of different social situations are seen only as members of gender groups. In the sense of an abstract negation, the men are representatives of patriarchy; the women are – undifferentiated – nothing else than both their victims and their positive contra-image. Although as a rule, male gender membership in fact implies privileges at all social levels, not all men have power; and although women almost everywhere are discriminated against in favour of men, there are indeed considerable differences in the degree to which they are affected by this discrimination. In addition, poor women are subordinate to wealthy women.

Apart from exceptions like Dorothy Dinnerstein and Shulamith Firestone, in radical feminism there are scarcely any elaborated subject-theoretical approaches which could explain how a pathological-phallocratical sexuality originates, how men become patriarchs, by which conflicts the male wish to oppress women is fed. The individual 'man' appears as identical in himself – without contradictions and ambivalence: male subjectivity stands in a negative relationship to motherhood; it has not been shaped by a childhood embedded in a culture which was also moulded by women, and in which identification with both feminine and masculine patterns occurred. The radical feminist image of female subjectivity has been similarly cleansed of mediations which also embrace opposite identifications. What is not mentioned is that women have also internalized aspects of persons of both genders, that they are entangled in a dominant culture that is both familiar and, in part, alien to them, that they have been shaped by a history in which they again find themselves as agents, as the oppressed, and as rebels. They share responsibility for the state of a society into which, on the one hand, they have been integrated, and within which, on the other hand, they are marginal.

That which must be kept apart – because it refers to different genesis – is treated as though it were situated at the same level. The subjective and the objective are understood neither as developing in mutual dependence, nor as maintaining their own logic in their mediation. Behaviour and conditions of acting, agents and agencies, personal and impersonal interactions, relationships and the structural prerequisites of social processes of separation and exchange in society, become blurred in radical feminism.

This conceptual mixture leads to patterns of argumentation that support each other tautologically: the construction of masculinity according to identitarian logic serves to personalize power (patriarchy is more an organized behaviour syndrome for men than a feudalistic system) as well as to depersonalize men: each individual is nothing more than a representative of his gender group. Femininity, thought to be completely different, also remains fixated on that from which it should stand out qualitatively: womanculture, the expression of femininity, constitutes nothing more than the reversal of the world of men; it is the positive equivalent of a negative contra-image – nothing above and beyond this.

Radical feminism is entangled in a paradox of identitarian logic. According to Adorno, this paradox permeates all emancipatory aspirations which attempt to disregard their historical bonds. Real freedom can only come into being where there is no mediation. Mediation always taints the newly anticipated with that from which it wants to detach itself.

As gender relations are linked with comprehensive relations of power, an exodus of the women's movement out of the gender order cannot lead to the attainment of utopia: there is no neutral ground on which communities of women might prosper autonomously. Society, together with its male institutions, undisputedly continues to exist. Because self-sufficient enclaves are hardly conceivable in social systems which are differentiated and function according to principles of the division of labour, the formation of female communities would have to be carried out within existing social structures. Global dependencies between world markets, differences in power between the metropolises and the periphery, and the international division of labour even between female gender groups all lead to the drawing of lines of separation amongst women due to class- and ethnic-specific disparities. If feminists want to create an entirely new world, they will have to intervene in the old one. Otherwise their radicalism is based on nothing more than an abstract negation of dependencies, to which they turn a blind eye in their creation of a womanculture.

Equality and difference in the liberal feminism of the women's movement in the USA

It is understandable why approaches based on the theory of difference are more likely to fall back on premises of identitarian logic than do approaches which orient themselves towards equality of the genders. Radical feminists have demonstrated just this: only when opposites have been standardized can separation and dissociation be strictly maintained. In comparison, demands for equality can only be formulated if the phenomena of inequality which are to be eliminated have been identified. The notion of 'equality' refers to the notion of 'difference'. This, in turn, can be seen in the attitudes of liberal feminists in the women's movement in the USA. There, ideas about equality are first of all bound to the determination of social differences in the social position of the genders. Demands for equal rights, equal status and equal value are ignited by the structural disadvantages of women: claims are made for the parity of women under the law, as citizens, and as working persons. Because the private sphere was seen as a space for the unrestricted development of the individual, sexual oppression was ignored for a long time. This has changed.

And yet in the liberal feminist movement in the USA, which has taken up the cause of equality, one encounters premises based on identitarian logic. They result from an abstract conception of 'free and equal individuality', which is rooted in the liberal tradition of natural rights.

Because, according to this approach, men and women have the same potential for qualification, the barriers against securing a social existence and against social advancement are erected by those from outside. The premise of identitarian logic that maintains a free individuality, conceived as gender neutral and independent of class or ethnic membership, levels out, for one thing, the differences between women with different social statuses and differing cultural orientations.

It is assumed that all women find the same things good and proper. Seen from this perspective, equal opportunity could only be achieved if the state controlled and punished all violations of the law of equality. A.M. Jaggar comments: 'Several writers have pointed out, however, that, if liberal feminists were to follow their own logic through to the end, the notion of equal opportunity could be used to justify state control of every aspect of life' (1983: 195). With the consequence that women from different social strata and differing cultural contexts would be exposed to social control in different ways. For example, both Onora O'Neill and D.A. Lloyd Thomas argue that genuine equality of opportunity would require that children be removed from their parents' care and control to be reared in state nurseries. Only in this way, they argue, would it be possible to guarantee to each child the equal 'distribution of health care, diet, socialisation, consideration and respect, as well as of schooling, which would ensure the same distribution of competences' (quoted in Jaggar, 1983: 195).

Liberal feminism is not concerned with the separation of the genders; determinations of difference do not serve the purpose of dissociation in order to enhance the female gender group and devalue the male. Women should be integrated into an existing society, which is accepted as being meritocratic, and equal rights should cancel out inequality. However, what is overlooked is that, for historical reasons, men and women are not individuals with equal opportunities. Non-synchronicities in the development of society – for instance the retention of unpaid forms of labour in relations otherwise mediated by the market – have created exceptional circumstances in women's lives which cannot be generalized to men: for example the dual burden of housework and employment, caring for children and pursuing an education. Only special measures can help in this case – measures which are designed to solve such specific problems.[3]

A feminist politics of supporting women which unites both – the effort of compensating for existing inequalities between the genders through special measures; and the achievement of equal treatment in order to eliminate discrimination against women – can be considered paradigmatic for an understanding of democracy in societies in which heterogeneous sections of the populations have unequal opportunities for participating in society. In view of economic and cultural disparities, in such constellations there are no systems, public welfare or uniform justice that can be called upon and into which all justifiable group interests could possibly be integrated. In such circumstances, 'equality' cannot mean *Einerleiheit* (one identity), but rather equality in spite of difference. Only under this premise does the observance of social differences cease to imply the exclusion and devaluation of others, and instead mean the tolerance of exceptional circumstances.

This position is also represented by those feminists who demand a voice in political decision-making processes for every group, regardless of whether they constitute a unit within themselves under the aspect of cultural solidarity, or have corresponding political interests. Above and beyond this, this conception of variety with equal rights should keep open the possibility of flexible coalitions (Fraser, 1974; Young, 1989).

It is a reasonable proposition to want to give every social unit a political voice in order to create a counterbalance to the general claims of traditional parties concerned with their own authority, but its weaknesses become all the more obvious if one looks at it from a sociological point of view. While liberal feminists hypostasize the equality of individual needs according to natural law, in this case it remains vague how social identity or, more precisely, how the social homogeneity of groups formed according to cultural proximity or corresponding interests is constituted.

Cultural group identity does not necessarily mean social equality or political solidarity based on mutual interests. Even beyond the cohesion of the group, it does not bring about the equality of those treated unequally by society.

Applied to the question of equality and difference in gender relations, this means that we cannot consider 'women' a social interest group until we have succeeded in determining common characteristics of oppression *qua* gender membership; however, in view of ethnic and class-specific differences, this does not allow us to speak of a 'group identity'.

Now where can common characteristics be found that exist despite 'differences'? The majority of women are situated in gender relations which are characterized by hierarchical structures. Gender orders may vary depending on the historical formation of the society in which they are embedded. However, at least for Western industrial societies we are able to make out a correspondence between the modes of societal reproduction and the organization of gender relations, which concern women collectively. This will be pursued in the following section by considering Adorno's theory of society.

On the hegemony of societal spheres and the social dominance of the male gender group

Adorno regards the tendencies of society as a whole. His notion of society therefore embraces two perspectives which belong together: on the one hand, there is the contradictory apparatus of economic, administrative and political domination, sustained by science and technology; on the other hand, 'society' stands for the unity of conflicting social forces. The category 'totality' reflects this twofold complexity: the objectifications represented by institutions and potentials of subjectivity, which have arisen out of history and which may alter social constellations. The notion of totality does not affirm a preponderance of the social apparatus over the individual, reducing society to a closed system. Rather, for Adorno '[t]otality is a category of mediation, not one of immediate domination and subjugation . . . societal totality does not lead a life of its own over and above that which it unites and of which it, in turn, is composed. It produces and reproduces itself through its individual moments' (Adorno, 1976: 107).

But in his analysis of society, Adorno encounters the dominance of technocratic institutions over the vital life process of human beings. Within these power relations, individuals and social groups are socialized and situated within societal hierarchies. We refer to them as conditions of social life: *Verhältnisse*. It is within these conditions that social groups, for example classes, are placed in relation to one another.

Analogous to this, gender order can be understood as an institutionalized structural system. It is an ensemble of objective conditions under which the genders – despite their separation – are related and refer to each other socially. Gender order represents the sum total of those relations according to which the division of labour in society is organized, access to cultural and economic resources as well as to power is regulated, the processes of sexual exchange are standardized, and generative reproduction is arranged. Constitutive of hierarchies within the gender order is the inferior social value of the female as opposed to the male gender. However, this process of evaluation implies the sedimentation of social structures which confirm inequality. Discriminatory relating generates a gender relationship based on dominance and subordination. Assessing genders goes together with estimating fields of practice assigned to women and men. By gendering social areas, an evaluation that privileges men turns into a classification that degrades women. This has consequences for a woman's social status.

I would like to elaborate these statements by analysing the correspondence between hierarchical structures in gender orders and the state of industrial nations as described by Adorno.

According to Adorno, modern industrial societies are characterized by sectoral differentiation. The societal whole reproduces itself by means of the association of functional areas based on the division of labour. These areas are separate; however, they nevertheless stand in interdependent relation to each other: private lives, education, spheres of production, the service sector, the state.

But unlike system-theoretical approaches, Adorno's analysis pursues the antinomies and conflicts under which late capitalistic, technocratically hardened societies reproduce themselves.

The association of differentiated social spheres is not carried out in a balloting process which takes into account reciprocal dependencies as they exist, for example, between the private sphere, and the spheres of industrial production and the labour market. The sphere of employment needs the labour force, which is regenerated within the family. Families, in turn, rely on the labour market to meet their existential needs. Despite such dependencies, there are hierarchies amongst the various sections of society: some have at their disposal tremendous power to shape society, while others can scarcely influence the direction of societal development. In industrial-capitalistic systems, economic and government sectors occupy a dominant position. In contrast to this, family or cultural institutions have less opportunity to exercise influence – they have virtually no impact on the development of official policies in the areas of work, technology or education.

In view of the hierarchy of societal spheres – which exist despite the reciprocal dependency of all sections of society – and in view of the claim to dominance by a few of these sectors – although essentially all of them are necessary for maintaining the whole – we can say that the formation of Western industrial nations is contradictory. This finds expression in the principles of organization with which the system (regardless of how crisis-prone it is) is held together: separation of the spheres, making their reciprocal dependency invisible, goes along with their connections, enabling the exercise of influence on, and interference with, other spheres; the claims to hegemony of individual segments, which in turn subordinate others, are connected with relative independence, because this is necessary for the realization of social tasks specific to the respective area. This synchronicity of separation and relatedness, of hegemony and relative autonomy, can be most clearly seen in the relation between the spheres of employment and the family: private life is a separate area – this is called for by the specific demands of procreation, regeneration, housekeeping and childrearing; yet its time structures and standards of behaviour and discipline are geared towards a working world mediated by the market – the restrictions of employment are carried over into the private sphere. The laws of the market take precedence over the immediate living process.

This societal contradiction can be found again in the organization of gender relations. The hierarchy of the spheres of society, primarily the dominance of the area of employment over the institution of the family, is reflected in the hierarchy of the genders. The sphere of labour, like other public forums, has traditionally been a domain which favours men over women. In the life of a man, his career continues to have absolute priority over housework. Male participation in employment is, above all, considered to be the foundation that secures the livelihood of the family. Because of his monetary achievements, the man is the breadwinner of the family. That women participate to a great degree in the labour force and that this carries significance for the maintenance of the family has done little to change the self-image of the male as the provider, a norm which persists to this very day. Social situating of the genders runs parallel to the societal construction which says that work outside of the home is more valuable than housework and, in addition, that men's work exclusively means paid work. In contrast, housework is viewed as 'women's work'. The lesser value of housework as compared with professional work even extends into the devaluation of work performed by women that is mediated by the market: as a rule, it is more poorly remunerated, offers less opportunity for advancement, and is afforded less union protection. Men occupy a master status in both spheres: within the family they are the heads of the household; within the labour market they are considered a class above women (Krüger, 1995).

Even fathers in families in which the wives are the breadwinners profit from this dual master status. These family men do not participate in housework, because this is viewed as a female matter. They profit from the greater value of male labour although this value in the world of employment is not achieved by virtue of special qualifications, but which can be attributed to their gender membership. This normative orientation is upheld even if the man is unemployed: he is still not responsible for reproductive work in the home.

Women are socialized in two respects: they are responsible for private reproduction, and they participate in the labour force. However, this dual social involvement does not afford them any advantages; on the contrary, it yields them structural disadvantages in comparison with men. The problems associated with combining a family with professional ambitions are typical conflicts which men are rarely confronted with. Because gender hierarchies cut through all areas of society, many women also experience an accumulation of discrimination. As a rule, their possibilities of livelihood are generally more limited than those of men. This is indicated, for example, by the femininization of poverty. 'Gender' is therefore a structural category in the sense of a stratification criterion which indicates social inequality.

These structural conditions I have demonstrated, derived from the correspondences between organizing gender hierarchies and arranging societal hegemonies, are primarily – and *generally* – applicable to the female gender. Individual privileged women or groups of women may be able to modify them; however, they continue to be confronted with the phenomenon of other members of their gender being measured against male standards. This also affects the perspectives of their (own) emancipation: their gender has not been liberated.

Notes

I would like to extend my gratitude to Rebecca van Dyck for the translation of my contribution from German into English.

1 Compare Bunch and Myron (1974).
2 Not all radical feminists speak in a universalistic way about women, as is the case with e.g. Susan Griffin or Mary Daly. There are voices which maintain the different interests between women and which also consider particular coalitions between women and men legitimate – in light of unequal treatment based on class, race or religion. However, the opinion that social inequality does not play a role in womanculture is predominant: 'Race, class and national oppressions come from men, serve ruling class white men's interests, and have no place in a woman-identified revolution' (Bunch and Myron, 1974).
3 These problems characterize the emancipation politics of those Turkish feminists who support Kemalist positions. Their commitment to the reform programme of Ataturk, which enabled the integration of upper-class Turkish women oriented towards the West into public spheres, implies the assumption of a fundamental equality of the genders. The traditional patriarchal role distribution in the private sphere is not discussed.

References

Adorno, Theodor W. (1976) 'On the logic of the social sciences', in Theodor W. Adorno et al., *The Positivist Dispute in German Sociology*, trans. Glyn Adey and David Frisby. New York: Harper & Row. pp. 105–22.
Becker-Schmidt, Regina (1991) 'Identitätslogik und Gewalt. Zum Verhältnis von Kritischer Theorie und Feminismus', in Joachim Muller-Warden and Harald Welzer (eds), *Fragmente kritischer Theorie*. Tübingen: edition diskord.
Becker-Schmidt, Regina (1992) 'Verdrängung Rationalisierung Ideologie', in Gudrun Axeli Knapp and Anglika Wetterer (eds), *Traditionen Brüche: Entwicklungen feministischer Theorie*. Freiburg: Kore Verlag.
Bunch, Charlotte and Myron, Nancy (eds) (1974) *Class and Feminism: A Collection of Essays from the Furies*. Baltimore: Diana Press.
Fraser, Nancy (1974) *Widerspenstige Praktiken: Macht, Diskurs, Geschlecht*, trans. Karin Wordemann. Frankfurt-on-Main: Suhrkamp.
Gerhard, Ute (1978) *Verhältnisse und Verhinderungen: Frauenarbeit, Familie und Rechte der Frauen im 19 Jahrhundert*. Frankfurt-on-Main: Suhrkamp.
Gerhard, Ute (1988) 'Sozialstaat auf Kosten der Frauen', in Ute Gerhard, Alice Schwarzer and Vera Slupik (eds), *Auf Kosten der Frauen. Frauenrechte im Sozialstaat*. Weinheim and Basel: Beltz.

Jaggar, Alison M. (1983) *Feminist Politics and Human Nature*. Totowa, NJ: Rowman and Allanheld.

Koedt, A., Levin, E. and Rapone, A. (eds) (1973) *Radical Feminism*. New York: Quadrangle Books.

Krüger, Helga (1995) 'Dominanzen im Geschlechterverhältnis. Zur Institutionalisierung von Lebensläufen', in R. Becker-Schmidt and G.A. Knapp (eds), *Das Geschlechterverhältnis als Gegenstand der Sozialwissenschaften*. Frankfurt-on-Main and New York: Campus.

Maihofer, Andrea (1995) *Geschlecht als Existenzweise*. Frankfurt-on-Main: Helmer.

Rosaldo, M.Z. (1989) 'The use and abuse of anthropology. Reflexions on feminist and cross-cultural understanding', *Signs: Journal of Women in Culture and Society*, 5 (3): 392–5.

Young, Iris M. (1989) 'Humanismus, Gynozentrismus und feministische Politik', in Elisabeth List (ed.), *Denkverhältnisse. Feminismus und Kritik*. Frankfurt-on-Main: Suhrkamp.

6 Fragile Foundations, Strong Traditions, Situated Questioning: Critical Theory in German-Speaking Feminism

Gudrun Axeli Knapp

Since feminist theoretical debates on equality, difference and deconstruction have become more international, an inter-discourse has emerged which appears curiously aloof. Specific cultural backgrounds of experience and traditions of thought are rarely made transparent in contributions to this debate; arguments are mostly formulated in a very general mode.[1] At the same time, however, and in reaction to this trend, there is a growing awareness of the various ways in which theories and terminology are tied to contexts, and of the 'transformations' theories undergo 'in their travels' (cf. King, 1994).[2] Recontextualization and translation become more urgent the more we enter into an exchange and the more the contours of what may be considered to be common experiences become blurred.

My attempt to outline some of the trends within the German feminist reception of critical theory has to be seen against this wider background. What puzzled me was to notice that the theories of the early Frankfurt School have so far hardly played a role in the lively theoretical debates in English (this holds true although central texts are by now available in translation), while critical theory is associated, almost self-evidently it seems, with the name of Habermas. It is not my suggestion that there has been a wide reception of critical theory among German-speaking feminists. However, where this tradition has been referred to, it is the texts of Horkheimer and especially those of Adorno that are taken up. Noticing this discrepancy induced me to take a closer look at the specific ways in which critical theory has been received in German feminist writing.

My argument is that the seemingly contradictory way in which feminists refer to Adorno and Horkheimer, as well as the contours of their reformulations of critical theory, to a certain degree are shaped by the ways in which feminists in Germany are politically and historically situated.[3] The tense relationship feminists have developed towards critical theory – tense in that they at the same time refer to and distance themselves from this theory – carries the potential for a further development of feminist theory. This would imply a crossing of the usual barriers between advocates of critical theory and those of French post-structuralist thought, and an exploration of the specific explanatory potentials of both theoretical strands for more complex analyses (cf. Fraser and Nicholson, 1990).

Appropriation through critique

In order to explain why the feminist interest in the texts by Adorno and Horkheimer increased in the 1980s, some authors have pointed to the political relevance of these texts as a means to analyse the past as well as the present. Irmgard Schultz writes: 'The rediscovery of Horkheimer's and Adorno's *Dialectic of Enlightenment* by feminists in this country has to do – at least I can say this for myself – with a belated readiness to tackle the issue of German Fascism as a German and as a feminist 44 years after this book was written and 43 years after the camps were opened' (Schultz, 1992: 38). Ursula Beer notices 'that the sudden interest in Critical Theory coincides with a boom of mythical thinking . . . which also affected the women's movement and with the general renouncement of "reason" – publicly deplored in feuilleton writing' – which, supposedly, has to be seen in direct relation to society's general state of crisis (Beer, 1988: 17).

The reappropriation of critical theory became possible only after this theory was thoroughly examined and scrutinized. It was necessary thus to clarify the limits of adopting its propositions for a feminist analysis of society and critique of modernity:

> To choose gender differences as the central focus for a critical analysis of society means going beyond the Frankfurt School. It will not suffice to simply supplement the picture the Frankfurt School created of modernity. Rather, from a perspective that uses gender as the category of analysis one can highlight Critical Theory's own androcentric traits. (Nagl-Docekal, 1990: 2)

Discussions of critical theory in German-speaking feminism have primarily focused on the connection established in *Dialectic of Enlightenment* between instrumental reason and the domination of nature, the history of the civilization of the 'Self', the 'identical, purposive, virile character of [hu]man[kind]' (Horkheimer and Adorno, 1972: 33), the emergence of stereotypes of 'others' who serve as a target for venting hatred of one's own subordination and identity constraints.

While feminist debates have centred fairly intensively on the exemplary socio-philosophical analyses of the connection between instrumental reason, self-preservation and subordination, there have only been marginal references to the – in a narrower sense – social-theoretical assumptions of critical theory.

The first and most obvious reason for this hesitancy is critical theory's insufficient analysis of the 'gender system' (*Geschlechterverhältnis*). Significantly, there is a high degree of congruence between various authors of the Frankfurt School concerning their view of women's societal integration (*weibliche Vergesellschaftung*), a congruence which – despite accentual differences on details – stretches from Horkheimer and Fromm via Marcuse to Negt and Habermas. These scholars all tend to neglect the contradictions of women's societal integration and socialization in favour of an idealized notion of the family (Horkheimer) or of the 'contrasting virtues' of women (Habermas).

The second barrier to the reception of critical theory lies in its strong conceptual emphasis on the preponderance of societal conditions over individual behaviour, which remains dominant despite its explicit claim to a dialectical analysis of historical constellations of individuals and society.[4]

Taking into account the atmosphere of liberation and the diverse activities of the women's movement – particularly during the 1970s and 1980s – as well as the experienced and theorized contradictions of women's life contexts, there were at first hardly any points of connection between feminists and critical theory.

Adorno and Horkheimer's analysis of society is clearly marked by a fear of affirming and harmonizing societal conditions. Their critique is directed at the supremacy of the general in which specific interests gain a systemic quality which dominates that which – in the course of this historical process – is constituted as the particular. Since they perceived the social relations of reproduction as complicit with relations of dominance and thus as a 'falsely' composed whole, a 'negative totality', there was little room for a categorial identification and exploration of asynchronicities, contradictions and potentials of conflict. It is this aspect which rendered critical theory somewhat unwieldy for feminist reception.

At the same time, however, Adorno and Horkheimer's statements on the irrationality and coerciveness of an increasingly economized and rationalized society are path-breaking for feminist enquiries. Adorno's lecture, held in 1968, on 'Spätkapitalismus oder Industriegesellschaft' (Adorno, 1990) in passages reads like a diagnosis of the present and an early comment on some strands of 'postmodern' discourse: 'The system has taken a momentum of its own against all of us, even those in charge. It has become a fatality which finds expression in an omnipresent – according to Freud – free-floating anxiety' (Adorno, 1990: 364). 'As far as contemporary talk evolves around plurality, there is due suspicion that this pluralism, in the course of the expanding dominance of the system as a whole, has turned into ideology. The critical effort consists of breaking up totality's supremacy instead of pretending that pluralism already exists' (Adorno, 1990: 586; quotes translated by G.A. Knapp). Current social developments, in particular the increasing global interdependencies which go hand in hand with apparent uncontrollability of their economic, socio-political and ecological consequences, seem to confirm the relevance of the tendencies he diagnosed in the 1960s.

In line with probably most feminist scholars, Adorno considered it possible 'that contemporary society escapes from any coherent theory' (Adorno, 1990: 359). However, in contrast to the growing number of those who have responded to this development by doing without social theory,

Adorno continued to insist on the analysis of individual phenomena in the context of the socio-cultural system in which they are embedded. He furthermore emphasized the need to understand barriers of insight as an epistemological problem and ideology critique as a problem of socio-cultural and historical developments. I consider it worthwhile to pick up the threads of both these arguments.

The current trend towards reductionist approaches in parts of feminist theoretical debates is linked to the increasingly dominant role ascribed to questions of culture and language which, indeed, did not receive sufficient attention previously. The notion of society tends to be replaced by the notion of culture, and post-structuralist or 'postmodern' theories can nowadays be seen to play a distinctly larger role. By referring to Lacan, Irigaray and Derrida, for example, feminist theory has gained valuable inspiration but also has had to take on board a host of problems resulting from the legacy of a structuralist theoretical tradition. I consider its nominalism and the ahistorical treatment of the symbolic order to be the biggest problems in this respect.

Paradoxically this development has, however, also lent a renewed and unexpected relevance to such radical (pre-post)modern theories as that of Adorno. It is the concurrence of a thematic affinity between central ideas of post-structuralist or 'postmodern' theory (critique of instrumental reason, significance of aesthetics for the formation of theory, critique of identity, critique of the subject's illusion of autonomy) and their articulation in the context of Marxist-oriented social theory and psychoanalytic theories of the subject, which has kindled a renewed interest in this variant of critical theory. This is the more so as the inherent difficulties and limits of 'postmodern' and post-structuralist positions have become more apparent (Dews, 1994; Jay, 1995; McCarthy, 1991).

In recent feminist debates on the sex/gender differentiation the problematics of nominalistic and discourse-ontological tendencies have become particularly apparent. It therefore seems useful to me to study Adorno's dialectical critique of cognition more closely.[5] In the following section I will briefly outline its major features, focusing on Adorno's notion of mediation (*Vermittlung*).

Turning against positivism and a naive realism, Adorno emphasizes that there are no conceptually unmediated 'facts'. And vice versa: turning against Hegel's hypostatization of the *Geist*, Adorno states that all concepts necessarily refer to something beyond themselves: the subject matter of thought. There is no basis, no original signified, the relationships are mediated. In using the concept of mediation, which he specified explicitly in a critique of Hegel's understanding of *Vermittlung*, Adorno outlines the non-existence of ultimate foundations, but does so differently from post-structuralist theory.

Structurally, 'mediation' implies that a subject matter gains its determinacy, identity, only in reference to a non-identical moment. While Hegel conceptualizes the notion of mediation emphasizing the *medium*, its syn-thesizing potentials, Adorno, in contrast, attempts to outline mediation without a reconciliatory 'third point of reference'. He wants to unravel and break up the polarizing extremes and their inherent contradictions to such an extent that a kind of 'mediation without synthesis' can be perceived. He demonstrates this aporetic movement of thought, in which there is no reconciliation, in his *Negative Dialectics* (Kager, 1988: 146).

Apart from the conceptual, subjective pre-formation of epistemological objects (objects mediated through the subject), which all critics of naive realism have emphasized, Adorno stresses the objective mediation of the subject. However, contrary to (neo-)structuralist thought, in his case the decentring of the cognitive subject is not based on the argument that the symbolic order exists prior to the subject although Adorno agrees that language has an inescapable, constitutive function. To state the objec-tive mediation of the subject means to relativize the subject and her epistemological potentials by positioning her as an ephemeral part of nature within historically and culturally conditioned contexts. This relativization is radical since it presupposes the object's preponderance (Adorno, 1973a: 183).

> Carried through, the critique of identity is a groping for the preponderance of the object. Identitarian thinking is subjectivistic even when it denies being so. . . . Due to the inequality inherent in the concept of mediation, the subject enters into the object altogether differently from the way the object enters into the subject. An object can be conceived only by subjects but always remains something other than the subject, whereas a subject by its very nature is from the outset an object as well. Not even as an idea can we conceive a subject that is not an object; but we can conceive an object that is not a subject. To be an object also is part of the meaning of subjectivity; but it is not equally part of the meaning of objectivity to be a subject. (Adorno, 1973a: 183)

In Adorno's theory the idea of the object's preponderance has two dimen-sions: the first the somatic character even of cognitive processes which he holds against any idealistic hubris. 'The fact that the subject's cognitive achievements are somatic in accordance with their own meaning affects not only the basic relation of subject and object but the dignity of physicality' (Adorno, 1973b: 193). The second refers to a historical dimension which epistemology has to take into account: namely, the historical change in the qualitative subject–object constellation of cognitive possibilities, that is the primacy of the social over the individual, and the growing opacity of societal totality.

Drawing on Nietzsche and Benjamin, truth is decisively historicized. What is maintained, however, is an emphatic claim to cognition in the sense of gaining insight and understanding contextual relations: 'the traditional Cartesian notion of truth as the adequacy of a notion in terms of the respective object [is] shaken. . . . The locus of truth is changed to a multi-faceted dependency, the mutual (re-)creation of subject and object, and it may no longer be perceived as a static correspondence' (Adorno, 1975: 141). Central terms which recur in the context of the formulation of this process-ual, explicatory concept of cognition are: exact imagination, constellative, micrological thinking which seeks a proximity to the factual and, in concretizing that which it accounts for, makes use of the mimetic,[6] the rhetorical elements of language,[7] in order to grasp it in an interpretive mode and construe it as the outcome of its history:

> Becoming aware of the constellation in which a thing stands is tantamount to deciphering the constellation which, having come to be, it bears within it. . . . Cognition of the object in its constellation is cognition of the process stored in the object. As a constellation, theoretical thought circles the concept it would like to unseal, hoping that it may fly open like the lock of a well-guarded safe-deposit box: in response, not to a single key or a single number, but to a combination of numbers. (Adorno, 1973b: 163)

According to Adorno, this procedure resembles that of composing in music: a composition can be seen to be successful only where its subjective production is submerged, and it becomes readable as a sign of objectivity. 'What resembles writing in such constellation is the conversion into objec-tivity, by way of language, of what has been subjectively thought and assembled' (Adorno, 1973b: 165).

The complex theoretical architecture of a subject–object dialectics formu-lated in this way provides a space which seems to have been abandoned by approaches focusing solely on language or text. This is the architectural aspect Fredric Jameson might have in mind when he characterizes post-structuralist approaches as having 'a certain flatness' (1983). The fact that the notion of constitution has been reduced to encompass the constitution of meaning only, as well as the common labelling of all and everything as an 'effect' of language, indicates the lack of a more differentiating vocabulary. I do not underestimate the systematic problems which inhabit the subject–object dialectics and which have led Critical Theorists such as Habermas to concentrate more strongly on questions of intersubjectivity, of language and on normative questions of the conditionalities of truth. Nevertheless, although one might sympathize with Habermas's motivation to pursue a rational reconstruction of critical theory, a comparative reading conveys a feeling of loss. The question seems open of whether it is possible to make use of the analytical advantages of the linguistic turn without losing the encompassing and penetrating moments of negative dialectical thinking. The common either–or answers as well as the strikingly insistent and defensive pathos detectable on both sides of the fence of pro-and-con rhetorics seem to indicate – as one could well learn from negative dialectics, psychoanalysis and deconstruction – that it could be worthwhile to pursue this path further. My proposition is that the aesthetic (socio)philosophical model of a constellative, micrological thinking which, in the above sense, continues to draw upon the relations of mediation between the particular and the general, subjectivity and social objectivity, contains a number of impulses, not only for the social sciences.

In summary, it is critical theory's epistemological and methodological orientations, rather than its substantial statements on society and the 'gender system' itself, which can usefully be appropriated in the context of a feminist analysis of society:

1   the anti-foundationalist critique of knowledge which tries to negotiate rather than to dissolve the tension between thinking and that which is thought, between epistemic and ontological questions;
2   the mutual relatedness of a critical (i.e. psychoanalytically oriented) theory of the subject and social theory;
3   the intention to understand all phenomena from within the historical context which constituted them;
4   the necessity to expose conditions of domination and the diverse mechanisms through which power is implemented in society, in the constitution of subjectivity, as well as in the media of thought;
5   the claim to analyse society as a structural complex marked by contra-dictions   and   unevenness   resulting   from   specific   historical developments;
6   an anti-positivist and non-empiricist perspective which envisages theor-etical work as an element of political practice and, in this context, attempts to understand theory and empirical studies as mutually con-cretizing and enriching each other (cf. Becker-Schmidt, 1992: 666).

Gender and society

The systematic point of departure for feminist theorizing in sociology theory was the question of how the 'gender system' is embedded in social processes of material, generative and (in a wider sense) cultural reproduction. How is one to explain that whereas historical changes in economy, technology, politics, culture and social relations, commonly summarized as moderniza-tion, have modified the 'gender system', one can at the same time observe a re-formation of phenomena of systematic segregation and inequality which cut across other forms of social inequality and domination? Why is it that overtly violent relationships between the sexes have not disappeared in the wake of an allegedly progressing civilization? How do structures of gender segregation, a disregard for the interdependencies of gender groups and cultural symbolizations of gender differences interact to perpetuate or undermine hierarchies? How does the highly ambivalent cathexis of gender differences relate to specific conflictual constellations in the constitution of subjectivity, to the formation of inner-psychic representations of the 'Other' and to the psycho-dynamics of anxiety and desire?

Among current anti-foundationalist sociological approaches which claim to read 'things in being as text of their becoming' (Adorno) one can broadly differentiate between the following:

- Discourse theories analyse the 'becoming' of gender differences and of gender relations in at least two ways: the first is a critique of forms of representation which investigates language-based, symbolic mechanisms of essentialization and asks how something is represented or constituted in language. The second variant adopts a 'genealogical' perspective which traces the historical configurations of disciplining, normalizing and subjectivizing practices in which subjects are gendered. In this case dispositions of knowledge and power form the analytical points of connection.
- The social-constructivist enquiry of the 'becoming' of gender primarily employs a microsociological approach to 'doing gender', to processes of ascribing meaning to and representing gender in interactions between individuals. Human beings do not 'possess' a particular gender, nor 'are' they simply women or men. On the basis of a binary classificatory system, they rather 'present' and 'perceive' each other as such. Grounded in the sociology of knowledge this interactionist perspective is at times broadened to include various gendered social contexts.
- Approaches which broadly refer to critical theory analyse the 'becoming' of gendered subjects and the 'gender system' in a dialectical perspective, generally focusing on tensions, on forces and counter-forces within society and individuals. Society is scrutinized in terms of its contradictions and unevenness; processes of subject constitution taking place under those conditions are studied with a critical view on notions of identity. Emphasizing the coercive and normalizing features of identity and, thereby, the ideological dimension inherent in all identity claims, feminist critical theorists investigate the conflicting processes of individuation, enculturation and socialization.

In this context two social-theoretical questions are crucial: what is the connection between the specific organization of a society and the form of its 'gender system'? And, to what degree can gender be considered a category which underlies the systematic structuring of social division and differentiation; what is the relationship between gender and other categories of social inequality such as class/strata, 'race' or ethnicity?

Especially with regard to this last question it is in my view necessary to combine the approaches of social theory, discourse analysis and theories of action and interaction. My argument is that critical theory not only allows for this combination but, being a dialectically oriented theory, in fact contains a specific potential for overcoming the misleading distinction between micro- and macrosociology as well as the reductionist segregation of political, economic, social and cultural spheres. In this context it is not my aim to outline a 'grand theory' but rather to extend the possibilities of concretizing the notion of society, the terms of mediation and the notion of constellation in the framework of sociological enquiries.

According to critical theory society is a historically constituted relationality of individuals, groups of people, institutions and functional spheres, a complex of mediations of individuals and society, subjectivity and social objectivity which is permeated by power and modes of domination. Consequently, it is impossible to gain an understanding of the whole of society by combining analyses of single social spheres in the fashion of a jigsaw puzzle. As Adorno emphasized, society is not a 'social map' consisting of land and people (Adorno, 1990: 210).[8] Nor can individuals, their behaviour and their interactions count as the irreducible basis or as sole points of departure for analyses, nor can one ontologize the notion of 'societal totality': society is a category of mediation (Adorno, 1990: 549), a functional and relational notion, and not an essentialist term the contours of which could be defined in a geographical sense only.

What follows from these premises is that neither micro- nor macrosociological approaches lend themselves to an understanding of the contradictory processes and constellations of societal reproduction and social change. In this respect critical theory operates within the same heuristic horizon as theories such as those by Bourdieu, Giddens or Elias which investigate the relations between social structures and processes of structuration. At the same time, however, it goes beyond these action-oriented social theories in that it asks how life conditions and modes of experience are affected by the specific interrelation of the different spheres of social reproduction itself (*Vergesellschaftung der Sphären*).

Sociologists widely agree (and this applies to those with a system-theoretical, a Weberian or a Marxist background) that modern capitalist industrial societies can be seen to be differentiated into functional spheres and that the division of labour between these spheres contributes to the reproduction of the dynamic whole. However, opinions deviate when it comes to analysing the relationships between these sectors (such as the sphere of production, the service sector, the state, the educational system, private life contexts/family) and when they are to be identified as historically constituted, contradictory and uneven relations of dominance and subordination. In what way are these differentiated spheres themselves interrelated and which socio-economic, political and cultural factors determined the development of this constellation? Which homologizing processes take place between the social subsystems, and where are their limits? This applies to historical developments of economization, rationalization, formalization, normalization and their primary media: technology, science and law.

These are the questions taken up by Regina Becker-Schmidt, one of the few German feminists working in the context of social theory. With reference to Adorno she suggests a conceptualization of the contradictory societal integration of women as well as social-theoretical heuristic perspectives which other feminist scholars have made use of, specified, modified and applied to other fields of research (cf. Becker-Schmidt and Knapp,

1995). I will use her approach as a point of departure and reference for some remarks on the discussion on the differences among women. Based on these, I will outline why I consider it necessary to combine theoretical approaches which have so far been separated or have been formulated in antagonism to each other and why I consider social theory indispensable in this context.

In her reflections on the contradictory interdependencies of the spheres of social reproduction in capitalist industrial societies in the West, Regina Becker-Schmidt presupposes that in the course of social history economic, military, national and androcentric claims to supremacy have amalgamated. These have an impact on the specific structural organization of the various societal sectors as well as on the hierarchical relations between them (cf. Regina Becker-Schmidt, Chapter 5 in this volume; 1991a, 1994a). Gender relations are tied into this social history as both constituted and constituting elements. Her position is thus directed against dual-system concepts, Marxist notions of gender inequality as a secondary antagonism and one-dimensional concepts of patriarchal domination. The term 'gender system' (*Geschlechterverhältnis*) as it is used here has to be distinguished from that of 'gender relations' employed in theories of action and interaction. In a meta-perspective, it denotes the whole of those institutional regulations within a social framework through which gender groups are relationally positioned towards each other. Thus the notion of *Geschlechterverhältnis* neither stands for two homogeneous gender categories that live with and next to each other in a complementary division of labour (as functionalist gender role theory suggests); nor does it signify two homogeneous classes of persons who are positioned towards each other in rigid forms of subordination and supremacy, as concepts of patriarchal domination suggest. Rather, as the term itself already indicates, *Geschlechterverhältnis* is a functional, positional and relational term that cuts across other categories of social divisions such as class, colour and ethnicity and thereby shapes them in a specific way, much as the latter in turn mark the 'gender system'.

This theoretical perspective does not envisage class, 'race', ethnicity, gender and sexuality as group characteristics, but as mutually mediated, yet distinctly organized, socio-cultural structures. These generally include legal conditions, property relations, the division of labour, the organization of generativity, kinship and sexuality, of social positioning and of access to resources, and the discourses which found, consolidate and legitimize them. These conditions are contradictory and interspersed with unevenness. Respective modes of regulation and forms of institutionalization are not to be located on the same analytical level. They are not historically contingent, as the powerful economic, social and scientific developments of the late eighteenth and nineteenth centuries demonstrate during which era scientific discourses of difference flourished in the wake of the establishment of bourgeois-capitalist and modern forms of patriarchal domination, of the formation of national identities, colonialist expansion and racism. The relationship between these categories furthermore varies depending on whether one attempts to determine it in the context of an analysis of societal processes of reproduction and social disparities, or whether one addresses it from a perspective which challenges notions of identity and normalization. This perspective makes a difference between differences.

In discussions on the differences among women, sexual orientation features as a relevant category related to specific experiences of discrimination, subordination and questions of identity. Beyond the horizon of specific experiences, this 'difference' points to a systematic dimension of conditions of power or domination: the organization of sexuality as phallocratic heterosexuality. There can be no doubt that homosexuality or trans-sexuality (marginalized positions of desire and identity within the 'gender system' which have stabilized the historically established power of 'normality') belong to those politically contested demarcations which have received enormous state, clerical and scientific attention. However, in analytical terms, it is necessary to distinguish between the background, consequences, structures and social functions of the condemnation of sexual deviation if one considers them not primarily in terms of a critique of identity or normalization, but in terms of their embeddedness in processes of social reproduction, that is from the perspective of social and cultural theory. Neither on principle nor necessity is the organization of sexuality constitutively intertwined with the social organization of kinship, as common sense and structural theory can be seen to assume. On the contrary, sexuality and generativity can be largely de-linked, as has been shown, for example, in studies on the significance of homosexuality in relation to the organization of generativity in Greek antiquity (Foucault, 1986; Siems, 1988). As the social anthropologist Maurice Godelier (1990) has pointed out, the relationship between sexuality, generativity and kinship as well as their importance for the life process of a society vary according to culture and historical situation.

In analysing instances of social inequality gender, class, colour and ethnicity display a greater impact than sexual orientation. However, this is not the case with regard to questions of normalization, violence and identity. In terms of the politics of order and identity – and this would have to be specified historically – sexual orientation can be a more determining category than class which (looked at from the same perspective) is characterized by different distinctions and modes of regulation. This difference becomes even more apparent when one resorts to a Marxist definition of class rather than to an empirical notion of social stratification. For Marx class does not denote specific group characteristics, milieux, identities, experiences or attitudes, but instead refers to the organization of society, 'the historically constituted objective contradictions in the mutually dependent relationship between capital and wage labor, to the division of labor, the separation of processes of production and reproduction' (Becker-Schmidt, 1996: 184).

This background casts a different light on the discussion about the dividing lines among women. In recent years feminists have criticized the essentialist allegation of the 'equality' of women as victims of patriarchal domination and have pointed to the differences between women. In *Gender Trouble* (1990) Judith Butler problematized the way in which such distinctions have been established. She considers the common elaboration of predicates of colour, sexuality, ethnicity and class to be the desperate and ultimately futile attempt of feminists to encompass a 'situated subject'. She reads the embarrassed 'etc.' at the end of such lines of characterization as a 'sign of exhaustion as well as of the illimitable process of signification itself' (Butler, 1990: 143).

It is no coincidence that this debate originated in the USA where identity politics, as efforts of suppressed groups to gain political and cultural recognition, represents a specific tradition, a tradition which has left its marks on forms of political organization as well as on the formation of theory. I agree with Judith Butler's accentuation of the problematic aspects of this 'identity politics' in which theoretical and political definitions of 'group-identities' as 'difference' go hand in hand with a renewed exclusion of the non-identical which then triggers new conflicts and demarcations – although political practice cannot do without the formulation of group interests (Fraser, 1995). At the same time, however, the talk of an 'illimitable process of signification' can be reductionist if it is generalized in an unspecified way. An analytical perspective which, in a critical or affirmative fashion, concentrates exclusively on the symbolic modes of construction and representation of 'difference' (as identity) runs the risk of levelling historically constituted 'factual' differences and thereby suppressing 'differences' on its own terms. Against this background, the tendency in recent feminist debates on the diversification of 'Woman', which draws the lines of distinction between women primarily with regard to social identity and representation, is in my view a decisive step backwards. What seems to be necessary is a kind of theory formation and research which accounts for the diverse conditions which gave rise to the constitution of differences as well as their historical interrelatedness. It is important to think more carefully about such historical interconnections if we want to avoid explaining current gender divisions and hierarchies with reference to one principle only, namely the politics of gender differences, as is done by social-constructivist approaches to 'gendering'.

Such a reconstruction can only succeed if the theoretical tools of feminist analysis become more complex, as can be illustrated by using research on racism as an example. An analysis of the language of racism will give important insights into the modalities of the construction and representation of difference. Yet, this approach by itself will not achieve the same kind of insight into the constitutional and functional relatedness of racisms as one that combines the analysis of language and speech with an enquiry into the historically sedimented discursive repertoires, related forms of institutionalization and psycho-social dispositions which induce people to make a distinction between themselves and others. And these complexes in turn have to be set in relation to more general developments in the realms of culture and society, of economy, politics, the public media and science. Racisms have a different function within a text or a discourse than within the psychic disposition of individuals who articulate themselves in a racist way. The subjective functions of racism differ from its social functions – for instance with regard to the perpetuation of social inequalities and exploitation or with regard to unifying categories such as 'nationality' or 'ethnicity'. However, they are connected in a fatal way, as German history in particular has taught us.

It is the complexity of such contexts of mediation which asks for an interdisciplinary integration of different theoretical perspectives. At the same time an awareness has grown that they cannot easily be combined. What I have in mind is that in interdisciplinary analyses the difference between these perspectives could be reflected on the level of presentation by organizing insights so that they elucidate each other. In doing so, the moment of construction inherent in every insight should be integrated into the presentation in a self-reflecting way. Such methods may appear unorthodox in terms of common academic, especially sociological, practices. It is, however, precisely this experimental and unorthodox moment which allows one to articulate most convincingly the epistemological potentials of such an understanding of feminist critical theory. This moment grows out of a reflection on the restrictedness of the ideal of an all-encompassing knowledge and a complete theoretical integration into 'grand theory', and yet it insists on the analysis of large-scale societal constellations.

This throws a new light on a line of divergence between Horkheimer and Adorno on the issue of interdisciplinarity. There is a certain tension between Horkheimer's approach of an interdisciplinary materialism geared towards society's totality, and Adorno's model of a micrological and constellative thinking which was inspired by Benjamin. Martin Jay states 'that a large proportion of the creative ambivalence to be found in Adorno's negative dialectics can be traced back to the irreconcilable tensions between these two impulses in his work. His own variation of Critical Theory can be understood as a non-identical "field of force" between the poles of Benjamin and Horkheimer' (Jay, 1982: 81). This tension in Adorno's work had an impact on his notion of interdisciplinarity. In the context of discussions on an interdisciplinary methodology and on the relationship between sociology and psychology, as well as in his remarks on the debate on culturalism, Adorno criticized the attempt to combine these disciplines systematically, for example by Fromm and, later, by Talcott Parsons: 'The dissonant oppositions between these disciplines were genuinely more critical for Adorno than their smoothly integrating harmonization' (Jay, 1982: 77).

Within feminist debates that draw on critical theory this dissonant relationship between disciplinary perspectives is not, as in Adorno, tied to a diagnosis of societal conditions in general and of internal processes of the subject's societal integration in particular (Knapp and Landweer, 1995). Nevertheless, it plays a role in the context of a theoretically as well as empirically based critique of specific attempts to combine sociological and psychological perspectives as, for instance, that of defining a 'female social character'. This applies specifically to the critique of Nancy Chodorow's model developed in *The Reproduction of Mothering* (1978), which is one of the widely discussed feminist texts of the 1980s (Becker-Schmidt, 1993; Knapp, 1993; Othmer-Vetter, 1989; Rumpf, 1989).

Jay's statement on the Institut für Sozialforschung, namely that the failure of its original ambitions 'could paradoxically be interpreted as the source of its ultimate strength' (Jay, 1982: 83), might form a criterion of evaluation for potentially 'strong sides' of feminist critical theory. This spectrum of feminism is at least comparatively sensitive towards homogenizing or over-systematizing concepts which even out the contradictory mediatedness of subjectivity and socio-historical objectivity ingrained in the 'gender system'.

My discussion of the feminist reception and reinterpretation of critical theory serves to highlight two things: on the one hand the need to criticize critical theory for its biased and androcentric concept of women's societal integration; on the other that in taking up some of critical theory's methodological and theoretical perspectives one can (re)gain a non-economistic, non-functionalistic, historically concrete and complex notion of societal objectivity which, in the wake of the belated 'microsociological revolution' and of the overheated climate of change that accompanies 'postmodernism', runs the risk of being lost in feminist debates of the 1990s.[9] At the same time, early critical theory, especially that of Adorno, is a type of theory which is open to questions of language, discourse and signification which have been raised by post-structuralism.

In the following résumé I want to relate the development of feminist theory outlined above to my point of departure: the specific ways in which critical theory has been appropriated by feminists in Germany.

Without guidance: on tradition

The specific way in which critical theory has been appropriated by feminists can be outlined against the background of arguments formulated by Wolfgang Bonß and Axel Honneth in their introduction to *Sozialforschung als Kritik* (1982). They describe the reassessment of critical theory in the context of the crisis of dogmatic Marxism as well as with reference to the changing spectrum of social experiences which are reflected, for instance, in debates on ecology and technological developments.

The reception of Adorno and Horkheimer's work has been informed by both strands of critical theory: the initial conception of an interdisciplinary materialism, which espoused hope for social progress, and the deeply pessimistic diagnosis of the *Dialectic of Enlightenment* and their continuation in a *Critique of Instrumental Reason* (Horkheimer, 1967).

Apart from these two basic trends clearly set apart from each other, Bonß and Honneth point to distinguished discipline-specific structures of reception. Whereas strong continuities can be found in philosophical discussions and in debates on art and aesthetics, few reverberations have emerged in the empirically oriented social and political sciences.

Although I generally agree with this assessment concerning the 1970s and the German context, current developments seem to call for an elaboration and partial revision of the argument. In the context of the feminist appropriation of critical theory a political and academic constellation has emerged which in various ways cuts across the lines of demarcation drawn by Bonß and Honneth:

- Although it cannot be denied that there are discipline-specific ways in which critical theory has been taken up, feminist theory, in terms of its immersion in academic structures and its politically motivated enquiries, is a genuinely interdisciplinary project, one that does not, however, follow Habermas's route of a systematic revision and rational reconstruction of critical theory.
- The political project of feminist criticism depends on an analysis of contemporary society which is empirically oriented. The contradictory and complex nature of women's socio-cultural integration and positioning demands an unorthodox approach to the diverse strands and methodologies of the social sciences which cannot accept the demarcations between diverse schools of critical thought.
- The dangers of idolizing and thus arresting critical theory mentioned by Bonß and Honneth are comparatively small in the context of its feminist reception. As outlined above, due to the marginality of feminist interrogations in the academic field, even in its declaredly critical branches, appropriation without critique seems rather unlikely. This implication of a genuinely feminist focus of interest is apparent in the German rereadings of critical theory summarized above as well as in American feminist discussions on Habermas's theory of which Nancy Fraser's text *What is Critical about Critical Theory* (German trans. 1994) may be taken as an example (cf. also Meehan, 1995).
- Feminist theory does not comprise a homogeneous direction of research. Although loosely held together by a political bond, in disciplinary and theoretical terms it is a very heterogeneous movement. It is my assumption that this simultaneous awareness of community, of differences and of the openness of the feminist critical project provides the basis for a certain tolerance of theoretical differences. Despite some vehement debates, in German women's studies there are no theoretical disputes reminiscent of the sharp controversies that erupted within the academic left during the late 1960s in which theoretical demarcations were strongly intertwined with political dogmatisms. This attitude of overt eclecticism which is geared towards the possibilities of synthesis,

coupled with an awareness of its limitations and its preliminary character, and which furthermore reflects the specific confines of the theorist's own mode of thinking, is characteristic, in my view, of current developments in feminist theory.

If I initially referred to the seemingly contradictory structure of the feminist reception of critical theory, its underlying appropriatory constellation should have become clear by now. It is marked by the ambivalent political and academic positioning of feminist criticism: between radical scepticism about progress and the insistence on the possibility of eradicating dominance and violence within and beyond gender relations, between a critique of instrumental reason and an interest in reasonable societal relations, between a critique of covert androcentrism and the Enlightenment's homogenizing universalism, and the unfeasibility of completely discarding this heritage; between a critique of identitarian thought and a politics depending on the articulation of common problems and overlapping interests among women; between equality, difference and deconstruction, between theory and practice, academia and politics.

The specifically German background of experience, which I referred to earlier on, is indirectly reflected in the vehemence of the feminist critique of technology, rationality and identity which has been fuelled by *Dialectic of Enlightenment*. Each of these terms bears the marks of the historical experience of the murderous National Socialist mania of 'unrestricted practicability'. However, this historical background of experience also seems to manifest itself in the understanding of history. Radical versions of a 'postmodern' critique of history, in particular, which declare as illusory the temporal nexus of past, present and future, seem to be taking things too far.[10] In their understanding the present becomes a *posthistoire* in which the memory of the past does not provide orientation for the present (Rüsen, 1993). I regard the enduring presence of the history of National Socialism as one of the thresholds such relativist approaches to history come up against. They certainly have some validity when it comes to questioning unifying approaches to history and teleologies of progress; and yet, relativisim itself is relativized by the specific historical and political context. Beyond individual involvement and responsibility there are political and cultural moments of focused and dispersed attention usually referred to as 'historical culture'. The latter is marked by the struggles over the interpretation and significance of recollections and social memory. Such historical relationality in which German feminists are enmeshed as participants in a political movement and as citizens, suggest a twofold 'li[e]ability' in the sense of being embedded within a historical culture and accepting responsibility for it. Against this background our point of view can become idiosyncratic; developments including those within feminist theoretical debates are observed and critically questioned in recourse to this context of experience. The so-called

Historikerinnenstreit (the dispute among female historians) on the 'complicity' of women in National Socialism documents the topicality of this past (Gravenhorst and Tatschmurat, 1990).

Adopting such a perspective no longer allows one, for example, to skim over sentences such as those formulated by the feminist writer Luce Irigaray, who in 1987 in her critique of patriarchy declared emphatically:

> We should . . . not tolerate that our mothers are accused of having been the pillar of Fascism! Were they in power? Did they have a say in the choosing of a regime? Rather it would be more appropriate to recognize that each patriarchal order, which ascribes to women no other function and value than that of motherhood, is potentially fascist. (Irigaray, 1987: 59; my translation)

The impetus of her critique of the confinement of women to motherhood here turns into an affirmative exculpation of 'our mothers' and an obliteration of the involvement of German women and collaborating women of other nationalities in the history of Fascism. The theoretical background to this suspension of discriminating capacity has to be seen in Irigaray's notion of the exclusion and otherness of 'women' within 'culture', which, without any empirical reference, is based on her structuralist concept of the symbolic order (cf. Knapp, 1994). It is her renunciation of a historically specified analysis of culture and society, of the 'gender system' and the life conditions of women, which makes this perspective possible.

I am increasingly irritated by the degree to which 'theories of difference' appear to be easily appropriated by declaredly right-wing politicians who – without going into detail – refer to 'postmodern philosophy'. I suspect that this fatal appropriation is facilitated by the explicit obliteration of possible claims to promises of equality – although they are implicitly suggested and even logically presupposed. I am wondering whether the dialectical linking of equality and difference is relatively more resistant to such political instrumentalization or whether this always remains a possibility. The interview published by the neo-right-wing paper *Junge Freiheit* with the founder of the 'Nouvelle Droite', Alan de Benoist, can serve as a case in point. Benoist uses a mixture of Gramscian terminology and the jargon of *différance* in a deliberately playful way to propagate the 'acknowledgement of difference' as the basic element of a right-wing cultural revolution (Benoist, 1982; Mohler and Stein, 1993).

Peculiar alliances such as the one described above bring us back to Adorno. As a radical critic of instrumental reason and identitarian logics and as an advocate of the right to difference he never left any doubt concerning the legacy inspiring his critique. In a metaphorical sense the title of his text *Without Guidance: On the Tradition of Enlightenment* evokes something of the socio-political positioning of those feminists who have referred to the Frankfurt School while at the same time critically interrogating it with its own tools of thought. Without guidance, joined by the impetus to criticize domination and identity constraints, against the background of a history of racist identity politics: 'There is nothing traditional to be resumed more fruitfully than the momentum of Enlightenment betrayed and disparaged in Germany, a subterranean tradition of the anti-traditional' (Adorno, 1977: 316).

Notes

1 My impression refers in particular to those contemporary diagnoses which are presented under the ambiguous label of 'postmodernism'. For example, Andreas Huyssen has pointed to the crucial differences between US-American and European discussions on 'postmodernism' which have been covered up by the unspecific usage of this term (Huyssen and Scherpe, 1986). However, this problem recurs in other areas as well. Thus, in the US the discourse on the term 'race' exists in a social, historical and political context which is completely different from that to be found in Germany. Respective accentuations in the usage and in the critique of this term cannot be understood without recourse to the specific historical background of each country (cf. Gümen, 1994).

2 This also applies to the cultural and etymological characteristics of the key feminist term 'gender' which are largely unexplored. De Lauretis (1987) has pointed to the fact that the linguistic connotations of the 'sex/gender' debate in English are hardly transferable into Roman languages. This holds true for its transference into the German language in which a categorical distinction between 'sex' and 'gender' cannot be made. The highly condensed German word *Geschlecht* lexically never refers to biology alone. Its Old Middle and High German etymological roots (*geslehte*; *gislahti*) originally denote a 'similar kind'; *Geschlecht* is furthermore associated with a genealogical component in the sense of 'descent'; it recalls notions of species and genus; it has been employed to signify 'humankind' (*Menschengeschlecht*) and refers to the binary classification system of gender identity (*Geschlecht*: 'female'/'male'). For 'feminine' and 'female' there is only one German term: *weiblich*.

Translation of certain key terms of the dialectical theoretical tradition tends to create enormous difficulties. This also applies to central notions of feminist theory. Thus, the German *Geschlechterverhältnis* is generally translated by the term 'gender relations' which in German corresponds to *Geschlechterbeziehungen*. The term *Geschlechterverhältnis* signifies more than just relations between 'men' and 'women': from a meta-perspective it is geared towards the entire institutionalized arrangement by which gender groups are positioned towards each other. The latter suggests a closeness to the notions of 'gender system' and 'gender order'. However, these terms tend to overemphasize the aspects of statics and order.

3 There is a striking, unorthodox pattern of reference which cuts across the phases commonly distinguished to outline the history of critical theory. Thus, certain claims of Horkheimer's early and politically optimistic programme of an inter-disciplinary combination of theory and empirical research ('interdisciplinary materialism') are taken up (e.g. Kuhn, 1992) as well as later radical critiques of reason and identity, particularly those formulated within the context of negative dialectics.

4 Regina Becker-Schmidt makes a similar remark in her critique of Adorno: 'I believe that in his view of society as "negative totality" Adorno overestimated processes of social uniformity. Contradictions and potentials for conflict which can provoke resistance remain undetermined in his critique' (Becker-Schmidt, 1991a: 387).

5 'In fact, dialectics is neither a pure method nor a reality in the naive sense of the word. It is not a method, for the unreconciled matter – lacking precisely the identity surrogated by the thought – is contradictory and resists any attempt at unanimous

interpretation. It is the matter, not the organizing drive of thought, that brings us to dialectics. Nor is dialectics a simple reality, for contradictoriness is a category of reflexion, the cogitative confrontation of concept and thing. To proceed dialectically means to think in contradictions, for the sake of the contradiction once experienced in the thing, and against that contradiction. A contradiction in reality, it is a contradiction against reality. But such dialectics is no longer reconcilable with Hegel' (Adorno, 1973a: 144).

6 The differences between post-structuralist and negative dialectical interpretations of the notion of mimesis are discussed in Jay (1995).

7 'The constellation illuminates the specific side of the object, the side which to a classifying procedure is either a matter of indifference or a burden. The model for this is the conduct of language. Language offers no mere system of signs of cognitive functions. Where it appears essentially as a language, where it becomes a form of expression, it will not define its concepts. It lends objectivity to them by the relation into which it puts the concepts, centred about a thing' (Adorno, 1973a: 162).

8 'There exists a social map of Hessen [a German federal state] which in homey little pictures shows that in one region pig breeding prospers and in another the growing of potatoes, and then there are cities such as Frankfurt which have been commercial towns for centuries but today have a strong industrial sector [yet, such an addition of single sectors, of regions and their social structure does not signify] anything essentially sociological . . . because in reality there exists a functional interdependency between all these sectors. Society itself does not consist of a mere co-existence of the concrete moments it is composed of. As a concrete totality or a concrete generality . . . society documents itself in the relations of dependency between these single parts. Within the dominant types of societal integration [*Vergesellschaftung*], within the conditions which are really setting the terms of contemporary society, these sectors which are here portrayed in peaceful co-existence differ entirely in their relative importance. Consequently, they cannot be equated in terms of their relevance for society as a whole' (Adorno, 1993: 106).

9 I do concede that 'postmodern' theorists have posed important questions of academic and social development. However, their rhetorics of a change of paradigm and circulating metaphors of relegation (the end of history, etc.) have more to do with the hermetic architecture of theories, the force of hopes and illusions and the dogmatism of parties and political groups, which one felt compelled to dismiss, than with what was 'real' in societal terms and what remains as a task for critical thought and practice.

10 'All of the latest proclamations of the end of history entail recourse to a totalizing philosophy of history which is once more enjoyed in reminiscence but discarded in terms of its possible significance for the future' (Niethammer, 1993: 40).

References

Adorno, T.W. (1973a) *Philosophische Terminologie*, vol. 1. Frankfurt-on-Main: Suhrkamp.

Adorno, T.W. (1973b) *Negative Dialectics*. London: Routledge.

Adorno, T.W. (1975) 'Zur Metakritik der Erkenntnistheorie', *Collected Writings 5*. Frankfurt-on-Main: Suhrkamp.

Adorno, T.W. (1977) 'Über Tradition', *Collected Writings 1o.1*. Frankfurt-on-Main: Suhrkamp.

Adorno, T.W. (1990) 'Spätkapitalismus oder Industriegesellschaft?', *Collected Writings 8.1*. Frankfurt-on-Main: Suhrkamp.

Adorno, T.W. (1993) *Einleitung in die Soziologie*. Frankfurt-on-Main: Suhrkamp.

138   *Feminism, culture and society*

Becker-Schmidt, R. (1991a) 'Identitätslogik und Gewalt: zum Verhältnis von Kritischer Theorie und Feminismus', in J. Müller-Warden and H. Welzer (eds), *Fragmente Kritischer Theorie*. Tübingen: edition diskord. pp. 59–79.

Becker-Schmidt, R. (1991c) 'Vergesellschaftung und innere Vergesellschaftung: Individuum, Klasse, Geschlecht aus der Perspektive der Kritischen Theorie', in W. Zapf (ed.), *Die Modernisierung moderner Gesellschaften, Verhandlungen des 25: deutschen Soziologentages in Frankfurt am Main*. Frankfurt-on-Main and New York: Campus. pp. 383–95.

Becker-Schmidt, R. (1992) 'Verdrängung, Rationalisierung, Ideologie: Geschlechterdifferenz und Unbewußtes, Geschlechterverhältnis und Gesellschaft', in G.A. Knapp and A. Wetterer (eds), *Traditionen Brüche: Entwicklungen feministischer Theorie*. Freiburg: Kore.

Becker-Schmidt, R. (1993) 'Ambivalenz und Nachträglichkeit: Perspektiven einer feministischen Biographieforschung', in M. Krüger (ed.), *Was heißt hier eigentlich feministisch?* Bremen: Donat.

Becker-Schmidt, R. (1994a) 'Geschlechterverhältnis, Technologieentwicklung und androzentrische Ideologieproduktion', in N. Beckenbach and W.v. Treeck (eds), *Umbrüche gesellschaftlicher Arbeit, Soziale Welt*, Special Issue 9. Göttingen.

Becker-Schmidt, R. (1994b) 'Homo-Morphismus: Autopoietische Modelle und sozialwissenschaftliche Rationalisierung', in B. Aulenbacher and T. Siegel (eds), *Wege aus der Krise?* Pfaffenweiler: Centaurus.

Becker-Schmidt, R. (1996) 'Transformation und soziale Ungleichheit, soziale Ungleichheit und Geschlecht', in S. Metz-Göckel and A. Wetterer (eds), *Voransdenken, Querdenken, Nachdenken, Texte für Aylâ Neusel*. Frankfurt-on-Main and New York: Campus. pp. 183–95.

Becker-Schmidt, R. and Knapp, G.A. (eds) (1995) *Das Geschlechterverhältnis als Gegenstand der Sozialwissenschaften*. Frankfurt-on-Main and New York: Campus.

Beer, U. (1988) 'Das Zwangsjackett des bürgerlichen Selbst – Instrumentelle Vernunft und Triebverzicht', in C. Kulke (ed.), *Rationalität und sinnliche Vernunft*. Pfaffenweiler: Centaurus. pp. 16–30.

Benhabib, S., Butler, J., Cornell, D. and Fraser, N. (1993) *Der Streit um Differenz: Feminismus und Postmoderne in der Gegenwart*. Frankfurt-on-Main: Fischer.

Benoist, A. (1982) *Die entscheidenden Jahre: Zur Erkennung des Hauptfeindes*. Tuebingen: Grabert.

Bonß, W. and Honneth, A. (eds) (1982) *Sozialforschung als Kritik: Zum sozialwissenschaftlichen Potential der Kritischen Theorie*. Frankfurt-on-Main: Suhrkamp.

Butler, J. (1990) *Gender Trouble. Feminism and the Subversion of Identity*. New York: Routledge.

Chodorow, N. (1978) *The Reproduction of Mothering: Psychoanalysis and the Sociology of Gender*. Berkeley, CA: University of California Press.

De Lauretis, T. (1987) *Technologies of Gender*. Bloomington, IN: Indiana University Press.

Dews, P. (1994) 'Adorno, post-structuralism and the critique of identity', in S. Zizek (ed.), *Mapping Ideology*. London: Verso. pp. 36–46.

Foucault, M. (1986) *Die Sorge um sich: Sexualität und Wahrheit*, vol. 3. Frankfurt-on-Main: Suhrkamp.

Fraser, N. (1994) *Widerspenstige Praktiken: Macht, Diskurs, Geschlecht*. Frankfurt-on-Main: Suhrkamp.

Fraser, N. (1995) 'From redistribution to recognition? Dilemmas of justice in a "Post-Specialist" age', *New Left Review*, 212: 68–93.

Fraser, N. and Nicholson, L. (1990) 'Social criticism without philosophy: an encounter between feminism and postmodernism', in L. Nicholson (ed.), *Feminism/Postmodernism*. New York and London: Routledge. pp.19–39.

Godelier, M. (1990) *Natur, Arbeit, Geschichte. Zu einer universalgeschichtlichen Theorie der Wirtschaftsformen.* Hamburg: Argument.

Gravenhorst, L. and Tatschmurat, C. (1990) *Töchter Fragen.* Freiburg: Kore.

Gümen, S. (1994) 'Geschlecht und Ethnizität in der bundesdeutschen und US-amerikanischen Frauenforschung', *Texte zur Kunst*, 4 (15): 127–39.

Horkheimer, M. (1967) *Kritik der instrumentellen Vernunft.* Frankfurt-on-Main: Suhrkamp.

Horkheimer, M. and Adorno, T.W. (1972) *Dialectic of Enlightenment.* New York: Verso.

Huyssen, A. and Scherpe, K. (eds) (1986) *Postmoderne: Zeichen eines kulturellen Wandels.* Reinbek bei Hamburg: rowohlt.

Irigaray, L. (1987) *Zur Geschlechterdifferenz: Interviews und Vorträge.* Vienna: Frauenverlag.

Jameson, F. (1983) 'Postmodernism and consumer society', in H. Forster (ed.), *The Anti-Aesthetic. Essays on Postmodern Culture.* Washington, WA: Bay Press.

Jay, M. (1982) 'Positive und negative Totalität: Adornos Alternativentwurf zur interdisziplinären Forschung', in W. Bonß and A. Honneth (eds), *Sozialforschung als Kritik.* Frankfurt-on-Main: Suhrkamp. pp. 67–86.

Jay, M. (1995) 'Mimesis und Mimetologie. Adorno und Lacoue-Labarthe', in G. Koch (ed.), *Auge und Affekt: Wahrnehmung und Interaktion.* Frankfurt-on-Main: Suhrkamp.

Kager, R. (1988) *Herrschaft und Versöhnung: Einführung in das Denken T.W. Adornos.* Frankfurt-on-Main and New York: Campus.

King, K. (1994) *Theory in its Feminist Travels.* Bloomington, IN: Indiana University Press.

Knapp, G.A. (1992) 'Macht und Geschlecht: Neuere Entwicklungen in der feminist-ischen Macht- und Herrschaftsdiskussion', in G.A. Knapp and A. Wetterer (eds), *Traditionen Brüche: Entwicklungen feministischer Theorie.* Freiburg: Kore. pp. 287–325.

Knapp, G.A. (1993) 'Der weibliche Sozialcharakter – Mythos oder Realität? Soziologische und sozialpsychologische Aspekte des Sozialcharakter-Konstrukts', in M. Krüger (ed.), *Was heißt hier eigentlich feministisch? Zur theoretischen Diskussion in den Geistes- und Sozialwissenschaften.* Bremen: Donat. pp. 93–121.

Knapp, G.A. (1994) 'Politik der Unterschiedung', in Institut für Sozialforschung (ed.), *Geschlechterverhältnisse und Politik.* Frankfurt-on-Main: Suhrkamp. pp. 262–88.

Knapp, G.A. and Landweer, H. (1995) 'Interdisziplinarität in der Frauenforschung. Ein Dialog', *L'Homme. Zeitschrift für feministische Geschichtswissenschaft*, 6 (2), Schwerpunktheft 'Interdisziplinarität': 6–39.

Kuhn, A. (1992) 'Kritische Theorie und Frauenforschung', *Neue Gesellschaft, Frankfurter Hefte*, 39: 1008–18.

Kulke, C. (ed.) (1988) *Rationalität und sinnliche Vernunft. Frauen in der patri-archalen Realität.* Pfaffenweiler: Centaurus.

Kulke, C. and Scheich, E. (eds) (1992) *Zwielicht der Vernunft: Die Dialektik der Aufklärung aus der Sicht von Frauen.* Pfaffenweiler: Centaurus.

Löwenthal, L. (1983) 'Erinnerungen an Theodor W. Adorno', in L. v. Friedeburg (ed.), *Adorno-Konferenz 1983.* Habermas. Frankfurt-on-Main: Suhrkamp. pp. 388–402.

McCarthy, T. (1991) *Ideals and Illusions: On Reconstruction and Deconstruction in Contemporary Critical Theory.* Cambridge, MA: MIT Press.

Meehan, J. (ed.) (1995) *Feminists Read Habermas: Gendering the Subject of Discourse.* London: Routledge.

Mohler, A. and Stein, D. (1993) 'Im Gespräch mit Alain de Benoist', in *Junge Freiheit, Interview-Reihe*, 3, Freiburg: Potsdam.

Nagl-Docekal, H. (1990) *Kritische und feministische Theorie*. Vienna.

Niethammer, L. (1993) 'Die postmoderne Herausforderung. Geschichte als Gedächtnis im Zeitalter der Wissenschaft', in W. Küttler, J. Rüsen and E. Schulin (eds), *Geschichtsdiskurs*. Frankfurt-on-Main: Fischer.

Othmer-Vetter, R. (1989) *'Muttern' und das Erbe der Väter: Eine neuere Affäre zwischen Feminismus und Psychoanalyse?* Feministische Studien, Zwischen Tugend und Affären, Heft 2/89, Weinheim: Deutscher Studien.

Rauschenbach, B. (ed.) (1992) *Erinnern, Wiederholen, Durcharbeiten: Zur Psycho-Analyse deutscher Wenden*. Berlin: Aufban.

Rumpf, M. (1989) *Spuren des Mütterlichen: Die widersprüchliche Bedeutung der Mutterrolle für die männliche Identitätsbildung in Kritischer Theorie und feministischer Wissenschaft*. Frankfurt-on-Main and Hanover: Materialis.

Rüsen, J. (1993) 'Moderne und Postmoderne als Gesichtspunkte einer Geschichte der modernen Geschichtswissenschaft', in W. Küttler, J. Rüsen and E. Schulin (eds), *Geschichtsdiskurs*. Frankfurt-on-Main: Fischer. pp. 17–31.

Schultz, I. (1992) 'Julie and Juliette und die Nachtseite der Geschichte Europas: Naturwissen, Aufklärung und pathische Projektion in der "Dialektik der Aufklärung" von Adorno und Horkheimer', in C.Kulke and E. Scheich (eds), *Zwielicht der Vernunft*. Pfaffenweiler: Centaurus. pp. 25–41.

Siems, A. (ed.) (1988) *Sexualität und Erotik in der Antike*. Darmstadt: Wissenschaftliche Buchgesellschaft.

7 Adorno: The Riddle of Femininity

Juliet Flower MacCannell

Love you will find only where you may show yourself weak without provoking strength.

(Adorno, 1974: 192)

Favorite virtue in a woman: weakness.

(Karl Marx, 'Confessions', in Marx and Engels, 1978: 436)

Woman doesn't exist

My themes as a cultural critic and analyst have more than overlapped with those of Adorno. His larger insights into totalitarianism, anti-Semitism, and the newer forms of damage inflicted by contemporary civilization have always guided my speculation.[1] These matters he raised so often and so urgently have shaped my own assimilations of deconstruction, semiotics and psychoanalysis, if not my feminism. Like him, I have an abiding concern for uncovering the sources of Fascism and the recurrence of repressive author-itarianism in the midst of bourgeois forms of social and cultural life; for the meaning, role and possible refunctioning of art and aesthetics; for the problematic heritage of the Enlightenment; and for the desirable, if failed, synthesis of Kantian (for me rather Rousseauesque), Freudian and Marxist analytic theories.[2] And like him, I would like to see those philosophies that claim disinterestedness called to account when they unknowingly rationalize existing power arrangements.

As a 'politicized' student in the 1960s, present at May '68 in Paris and participant in resistance to the Vietnam War, I was also at that time a student of a deconstruction oriented to German philosophy. So I, too, traced some of the same paths as Adorno, through Husserl, Heidegger, Hegel, Kant, Freud, as extremely turbulent political events took place all around. Like him, I can imagine no better or alternative way of access to 'society' and its darker secrets – its unresolved antagonisms – than through the individual who is imbued, structured and shaped (that is, alienated) by them (Adorno, 1974: 17). My interest in psychoanalysis has been marked by the same demand as Adorno's – that it prove its worth by offering access to these hidden sides of a damaging social order, rather than by fulfilling a mission of better adjusting the individual to that order.[3]

Why, then, have I never felt a personal affinity with Adorno's writing? I have tried to sort out why Adorno, with his brilliant insights and *aperçus,* and whose theories I am so often more than ready to second and support, to applaud and to quote, never drew me intimately toward him. Each contact with him sent me off in search of others who agreed with him, but who expressed themselves differently. My preferred portions in Adorno's work, for example, are those that resonate with Benjamin; my favourite piece of Adorno's writing is his epitaph/essay for his troubled colleague.[4] I've even elected to make my way through Lacan's, rather than Adorno's, complicated syntheses of Kant and Freud (which, all told, must owe a great deal to Adorno's insights), not least because Lacan articulated them in so singular and intriguing a manner. Hannah Arendt's closely worked analysis of Eichmann has inspired my writing more than all of Adorno's brilliant analyses of anti-Semitism.[5] Bakhtin's aesthetics, Barthes's deciphered bits of modern culture – these speak more directly to me than Adorno. Why?

Is it because of Adorno's taste for German over Anglo-American and French culture? for classical music over jazz? for the dialectic? Is it my resistance to his darkest cynicism about art and the role of sublimation in it ('Every work of art is an uncommitted crime'; 'Talent is sublimated rage'),[6] a sublimation he restricts to an individual artist's capacity to exhibit and yet forgo murderous enjoyment? Or does it have something to do with women and his general absence of recognition of a special significance to female human existence? Perhaps in unravelling the secret of my resistance to him, of what has kept him from my fullest embrace, I will learn something more about 'woman', and not only in his work.

Feminist Adorno: I

Adorno contrasted the 'bad equality of today' (Adorno, 1974: 102–3), the quantitative egalitarianism of contemporary society and its demand to eradicate differences, with a potentially 'better state' in which people could be different without fear.

> That all men are alike is exactly what society would like to hear. It considers actual differences as stigmas indicating that not enough has yet been done; that something has been left outside the machinery. . . . The spokesmen of unitary tolerance are always ready to turn on any group that remains refractory. . . . An emancipated society, on the other hand, would not be a unitary state, but the realization of universality in the reconciliation of differences. Politics that are still seriously concerned with such a society ought not, therefore, [to] propound the abstract equality of men as an idea. . . . The melting pot was introduced by unbridled industrial capitalism. The thought of being cast into it conjures up martyrdom, not democracy. (1974: 102)

In such a 'better state' no one should have to sacrifice their specific difference, their 'thing'. Where would women fit? Adorno criticized in women submissive 'femininity' and sadistic coldness alike. But what, if not femininity and its flip side, the dominatrix, is the specific difference of 'woman', her 'thing'? Adorno framed a utopia here – 'emancipated society'; 'the realization of universality in the reconciliation of differences' (1974: 103) – yet specified no space for woman as a particularity, a particularity which, for Adorno, alone yields access to the universal.[7] This, then, is one stake of my game: the adequacy or inadequacy of *woman* to the universal subject of Adorno's dream.

It is the only real reason to ask the 'Woman Question' of Adorno because there is very little to find fault with in him, and much that we would today call 'political correctness', where woman is concerned. His critical theory is virtually gender-blind, his aphorisms about women are almost always proto-feminist – such as his pronouncement that 'The feminine character, and the ideal of femininity on which it is modeled, are products of masculine society' (1974: 92). Long before the woman's movement he assailed women's abuse, archaic as well as contemporary (1974: 90). While he mainly ascribed this abuse to the bourgeois social order (from the Renaissance on) that drew his theoretical Marxist and personal antipathy, he also extended it to prehistory. Commenting on a play by Schnitzler, Adorno speaks of an 'agreeably non-puritanical wench' who nonetheless verbally chases off a suitor while accepting his advances:

[She] voices an archaic frigidity, the female animal's fear of copulation, which brings her nothing but pain. Pleasure is a late acquisition, scarcely older than consciousness. . . . Females . . . undergo love in unfreedom, as objects of violence. Women have retained a consciousness of this, particularly among the petty bourgeoisie, down to the late industrial era. . . . No man, cajoling some poor girl to go with him, can mistake, unless he be wholly insensitive, the faint moment of rightness in her resistance, the only prerogative left by patriarchal society to woman . . . as the giver she has from time immemorial been the dupe. (1974: 90–1)

He heaped scorn on the way women fared under the *petit bourgeoisie* – as when he glimpsed the entire battle of the sexes in the way a housewife holds her husband's coat for him:

The domestic tyrant has his wife help him on with his coat. She eagerly performs this service of love, following him with a look that says: what else should I do, let him have his little pleasure, that's how he is, only a man. The patriarchal marriage takes its revenge on the master in the wife's indulgent considerateness. . . . Beneath the lying ideology which sets the man up as superior, there is a secret one, no less untrue, that sees him as inferior, the victim of manipulation, manoeuvring, fraud. . . . In the incongruity between his authoritarian pretensions and his helplessness. . .there is something ridiculous. . . . Hegel's dialectic of master and servant applies. . . . As the repressed matriarch she becomes the Master precisely where she has to serve, and the patriarch needs only to appear as such in order to be a caricature. This simultaneous dialectic of epochs has presented itself to individualistic eyes as the 'battle of the sexes'. Both opponents are in the wrong. In demystifying the husband, whose power rests on his money-earning trumped up as human worth, the wife too expresses the falsehood of marriage, in which she seeks her whole worth. No emancipation without that of society. (1974: 173)

But his strongest criticism of woman's problem is reserved for the liberated condition in which the modern woman labours. Even more than prehistoric sexual relations, the patriarchy and its degraded petty bourgeois households, women's new emancipation has only a mere 'appearance' of life:

> Young people no longer have the family as the horizon of their developing lives; the autonomy of the father disappears, and with it resistance to his authority. Before, thralldom in her father's house would awaken an emotion in a girl which seemed to point to freedom, even though it was actually realized either in marriage or somewhere else outside. But now that a girl has the prospect of job before her, that of love is obstructed. The more universally the modern industrial system requires everyone to bind himself to it the more everyone . . . will tend to become the smalltime expert, the creature who has to fend for himself. As qualified labor, the independence of the entrepreneur . . . envelops all (including the 'professional' woman) as their nature. (Horkheimer and Adorno, 1982: 107)

Nothing seems to be missing from this extensive inventory of woman's existence. *Except* some kind of adumbration of *woman-beyond-the-bourgeoisie*, Adorno leaves us precious little of an anticipatory sort where a future woman is concerned. Granted, he argued vociferously against attempts to provide concrete images of a post-revolutionary world. He claimed to be giving us only the essence of woman's restricted choices both before and after the patriarchy. But if we want to imagine or dream ourselves beyond both the family and capitalist society *as women* we do not get much help from him.

Is there, notwithstanding, a feminist utopian horizon lurking in Adorno? Are the 'correct' attitudes he so eminently exhibits the upper limit of what we can discover about his understanding of *women* (not to mention the 'feminine' he held in such disdain as a bourgeois concept)?[8]

Let us look back at the last passage cited above. The crucial thing woman has 'lost' under advanced capitalism, if we read closely here, is 'an *emotion* which seemed to point to *freedom*' (my italics). Adorno constantly points out woman's absence of freedom, economic, social, and now even of the heart. Prior to capitalism, emotional freedom (and the emotion of freedom) had found its last resort in woman, in the pre-romantic form of 'pity' or compassion (Rousseau, 1964). 'The *rigor mortis* of society is spreading to the last cell of intimacy that thought itself secure' (Adorno, 1974: 138). With 'enlightened' self-interest, woman loses her link with the freedom of emotion – a 'freedom' that, in our time, can only be indirectly represented in the unconscious, that is, in hysteria (MacCannell, 1994b). Adorno will accuse today's woman of an almost complete absence of spiritual freedom.

At the same time he will also denounce the miserable circumstance that causes her accelerated sclerosis. Feeling's flight is the effect of her being torn between two opposing but unattractive forms: submissive femininity and fatal cruelty.

The horns of woman's modern dilemma he ascribes directly to Kant. Kant's virtuous (from the Roman for manly), rigorous duty of *apathy* was a first step on the path to Sade's erection of apathy to a principle of crime in the form of a beautiful, imperious woman, Juliette, the 'proficient manipulator of rational thought' (Horkheimer and Adorno, 1982: 95–6).[9] Kant, who barred the 'pathological object' from Reason and thus abetted the emotional destitution of woman, was doubly at fault: according to Horkheimer and Adorno, Kant's apathetic ethic was an unwitting apology for the industrial order, and it accidentally unleashed the full fury of a Sade – fury against, for and also *in* woman. It is no accident that in the last of the series of figures (1982: 85) for the bourgeois Master ('the slaveowner, free entrepreneur, and administrator') the prototype of the administrator, the 'professional woman', shows up first on the world stage as Sade's Juliette. The pernicious consequences seem unlimited to Horkheimer and Adorno: not only women's spiritual loss, but the growth of the administrative mentality and its late loathsome flowering in Fascism.

This imagery is disturbing on many levels. It is hard to think of Kant in this way, for one thing.[10] For another, the average pervert, as well as the average woman, obviously more than once resisted Fascism. Yet their choice of a fictional woman to stage the irrationality of reason and the originating moment of Fascism does contain a truth. For what prompts Horkheimer and Adorno to link Kant to Sade, Sade to Fascism, and Fascism to the female figure is their sense that *woman* as a formal entity is the weakest link. She is so unfree, so much an objectified (dominated) spirit, the very essence of spirit trapped by Reason's ruses, that she is the most susceptible to becoming what Lacan calls the instrument of the *jouissance de l'Autre* (see MacCannell, 1992). (The hallmark of the sadistic pervert in Lacan is that the subject makes itself the *object a* of the Other, the Other's means of *jouissance*.) The alarm Adorno and Horkheimer voice at the possibility of the existence of women like Sade's Juliette thus begins to allow us to *solve the riddle* (as Adorno himself might have phrased it) of 'femininity' in Adorno. These points remain to be considered at greater length:

- Enlightenment reason, and its relation to Adorno's view of woman;
- sadism, and particularly female sadism, manifested at the everyday interpersonal level, in love, and in the form of the bureaucratic order;[11]
- the 'Thing itself' (also termed 'matter' in Adorno's work). This is a question that ultimately involves the relationship to Adorno's desire to repair Hegel by putting the subject 'in the matter and not always beyond it', to 'penetrate into the immanent content of the matter' ('Dedication',

Adorno, 1974: 16). It is here that the least mentioned woman in Adorno, the Mother, perhaps returns.

Kant *avec* Sade: Enlightened reason and the loss of the object

Adorno attributed to Kant the epistemological construction of the Enlightenment subject. His deep knowledge of Kant, whom he read closely from the age of 15 on, did not prevent him from being ambivalent toward the German philosopher who both embodied and criticized the Enlightenment, and who was in his turn subjected to a critique by Hegel. (Hegel supplanted Kant in Adorno's affections.) *En route* to understanding the social and psychic roots of Fascism, Horkheimer and Adorno were convinced that Kant's philosophy predisposed the subject to Fascism. In their 1949 'Excursus II', where they made their shocking link of Kant to Sade, and to the subject inclined to Fascism, they insisted on woman's part. That their analysis had its Kant-Sade themes taken up even more radically by Lacan in 1963 and more literally by Hannah Arendt's study of Eichmann that same year without any particular link to 'woman' may be telling. It is worth touring through this chapter to revisit its cardinal points.

The authors argue that an accelerated loss of the object occurs with Kant, who split the subject in such a way as to double its power over the object.[12] (A transcendental half, free supraindividual universal Reason corrected and guided the perceptions structured or schematized in accordance with the other half, the Understanding, whose subjective judgement of objective qualities was invalid without Reason's correctives; it had no direct, unmediated experience.) The senses were not to be believed, as in Descartes, and as in Descartes, they needed correction by the *ratio*. To establish a calculating, mathematizing, conceptual or symbolic Reason (not excepting language, even figurative language, itself), to shape Understanding *before* it could apprehend the object, was tantamount to falling in line with the developing industrialization process of Kant's time. This process assigned not only a name and address but a *value* to everything:

> Being is apprehended under the aspect of manufacture and administration. . . .
> The conceptual apparatus determines the senses, even before perception occurs; *a priori*, the citizen sees the world as the matter from which he himself manufactures it. Intuitively, Kant foretold what Hollywood consciously put into practice . . . images are pre-censored according to the norm of the understanding. (Horkheimer and Adorno, 1982: 84)[13]

Kant's Reason, innocently harmonizing alienated judgement with the universal concept, and consciously acknowledging the untouchability and unknowability of the thing, did much more. Its 'cold' calculated distance from the Thing did not merely serve to prepare the object for subjugation *before* it could become an object of the senses. It had to devour that Thing, if only in secret, in order to survive it. For Horkheimer and Adorno, both scientific and universal conceptualization and paranoid projection (the return or revenge of the Thing) are equally logical outcomes of the schematism of Kant. To ascribe such consequences as paranoia and Fascism to the Enlightenment's systematic devaluation of the object in favour of its rational reproduction rings true, even as it demands further explanation.

Subjective appropriation of the object expropriates the subject. For Adorno this is the essence of Fascism adumbrated by Kantian philosophy: reification, or thought without a subject. The magnitude of the subject's command over the object indexes the extent of its loss of that object, for it no longer has any existence separate from the subject. But beside that object, what also gets lost under the pressure of social alienation and rational calculation is *the subject*, that which should be able to be 'in the matter, and not always beyond it'. An objectified or reified subject is 'no longer able to return to the object what he has received from it'. Its gains over the object make it 'poorer rather than richer' (Horkheimer and Adorno, 1982: 189).

The 'objectification' of the subject makes the link with sadism. Adorno's 'reified subject' bears no small resemblance to Lacan's later analysis of the sadist as identifying him or herself *as* the *object a*, that is, as the object of the Other's enjoyment, rather than as the subject of their own desire. The 'logical subject of the Enlightenment' ('mature' in Kant's sense of being capable of using 'one's understanding without the guidance of another person' to survive, and historically figured as 'the burgher, in the successive forms of the slaveowner, free entrepreneur, and administrator' (Horkheimer and Adorno, 1982: 83) would seem to be autonomous, a Master subject. The opposite is the case. The logical, reified subject of the Enlightenment is the one most at the disposal of the Other, of those 'social tendencies' or 'prevailing forms' s/he serves: Adorno calls Hitler history's 'drummer boy'. Of this parade of 'proto-sadists' if not 'proto-Fascists', his modern 'administrator' in feminine form is almost the most sinister.

Sade *avec* Kant: Juliette and the courtly perversion

To Adorno and Horkheimer, Kant's philosophical hand wrote the beautiful and criminal Juliette's figure 'on the wall' before Sade gave her account in detail (1982: 86). Ironically, the choice Horkheimer and Adorno made of this particular female sadist throws as much light on Adorno's hostility to beauty and poetry as on the roots of Fascism. For *Juliette* happens to be a parody of courtly love, that poetic form wherein 'the woman', 'the object', 'sublimated violence', 'art' and 'culture's damage' are historically tied together. It is also the original source of 'the ideal of femininity' Adorno so derided (1974: 95).

Historically, the courtly paradigm suffused the original novel that Sade's *Juliette*, like Laclos's *Liaisons Dangereuses*, parodies: Rousseau's *Julie, ou La Nouvelle Héloïse*. (Rousseau's principal female characters, for example, are Julie and Claire, as compared with Sade's Juliette and Clairwil; and the bourgeois Julie, forsaking her heart's passion, is left with control in only one part of her life, her garden, but over that her rule is absolute: '*Il n'y rien là que je n'aie ordonné*'.) Petrarch's original love object, Laure de Sade, may have been a direct ancestor of the Marquis, whose family domain was in Provence, the historic seat of courtly love.

Recent analysts have reminded us that the Lady can be seen as a figure of the maternal superego, the cardinal point of contact between the individual and a distorted social order (see MacCannell, 1994a; Žižek, 1994). It is the superego who issues – as the voice of conscience – society's increasingly irrational but nonetheless despotic demands. If Adorno hated femininity so much, it has as much to do with an abstract resistance to authoritarian society as with its peremptory mouthpiece, the arbitrary feminine superego. It converts the maternal breast into its opposite, the perverted social order.

Lacan credited the structure of the Lady's impossibility of access with the recurring origination of poetry, with the continued possibility and need for (re)inventing poetry (Lacan, 1992: 139 ff.). Freud, too, claimed that wherever love found no obstacles, it created them, and this making or *poeisis* was necessary to happiness. But in *poeisis*, Adorno saw little more than the mirror of production or its perverse incipience. We might wonder if his impatience with mediation – *poeisis*, alienated social exchange – is cause or effect of Adorno's understanding of the relation between the sexes.

If we compare Adorno's *Aesthetic Theory*, and its view of the object in the work of art, with the way he discusses the exploitation of the object in the *Dialectic of Enlightenment*, we can gauge more clearly the extent of Adorno's anger at the objectification of 'woman' in the industrial/Kantian/Sadean moral order. We can also start to clarify what he has in mind for 'the sex'. We will get the barest hint of what he might wish for a truly liberated female subject.

Poetry, beauty, or making courtly love

> The contradiction between what is and what is made, is the vital element of art and circumscribes its law of development, but it is also art's shame; by following, however indirectly, the existing pattern of material production and 'making' its objects, art as akin to production cannot escape the question 'what for?' which it aims to negate. The closer the mode of production of artefacts comes to material mass-production, the more naively it provokes that fatal question. (Adorno, 1974: 226)

Extending his critique of the (Kantian) grid that inserts itself between the subject and object to the realm of art Adorno found yet another regional problem, significant for woman, created by enlightened Reason: *beauty*.

> The ideology of cultural conservatism which sees enlightenment and art as simple antitheses is false, among other reasons, in overlooking the moment of enlightenment in the genesis of beauty. Enlightenment does not merely dissolve all the qualities that beauty adheres to, but posits the quality of beauty in the first place.

The disinterested pleasure that according to Kant is aroused by works of art, can only be understood by virtue of historical antitheses still at work in each aesthetic object. The thing disinterestedly contemplated pleases because it once claimed the utmost interest and thus precluded contemplation. The latter is a triumph of enlightened self-discipline. (1974: 224)

The perception of beauty was once due to a magical mode of thinking which tied beauty to dreadful and fascinating power over nature:

Jewels were seen as instruments for subjugating the course of the world by its own cunningly usurped power. The magic adhered to the illusion of omnipotence. This illusion was dispelled by mind's self enlightenment, but the magic has survived as the *power of radiant things over men*, in whom they once instilled a dread that continues to hold their eyes spellbound, even after they have seen through its claim to domination. (1974: 224; added emphasis)

This 'radiance' Adorno sees transferred to art as its magical claims to domination are renounced. Art is reoriented from domination toward 'purposiveness without a purpose'. In its negative mirror to the 'totality of purposefulness in the world of domination',

radiant things give up their magic claims, renounce the power with which the subject invested them and hoped with their help himself to wield, they become transformed into images of gentleness, promises of a happiness *cured of domination over nature*. This is the primeval history of luxury, that has migrated into the meaning of all art. In the magic of what reveals itself in absolute powerlessness, of beauty, at once perfection and nothingness, the illusion of omnipotence is mirrored negatively as hope, it has escaped every trial of strength. (Adorno, 1974: 224; added emphasis)

This negation of feverish productivity would merely reinforce the established order, however, were it not for the moment of 'contemplation' it evokes in the subject for whom 'bliss' consists in 'disenchanted charm'. Rejoining Aristotle and a bit of Husserl here, Adorno's 'contemplative moment' is both a respite from incessant labour and a relief for a nature momentarily released from domination by the technologies (industrial or linguistic), the 'makings', that subject her. Thus, while art's first drive is to master the object, the Kantian turn in art toward purposiveness without a purpose (which, for Adorno was ultimately to serve the alienated social order of domination) opened a brief window of opportunity to a renunciation of this drive. Adorno formed in his paradigm or parable of useless beauty a *laissez-aller* for the natural object and for the subject who contemplates it: an idea of what a pure subject–object relation, devoid of arbitrary forms of domination, might be like. (No place for the dominating Lady, whose beauty attracts the lover, yet is designed to send the lover off, away from the object, causing him to desire it all the more.)

Adorno's utopia of an undisturbed object providing that unique moment where the subject might be 'in the matter, and not always beyond it', wilfully excludes the intersubjective foundation of art, or what Lacan called later the lack of sexual relation. For human being it is less the subject–object relation than the intersubjective relation that is the crucible and realm of power and domination. At the limit, the intersubjective for Adorno – and this surely implicates sex – is the problem in need of elimination.

His notable resistance to Walter Benjamin's Baudelaire essay demonstrates this (see Bloch et al., 1977: 110–34). Benjamin, whose criticism is a *Kunstprosa* of the first water, faced an almost didactic, hard-line philistinism in Adorno's response, precisely because Benjamin had devoted himself to revealing the hidden subject inhabiting the architecture, the landscaping, the city's plan – all that Lacan would later sum up as 'unconscious as Baltimore in the early morning' (Lacan, 1970: 189). The 'frozen dialectic' Benjamin found congealed in the figure of the whore (saleswoman and wares in one) was precisely what Adorno wanted to get past – that 'bad' moment where the iniquitous social order has injured the object and imprisoned the subject. To start with the bad new things, not the good old ones meant a traverse through them, analysing them in detail in a way not to Adorno's taste, as it was to Benjamin's and Brecht's. Benjamin made tarrying with the negative too attractive.

If we cast, for one moment, our eyes toward the psychoanalysis Adorno both drew upon and reviled, we can reconsider his vision of the 'contemplative' moment from yet another angle. Is there not in Adorno's utopia of the subject–object relation something exceptionally maternal – in his intimation of an abiding element ('the matter') remaining at large, not captured, nor captivated, nor organized, nor exploited, nor ventriloquized (for example, as the maternal superego) by an iniquitous system of social relations – what Lacan would call 'the superego pressure' and Adorno 'the prevailing forms'. If all symbolic grids – linguistic, mythic, rational – are the domain of subjection for Adorno, who attributed their interference between subject and object to Kant, that is nonetheless a virtually indelible feature of all known forms of human life, which is the realm of domination and subjection, to be sure.

Feminist Adorno: II

Art and the resistance to beauty

Adorno claims art is irretrievably flawed, although it is a step toward a *critical* theory, an invaluable resource against reification when it is energized by fantasy. Yet it cannot really ever escape its roots in social mediation, which demands from the start the domination and exploitation of the object. Art begins, he tells us, in (socially determined) human oral and sexual appetites: 'cuisine and pornography' – that is, food and sex culturally shaped. The artist must forgo these appetites, in a first 'disinterested' moment, to preserve the openness of his desire against the commands of society, against his 'open-air' imprisonment by an increasingly reified civilization. For *art* to assist critical thinking, its basis in the temptation to destroy the object and exalt the subject (which in its turn only leads to the subject's reification) must be renounced.[14] Preservation of the object against a culturally calculated desire is necessary to preserve the subject.[15]

Art renounces *enjoyment*. But resisting this 'enjoyment' brings out the deepest antagonism of art, for art originates in a desire to dominate and assimilate: 'to devour or otherwise subjugate (the object) to one's body'. Adorno sees a *defence against enjoyment* as crucial to the subject, and makes it truer of his aesthetic than of Kant's because Adorno saw through, as did the later Lacan, to a secret enjoyment hidden in its 'disinterestedness'. (Adorno reminds us that the stronger the taboo against enjoyment in Kant the more it must be matched by a repressed urge for its opposite.[16]) Kant goes only halfway toward what is needed because, like Freud, he was unwilling to see the 'thorns pointed at' the non-subjective by works of art. If Adorno means that the enjoyment to be resisted is that of the Other in expectation of recovering your own lost enjoyment, that would be one thing. But Adorno disappoints precisely here. What his extremely interesting phrasing promises – an extraordinary or unheard of relation to the real of enjoyment – produces, instead, only a sense of art's resistance to the primary capitalist definition of happiness as bound up with production and the possessions it enables. Art is there chiefly to indicate that 'happiness lies beyond praxis', or, we might conclude, beyond art and work themselves.[17]

Where for Adorno does there exist an art capable of keeping 'a hold on the negativity of the real' and entering 'into a definite relation with it' (Adorno, 1984: 17) to gain the power to 'transcend mere existence'? Art can at best function to point thorns at alienated *subjective* life: 'Art is like a plenipotentiary of a type of praxis that is better than the prevailing praxis of society', whose predations against the objects are legion.

Compared to Benjamin, Adorno's stance on art is incomparably less 'political'. Benjamin saw the socially determined portion in art, but, unlike Adorno, he also saw it *politically*, as in his militant stance that every 'great' work of art is a monument to the victors, and silent witness to those trampled underfoot (Benjamin, 1969: 256). Benjamin's pronouncement evokes in his poetic, artful prose at one and the same time the servility of an art in thrall to the Masters, the envious symbolic theft and murder of the artist's rivals within the work, and also the anonymous labour of those who create the ordinary culture from which artwork springs. Adorno's does not.[18] Nor could it, given his Freud-derived belief in the damage that culture does to human life, his opinion of 'low' culture as exhibiting this damage to the most extreme degree, and his sense of the feebleness of culture's own efforts against that damage.[19] Adorno, the schoolboy beaten for his artiness by bullying uncultured classmates, could hardly see otherwise (Adorno, 1974: 193).

Adorno gave politics *in* art a slight nod by recognizing the class interests served by certain works (for example those of Proust or Anatole France), or by showing the Nazifying background to Kafka's fantastic tales of bureau-cracy run amok. But for Adorno, in the end art could only reflect, it could not effectively counter or participate in those struggles, intersubjective in character, which are *also* at the aesthetic root – struggles between master and slave, between fraternal rivals, but which Adorno did not locate as intrinsic to the artwork. To him, art's first and only real struggle is against its rival, nature. Its first duty is overcoming the temptation to destroy the object in that nature, by consumption and by technical dominion. This is the struggle that is 'immured' in art from first to last, from kitsch to the 'oldest works' (1974: 226).

Hence the undeniable poverty in Adorno's *specific* analysis when it comes to art – once his object is specified, and theory applied to it, Adorno seems to fail as often as he hits the mark. When I think of his theses on jazz and the 'castration' it represents to him (Adorno, 1967: 130), I feel uneasy largely because, as a product of one of the deepest social antagonisms – racial division, and its prior conditioning by a real master/slave relationship – jazz seems singularly suited to being analysed as one of those forms which could reflect and refract almost completely a very particular kind of repair (or to use Benjamin's term, redemption) of societal 'damage' to life. Jazz gets no recognition from him on this level, because he restricts his analysis of art to the basic theme of the need for artistic restraint before the object. Ironically enough, he rebels against this renunciation in this specific instance, calling its musicians victims of castration. For Adorno, this castration was even worse than that imposed by 'civilization', for it indicated the player's impotent capitulation before capitalist society's distortions. (Castration's Lacanian meaning, as the subject's dispossession by the signifier, might have altered Adorno's opinion of jazz.) When he claims that art-beyond-disinterestedness 'reproduces, in different form, the interest inherent in disinterestedness' (Adorno, 1984: 18) he doesn't seem to leave room for that interest ever to be anything other than the interests of the master.

Except, perhaps, the Mother's. The real mother, the mother behind or beyond the false schematizations that distance her yet secretly enjoy her. The mater, the matter (a false etymology, of course), the *mater dolorosa* of love for her son. Or perhaps, in a more modern idiom, the aunt – Agathe, who taught him four-handed piano, and over whose death Adorno wept the bitterest tears.

Fantasy, art and power

Interestingly, psychoanalytic theory does provide an alternative to Hegelian and Kantian (social and cultural) 'mediations' of the relation of subject to object. In Freud, the symbolic gridding of nature necessary to the formation of human desire (which is the same as saying human mental life) is preceded by a moment of *fantasy* and *hallucination*, the first of the 'two principles of mental functioning' (Freud, 1911: 215). The baby hallucinates the satisfaction of his needs whenever those needs are not immediately fulfilled: he or she literally *enjoys in fantasy* the unavailable mother's milk.

As an object without objectivity, referring both to the real of need and the real of enjoyment while being neither, the breast's *appearance* to the infant is not that of 'mere life' – the phoney attraction trumped up by an unjust social order. Nor is it purely *real*. As an *object*, it participates in both the real and the non-real, the mind's hallucinating a satisfaction that the real breast could also in fact provide. Lacan will call such objects *objects a*. They are at the root of fantasy, the asymbolic, non-linguistic original mode of subjective thought. And of intersubjective thought: think of Melanie Klein's infant, torn by fantasies of absolute aggressive orality against the mother's breast and loving, guilty dreams of repairing it.

This *fantasy* dimension cannot be restricted to the realm of myth, of the gods, the infancy of humanity, it can never be removed by 'enlightenment'. Adorno knew this, too:

> Fantasy alone, today consigned to the realm of the unconscious and proscribed from knowledge as a childish, injudicious rudiment, can establish that relation between objects which is the irrevocable source of all judgement: should fantasy be driven out, judgement too, the real act of knowledge, is exorcised. But the castration of perception by a court of control that denies it any anticipatory desire, forces it thereby into a pattern of helplessly reiterating what is already known. (1974: 122–3)

Fantasy emancipated can become a realm of freedom, the play of musement. But its freedom must be won by patient analytic labour, the kind Adorno tended to short-circuit. He admired this labour in Benjamin who was able to 'atomize' the object, as Adorno put it in his essay. For fantasy is most often for human beings a personal ideology or myth – or psychosis. Its 'pattern' is that of a repetition of a trauma – an arbitrary and unjust exercise of power by one subject over another. This arbitrary unjust visitation upon the subject Adorno calls Reason's (and the state's) 'court of control', but he refuses to assign *subjective* status to any force that so exercises its powers of domination. Those who would do so are already, in his eyes, magical monstrous hybrids, 'the gods', the evil subjects-become-objects. Lacan made it much easier: by calling this structure of oppression '*la jouissance de l'Autre*' he was able to implicate both the individual intersubjective relation and the general societal one as well. For Lacan, a subject traumatized by being made the imaginary object of the Other's enjoyment, will repeatedly restage their horror *as* that enjoyment in a fantasy adjusted to grant them relief from the abuse, and to return to them some of the enjoyment they lost to the Other.[20] True liberation can only come from a traverse of that fantasy. As psychoanalysis discloses the domination and objectification of the subject in fantasy, it can create the conditions for liberation from that scene of subjection.

For psychoanalysis, the mythic forms of fantasy will persist as long as intersubjective domination persists. This is precisely what Adorno protests against. In a way, Adorno could be said to want us to enjoy *in theory*. For him, we must go beyond an art that, like Freud's infant's fantasy, is only a compromise which still mediates between subject and object of desire. The full breast, the fantasy object insists inside Adorno's contemplative aspirations – it can remain full and yet satisfy thought, the subject, at the same time.

Beauty again: woman's cursed gift

Of all the woman's figures Adorno provides, the Beauty shows the least subjective freedom, the greatest conformity and acquiescence to her condition.

> Women of exceptional beauty are doomed to unhappiness. Even those favoured by every circumstance, who have birth, wealth, talent on their side, seem as if hounded or obsessed by the urge to destroy themselves and all the human relationships they contract. An oracle gives them a choice between calamities. Either they shrewdly exchange beauty for success. Then they pay with happiness for its condition. . . . Or the privilege of beauty gives them the courage and confidence to repudiate the exchange agreement. They take seriously the happiness that their person promises, and are unstinting with themselves, assured by the admiration of all that they do not need first to prove their worth. . . . [They marry early] and commit themselves to pedestrian conditions, forfeit the privilege of infinite possibility, abase themselves to human beings. At the same time, however, they cling to the childish dream of omnipotence with which their lives have beguiled them, and – unbourgeois in this – continue to throw away what tomorrow may be replaced by something better. Thus they are the type of the destructive character. (1974: 171)

Beauty in art, the mark of a happy weakness (the renunciation of domination) is, in woman, a destructive power.

Adorno's assignment of a 'destructive' character to the beautiful woman is not parallel to Benjamin's use of the same term. In Benjamin (or even Alissa in Duras's (1969) *Détruire, dit-elle*), the destructive character is the one who 'makes room', clears the field, and sees a way through and out of the forest, the constricted situation in which it and its fellows endure, but in which it cannot breathe. For Adorno, the destructiveness of woman's beauty of form is the very condition that limits her. Her mind and her matter are, as it were, *trapped* in her unlucky form. For her beauty destroys her absolute freedom from determination, excludes her from the unconditioned situation of which Adorno, rather like early democracy, dreamed. It is this unfreedom which leads her to destroy freedom in others.

Beauty is, for Adorno, a worse condition than *petit bourgeois* marriage, sadism (of which it seems to be an offshoot), and economic self-sufficiency for woman. While her beauty may be presumed as impotent, as is beauty in a work of art, this is not so. In no case does the beautiful woman choose to forgo the power to dominate others that her beauty promises. Indeed the reverse is true: not only does she not give this power up, it is *through* it that reified social conditions operate. In this way, the woman is herself impotent, since her beauty (produced by conventions of beauty) is in fact *imposed* by social conditions that make use of it.

Thus, the most beautiful woman in the world is powerless to create the terms of her intersubjective relations – her 'happiness'. In whose hands, then, would woman's 'happiness' lie?

In any woman's. She must become weak. The beautiful dominatrix most of all. She must yield 'the magical domination' ascribed to the beauty in natural objects; she must give up the dream of *omnipotence* her beauty had promised her. In this moment of renunciation, it appears that woman has to become the ultimate *object*, the object of pure contemplation, and, in her weakness, the *aim* of non-aggressive love ('Love you will find only where you may show yourself weak without provoking strength' (1974: 192).)[21] As with Adorno's 'better' side of art, woman must resist becoming an organ or instrumental function of the superego. In short, she must become a fully human being.

Or so it seems.

For Adorno drops a hint of something *beyond the human* in his analysis of useless beauties. Note that he calls their forfeiture of infinite possibility 'abas[ing] themselves to human beings' (Adorno, 1974: 171).[22] In this turn of phrase about 'abasing' themselves to human beings, Adorno suggests a special, if somewhat eerie, path toward the female *subject*. Her subjectivity will only come from releasing her from what has captivated and reified her – her beautiful human form. For the sake of becoming what? A *free spirit*.

Conclusion: Adorno and the thing itself

> Culture originates in the radical separation of mental and physical work. It is from this separation, the original sin as it were, that culture draws its strength. When culture denies the separation and feigns harmonious union, it falls back behind its own notion. Only the mind which, in the delusion of being absolute, removes itself entirely from the merely existent, truly defines the existent in its negativity. As long as even the least part of the mind remains engages in the reproduction of life, it is its sworn bondsman. (Adorno, 1967: 26)

To sum up: resistance to the duplicitous way 'enlightened reason' granted existence to nature, the object, and the Thing coloured much of Adorno's writing. In *Prisms*, Adorno allied himself with Hegel's critique of Kant: that, on the one hand, his cool, apathic Reason tabooed the Thing itself, closed it to all access, such that Reason must demand we willingly give it up. On the other, this very taboo on the Thing secretly (unconsciously) authorized the object's enjoyment by the subject – its exploitation, murder and subordination to the system of production. Hegel said that 'every method which sets limits and restricts itself to the limits of its object thereby goes beyond them' (Adorno, 1967: 31), that is, it silently licenses the violation of that object.

What, then, is Adorno's hope for getting beyond Kant?

It can be none other than that of a spirit freed, not from matter (the Christian notion), but from *form* and its corollary, *reproducibility*. For Adorno, the greatest injury to both subject and object stems from 'the subjugation of men to the prevailing form in which their lives are reproduced' (1967: 27). He rightly predicted culture's acceleration into its current formal glossiness, all the more subjugating the more it resembles 'liberation' from matter. Only dialectical energy, negatively charged, can disrupt this 'Hegelian' progress forward into abstract formal 'beauty' and show it as a progress into despair.

Adorno is not, however, dreaming, as Benjamin or even Brecht would, of redeeming the social, linguistic, economic and artistic orders from their capture by abstraction. At his most utopian, his is a dream of its complete unmaking, an unmaking that will release both spirit and matter from its grasp. This is no less than Adorno's return to the original scene of free fantasy – Freud's first (pleasure) principle of mental functioning.

At this, its deepest level, one has to wonder. Absolute freedom from mediation (society, form, language, metaphor, Lacan's big O Other) are improbable, at best, within the confines of *human* history. Women's release from 'subjugation by the prevailing form in which their lives are reproduced' would be impossible if woman is to remain 'woman'. Liberation would mean the end of woman as we know her. This is why, in Adorno, woman after the revolution, radical revolution, the passage beyond societal mediation, is without a figure.

Perhaps woman's release from capture by figuration *is* her last best hope.[23] But let us not decide this too hastily. There where the essential, free subject contemplates its quintessentially liberated object (matter, *mater*?), the Thing freed from the signifier, set free even from bearing society's demands (the maternal superego) – there little Adorno lies. He is face to face with a maternal breast beyond the mediation and intervention of the Other. His independence from it, without the aid of the Father (civilization, culture, language, technology), is nothing short of a miracle.

To the riddle of femininity is this the resolution devoutly to be wished?

Notes

1 See my book, *The Regime of the Brother* (1991)and two of my recent essays on Fascism: 'Facing Fascism' (1996a) and 'Fascism and the voice of conscience' (1996b).

2 Along with Lukács, Bakhtin and Benjamin. Of these, only Benjamin concurred with Adorno in making the Kantian problematic of the object a central concern.

3 Adorno's immanent critique, using the waning 'logical evidence of the senses', bears comparison with the materialists of the French theory of 'idéologie'. Adorno may have felt their influence via his philosophy teacher Professor Cornelius and also

Nietzsche. 'Idéologie' was an invention of Destutt de Tracy which came to be seen as the science of happiness as determined by the form of the state.

4 'A Portrait of Walter Benjamin', in Adorno (1967: 227–41).

5 See Susan Buck-Morss (1977: 136). While Benjamin left Germany in 1933 for Paris because he felt, as a Jew, that he could not even breathe there any more, Adorno assumed Nazism would blow over, and so even though he left in 1934, he did so in following practical advice to cover his bets, not so much out of a personal feeling that the situation under Hitler was unliveable. The recurrence of the forms of 'ethnic cleansing', fantasy formations, etc., are currently being analysed in ways that parallel those of Adorno, as in the recent book, *Radical Evil* (Copjec, 1996).

6 'The precondition for the autonomy of artistic experience is the abandonment of the attitude of tasting and savouring. The trajectory leading to aesthetic autonomy passes through the stage of disinterestedness, and well it should, for it was during this stage that art emancipated itself from cuisine and pornography, an emancipation that has become irrevocable. However, art does not come to rest in disinterestedness, it moves on. And in so doing it reproduces, in different form, the interest inherent in disinterestedness. In a false world all *hedone* is false. This goes for artistic pleasure, too. Art renounces happiness for the sake of happiness, thus enabling desire to survive in art' (Adorno, 1984: 18).

7 On this, please see Renata Salecl (1993).

8 'The fact that Nietzsche's scrutiny stopped short of them, that he took over a second-hand and unverified image of feminine nature from the Christian civilization that he otherwise so thoroughly mistrusted, finally brought his thought under the sway, after all, of bourgeois society. He fell for the fraud of saying "the feminine" when talking of women. Hence the perfidious advice not to forget the whip: femininity itself is already the effect of the whip' (Adorno, 1974: 96).

9 Horkheimer and Adorno cite this passage from Kant: 'therefore virtue, to the extent that it is founded upon inner freedom, also contains an affirmative commandment for men, which is to bring all their abilities and inclinations under its control [i.e. reason], which prevails over the negative commandment not to be ruled by one's emotions and inclinations [the duty of apathy]; because, unless reason takes the reins of government into its hand, emotions and inclinations will be in control' (Horkheimer and Adorno, 1982: 95).

10 Although Eichmann did, a fact that did not escape the ears of Hannah Arendt (1964).

11 Lacan's 1963 essay 'Kant avec Sade', as well as his chapter on 'Courtly love as anamorphosis' in *Seminar VII: The Ethics Seminar*, take up the relation of the idealist philosopher, Kant, and the rationalizer of sex, Sade, in a way worth comparing with Adorno. I have written on these relationships in two essays on Adolf Eichmann, 'Facing Fascism' (1996a) and 'Fascism and the voice of conscience' (1996b), as well as 1994b.

12 It would be important to compare this splitting of the subject into transcendental and empirical, with Lacan's similar-sounding subject split by language and given to desire. For Adorno with every split, there is a 'castration' (#79 1974: 123), a 'castration of perception'. Form distorts matter, 'logical perception' is destroyed. In Lacan, castration, by which he means subjection to language, is the necessary precondition for entry in all, not merely capitalist, societies. Castration for Lacan means the loss of an enjoyment of primary matter, of the body which is thereafter shaped by language and culture, though the enjoyment lost to language always returns to the body in various guises. Castration for Adorno is subjection, pure and simple, of the body, and distortion, pure and simple, of the mind.

13 Adorno's remarks on language as a system as also an instrument of domination can lead us to conclude that the system of signification, especially but not only under capitalism, is equally responsible for this loss for the object. (See 1974: 101.)

14 The structure applies to his analysis of the 'narcissism' in love. Here he follows the French line – La Rochefoucauld, Stendhal, Proust and Lacan – wherein the objectified ego is torn between the value it places upon itself and upon the beloved who becomes its competitor. Egotism eventually results in making its supposed object aloof and cold – the origin of the 'platonic' relationship. 'The frigid aloofness of the loved one, by now an acknowledged institution of mass culture, is answered by the "insatiable desire" of the lover. . . . Today the unprejudiced woman is the one who no longer believes in love, who will not be hoodwinked into investing more than she can expect in return. . . . Really, they no longer want ecstasy at all, but merely compensation for an outlay that, best of all, they would like to save as superfluous' (Adorno, 1974: 168–9).

15 The difference between his and Lacan's understanding of the relation to the object is that for Lacan, the object shields us from the Thing. Adorno makes it seem that the Thing itself is given to us by the object. The Thing for Lacan is the Mother, and likewise the maternal superego. It suffers from the signifier, as Adorno also sees. For Lacan it is a supremely human reflex to *turn away* from and shelter oneself from this thing. In contrast to Adorno, Lacan finds in the Thing both the Real and social reality's principle, the moral superego.

16 'If Kant's disinterestedness is to be more than a synonym for indifference, it has to have a trace of untamed interest somewhere' (Adorno, 1984: 16). He calls Kant's aesthetics 'castrated hedonism', which ignores the fundamental source from which art antithetically originates.

17 Of course he means beyond the alienated praxis of capitalism's alienation of labour. But is there to be any 'work' of any sort, art included, at all in a post-industrial Adorno world?

> The existence of trash expresses insanely and undisguisedly the factor that men have succeeded in reproducing from within themselves a piece of that which otherwise imprisons them in toil, and in symbolically breaking the compulsion of adaptation by themselves creating what they feared; and an echo of the same triumph resounds in the mightiest works, though they seek to forgo it, imagining themselves pure self unrelated to any model. In both cases freedom from nature is celebrated, yet remains mythically entrapped. What men trembled before, they have placed at their own disposal. (Adorno, 1974: 225)

18 'When he berates Benjamin's Baudelaire essay for failing to show the *mediation of total social processes* in his analysis of the arcades, he is basically criticizing him for too starkly (or too seductively) juxtaposing Baudelaire's poetic images with details of taxation, commerce, and political repression without retaining emphasis on the *processes of production and commodification* 'as primary facts of Paris life' (Bloch et al., 1977: 110–34).

19 'What escapes the jurisdiction of existence and its purposes is not only a protesting better world but also a more stupid one incapable of self-assertion. This stupidity grows, the more autonomous art idolizes its isolated, allegedly innocent self-assertion instead of its real one, guilty and imperious. The subjective act, by presenting itself as the successful rescue of objective meaning, becomes untrue. Of this it is convicted by kitsch; the latter's lie does not even feign truth. It incurs hostility because it blurts out the secret of art and the affinity of culture to savagery' (Adorno, 1974: 226).

20 I am most dependent here on the interpretations made of their research results by the Quebec group, Gifric, especially Willy Apollon, Lucie Cantin and Danielle Bergeron in their summer training session 1996, and in various articles in the journal *Savoir*.

21 Yet, isn't this *inutile beauté* not the very type of the intact, inviolable courtly woman?

22 Does Adorno mean an infinite number of lovers? I suspect that, rather than sexual licence, an option she never really has for she would quickly lose her value at any rate, Adorno has a deeper liberation in mind for woman.

23 She would be beyond the differentiations of the social construction of gender. This implication is currently being worked out by Hegelian philosophers like Judith Butler. In contrast, Lacan's recourse to the feminine–regressive from a Hegelian/ Adorno perspective – remains for me richly suggestive. As for Adorno, 'woman' doesn't exist. But she insists. The masculine feminine antinomy *in sexuality* (a topic Adorno usually skims the surface of) is that unreasonable relation not subject to the dialectic of Reason in Lacan.

References

Adorno, Theodor W. (1967) *Prisms: Cultural Criticism and Society*, trans. Samuel and Shierry Weber. London: Neville Spearman.

Adorno, Theodor W. (1974) *Minima Moralia: Reflections from Damaged Life* [1951], trans. E.F.N. Jephcott. London: NLB.

Adorno, Theodor W. (1984) *Aesthetic Theory* [1970], ed. Gretel Adorno and Rolf Tiedemann, trans. C. Lenhardt. London and New York: Routledge & Kegan Paul.

Adorno, Theodor W. (1994) *The Stars Down to Earth and Other Essays on the Irrational*, ed. Stephen Crook. London and New York: Routledge.

Arendt, Hannah (1964) *Eichmann in Jerusalem: A Report on the Banality of Evil.* Harmondsworth: Penguin Books.

Benjamin, Walter (1969) 'Theses on the philosophy of history', in *Illuminations*, trans. Harry Zohn. New York: Schocken Books.

Bloch, Ernst, Lukács, Georg, Brecht, Bertolt, Benjamin, Walter and Adorno, Theodor (1977) *Aesthetics and Politics.* London: NLB.

Buck-Morss, Susan (1977) *The Origin of Negative Dialectics: Theodor W. Adorno, Walter Benjamin, and the Frankfurt Institute.* New York: Free Press.

Copjec, Joan (ed.) (1996) *Radical Evil.* New York and London: Verso.

Duras, Marguerite (1969) *Détruire, dit-elle.* Paris: Minuit.

Freud, Sigmund (1911) 'Formulations regarding the two principles of mental functioning', in *General Psychological Theory: Papers on Metapsychology.* New York: Collier Books. (*Standard Edition of Writers of Sigmund Freud*, Vol. XII. London: Hogarth Press, 1958.)

Horkheimer, Max and Adorno, Theodor (1982) *The Dialectic of Enlightenment* [1949], trans. John Cumming. New York: Continuum.

Lacan, Jacques (1970) 'Of structure as an inmixing of an otherness prerequisite to any subject whatever', in Richard Macksey and Eugenio Donato (eds), *The Languages of Criticism and the Sciences of Man.* Baltimore: Johns Hopkins University Press. pp. 186–200.

Lacan, Jacques (1989) 'Kant avec Sade', English trans. James Swenson, in *October*, 51: 55–76, with annotations from 76–105 (Winter).

Lacan, Jacques (1992) *Seminar VII: The Ethics of Psychoanalysis*, trans. Dennis Porter. New York: Norton.

MacCannell, Juliet Flower (1991) *The Regime of the Brother: After the Patriarchy.* London: Routledge.

MacCannell, Juliet Flower (1992) 'Jouissance', in Elizabeth Wright (ed.), *A Critical Dictionary of Feminism and Psychoanalysis.* Blackwell: Oxford.

MacCannell, Juliet Flower (1994a) 'Love outside the limits of the law', *new formations* special issue on *Lacan and Love*, ed. Renata Salecl, August: 25–42.

MacCannell, Juliet Flower (1994b) 'Things to come: the hysteric's guide to the future female subject', in Joan Copjec (ed.), *Supposing the Subject*. London: Verso. pp. 106–32.

MacCannell, Juliet Flower (1996a) 'Facing Fascism', in Willy Apollon and Richard Feldstein (eds), *Lacan, Aesthetics, Politics*. New York: SUNY Press.

MacCannell, Juliet Flower (1996b) 'Fascism and the voice of conscience', in Joan Copjec (ed.), *Radical Evil*. London: Verso.

Marx, Karl and Engels, Fredrich (1978) *Marx and Engels on Literature and Art*. Moscow: Progress.

Rousseau, Jean-Jacques (1964) *Julie, ou la Nouvelle Héloïse* [1756], in Bernard Guyon, Jacques Scherer, and Charly Guyot (eds), *Oeuvres Complètes*, vol. 2. Paris: Bibliothèque de la Pléïade.

Salecl, Renata (1993) 'Woman as symptom of rights', in Juliet Flower MacCannell (ed.), *Femininity and Jouissance in the Politics of Postmodernity: Towards an Impossible Feminine Ethic*, and in *Topoi: An International Review of Philosophy*, 12(2) (September).

Žižek, Slavoj (1991) 'Why is Sade the truth of Kant?', in *For They Know Not What They Do: Enjoyment as a Political Factor*. London and New York: Verso. pp. 229–33.

Žižek, Slavoj (1994) 'From the courtly game to the crying game', in *Metastases of Enjoyment: Six Essays on Women and Causality*. London: Verso. pp 89–112.

8   Of Music and Mimesis

Barbara Engh

Luce Irigaray argues that if feminism is to make a difference, it must challenge philosophy, the 'discourse that sets forth the law for all others, inasmuch as it constitutes the discourse on discourse. . . . This domination of the philosophical logos stems in large part from its power to reduce all others to the economy of the Same' (1985: 74). Those familiar with the work of Theodor Adorno will hear resonances between their two projects, which share 'an awareness of the subterranean links between the metaphysics of identity and the structures of domination' (Dews, 1989: 2).[1] Irigaray concludes:

> What remains to be done, then, is to work at 'destroying' the discursive mechanism. Which is not a simple undertaking. . . . For how can we introduce ourselves into such a tightly woven systematicity? There is, in an initial phase, perhaps only one 'path,' the one historically assigned to the feminine: that of mimicry. One must assume the feminine role deliberately. . . . If women are such good mimics, it is because they are not simply resorbed in this function. They also remain elsewhere: another case of the persistence of 'matter,' but also of 'sexual pleasure.' (Irigaray, 1985: 76)

One of the most vexing problems of feminist cultural criticism concerns the signifier 'woman'. According to Irigaray's analysis, if feminism posits 'woman' as either the subject or the object of its discourse, it remains within and reproduces the dominant logic. But if instead it attempts to jam the theoretical machinery itself, it has a chance of outmanoeuvring that logic, 'suspending its pretension to the production of a truth and of a meaning that are excessively univocal' (Irigaray, 1985: 78). Historically, in Western culture 'woman' operates to signify not the sum of all woman as 'woman-kind' (as is the case with 'man'), but rather as something on the order of 'truth' – or its antithesis (Derrida, 1987: 195).

Since Plato, mimicry, or mimesis, has been associated with fraudulence. As imitation, it falls away from the ideal of authenticity embodied in an original. In order to grasp Adorno's theory of mimesis (insofar as this is possible – I think the notorious ungraspability of this concept in Adorno's thought is actually part of its 'message') – it will be necessary to try and get underneath the overwhelming sense of mimesis as imitation or copy. While this aspect does have a place in Adorno's theory, it is secondary. Adorno turns to the early Greek sense of mimesis in order to excavate 'the condition of the possibility of the less fundamental production of the copy' (Cahn, 1984: 34). It is this double character of mimesis that forms one of the central paradoxes of Adorno's thinking.

Before I turn to Adorno, a rehearsal of the Platonic position is useful. The musical performance – or 'poetry' in the Greek context, for Plato the chief enemy of philosophy – was mimetic to the core, in every aspect of its production and reception. 'Rhythm and harmony sink deep into the recesses of the soul and take the strongest hold there' (Plato, 1941: 90). Music is able to powerfully induce in its auditor the experience of others, of (according to Plato's enumeration) women railing, boasting, miserable, in love, sick, in labour – or of slaves doing their menial labour, or coarse drunkards, or madmen, or tradesmen, or 'horses neighing and bulls bellowing or the noise of rivers and sea and thunder' (Plato, 1941: 83–4). To stave off a free-for-all that would disregard not only the separations among human beings, but also those between humans, animals and inanimate nature, Plato declares that music cannot be allowed to function autonomously (*autonomos*: according to its own laws), but that it must be subordinated to the Logos, as accompaniment, and that only the music conducive to virility, suitable for marching into war or for politicking in peacetime, ought to be allowed. Eric Havelock contends that in order to make sense of Plato's passionate assault on poetic experience, which the latter denounces in the most extreme terms as a *femme fatale*, a siren that seduces, then poisons and cripples the mind ('we have our city of the soul to protect against her'), one has to understand its cultural status (Havelock, 1963: 5). Whereas *The Republic* is typically read as a document of utopian political theory, Havelock argues that its object is in fact pedagogy: it attacks the existing educational apparatus and demands urgent, non-utopian reforms. Rather than designating a particular literary or aesthetic practice, poetry referred to educational practice in its broadest sense, as a system of the storage and transmission of cultural memory and *savoir-faire*. Havelock points to the range of contexts in which the term mimesis, poetry's *modus operandi*, appears in *The Republic*: 'mimesis . . . [applies to] the artist's "act" of creation, the performer's "act" of imitation, the pupil's "act" of learning, the adult's "act" of recreation. . . . In short, Plato is describing a total technology of the preserved word which has since his day in Europe ceased to exist' (Havelock, 1963: 36). Havelock situates the origins of modern Western philosophy in the revolution in technologies of information storage and use that occurred as oral memory was supplanted by literacy. Between Homer and Plato, 'the method of storage began to alter, as information became alphabetized, and correspondingly the eye supplanted the ear as the chief organ employed for this purpose' (Havelock, 1963: vii).

> Preserved record . . . had to be carried continually in the living consciousness: it was itself a 'live recording'. . . . It could enlist the aid of only one sense, that of the ear, and the shaping of the material for presentation had therefore to be

governed by material which obeyed acoustic laws. The other senses were then involved as much as possible by devices of sympathetic association. (Havelock, 1963: 166)

Political power was grounded in the command of the technology of the effective utterance, 'which utterance is to be in the strictly technological sense "musical" ' – musical in a functional sense, so that the utterances were repeatable (Havelock, 1963: 108, 46). Havelock likens the situation to the contemporary reception of recorded popular music, to the acoustic advertising jingle, and to the nursery rhyme (1963: 147, 74, 84). 'In obedience to the laws of memorisation there was established in an oral culture an intimate linkage between instruction on the one hand and sensual pleasure on the other.' The activities of throat, larynx, lungs, tongue, teeth, hands, arms, legs and feet were engaged as *aides-mémoire*. The motor activity and the regularity of performance had hypnotic effects, arousing sympathetic reflexive responses akin to digestive or sexual pleasures (1963: 152–7). Havelock argues that the epic hero was not romantic, which is to say that the hero was not the paradigmatic individual whose agency might be enjoyed through vicarious, disembodied and solitary identification. Rather, the hero had a functional, technical, collective importance: 'The things they do will send out vibrations into the farthest confines of this society, and the whole apparatus becomes alive and performs motions which are paradigmatic' (1963: 166–7).

This then is the cultural apparatus that is the object of Plato's attack. The significance of mimesis cannot be understood if it is limited to imitation or impersonation, which the modern mind tends to 'picture' in visual terms, as a sort of mirroring.

Imitation in our language is governed by the presupposition that there is a separate existence of an original which is then copied. The essence of Plato's point, the raison d'être of his attack, is that in the poetic performance as practiced hitherto in Greece, there was no 'original.' (Havelock, 1963: 159)

Plato's task is to constitute an 'original': a subject capable of separating itself from the flux of mimetic experience and submitting the latter to rational analysis and evaluation. The earliest version of the dialectic, by Havelock's account, develops as an interruption, a method of wrenching the would-be 'singer' from the poetical/musical activity by asking them to reformulate habitual responses: 'What do you mean? Say that again' (1963: 209).

Most scholars have taken their own metaphysical presumptions to the study of early Greek philosophy and have assumed that this thought was metaphysical and abstract from the outset, as though, for example, the separation of the knowing subject from the known object were a universal and timeless attribute of thought. Against this assumption, Havelock argues that the capacity for abstract, conceptual thought was an effect of the displacement of mimesis, a shift in mnemotechnics (Havelock, 1963: ix).

The autonomous subject, 'who no longer recalls and feels, but knows', is now equipped not to dissolve noisily into multifarious experience, but to formulate 'a statement which will connect a subject and a predicate in a relationship which just "is", and is therefore permanent and unchanging' (1963: 219, 247).

If we accept Havelock's thesis that Plato's is 'a voice of revolution', then when Plato has Socrates declare on his deathbed that 'the supreme music is philosophy' (Havelock, 1963: 284), we can see that philosophy is now empowered, as Irigaray contends, 'to reduce all others to the economy of the Same'. One of the things fundamentally at stake in this reduction is the repression of the feminine. Pericles pronounced in his funeral oration words that are to Havelock's ears aphoristic: 'We philosophize without effeminacy' (Havelock, 1963: 281). Philippe Lacoue-Labarthe writes that philosophy has been particularly unable, indeed, perhaps even constitutionally unable to think about music. He also writes of the relation of music to the feminine:

> According to a very old, very profound, and very solid equivalence – perhaps indestructible – [music] is a *feminine* art, destined for women or for the feminine part of men. It is a *hysterical* art, in every sense. And for this reason, essentially, music *is* hysteria. At least, a particular music. . . . Here hysteria, or the aesthetic state, is to be understood as the height of passivity, that is to say as the height of plasticity, malleability, impressionability. (Lacoue-Labarthe, 1994: 105)

Now, given this history, and given the establishment of the discourse on discourse that allows one to stand back and posit essences, it is of course impossible to say what the feminine is, or indeed, what music is. However, we can say that they persist, as repressed contents inevitably do, and enter representation as symptoms, as traces of the archaic.

Nevertheless, there is music (as there are women) and it has a history. While we hear a range of musical expression much vaster than that prescribed by Plato, music continues to be subordinated to Logos, the best contemporary example of this being film music, where music almost always dutifully follows the action, the plot, the words, the mood. Underlying this is the assumption that music essentially imitates human affective states. When in the late fifteenth century, the period of the inception of Western musical modernity, the composers and musicians associated with the Florentine Camerata broke with the polyphonic style, they denounced it as aiming merely to 'tickle', rather than taking seriously music's power of moving the passions. They looked to the example of Ancient Greece, and fashioned the new style as a return to antiquity, taking up Plato's thesis that music imitates emotions or ideas (Galilei, 1965: 112–32). Ironically, the imitation of antiquity functioned in the absence of any original, as no scores of ancient music survived, if indeed there were any (Lacoue-Labarthe, 1994: xvi–xvii). Since the Renaissance, music has been understood to be mimetic: it imitates emotions or ideas. This concept of music has persisted through the centuries despite the best efforts of formalist musicology to dissociate music and emotion.

Alongside this persistence of a certain mimesis in art there has persisted, since Plato, a mimetic taboo with respect to human comportment. In the modern world, mimesis is the province of children.

> Children's play is everywhere permeated by mimetic modes of behaviour, and its realm is by no means limited to what one person can imitate in another. The child plays at being not only a shopkeeper or a teacher but also a windmill and a train. (Benjamin, 1979: 160)

Adorno describes the mimetic taboo, which functions both phylogenetically and ontogenetically, as follows:

> Civilization has replaced the organic adaptation to others and mimetic behavior proper . . . by rational practice, by work. . . . Uncontrolled mimesis is outlawed. . . . For centuries, the severity with which the rulers prevented their own followers and the subjugated masses from reverting to mimetic modes of existence, starting with the religious prohibition on images, going on to the social banishment of actors and gypsies, and leading finally to the kind of teaching which does not allow children to behave as children, has been the condition for civilization. Social and individual education confirms men in the objectivizing behavior of workers and protects them from reincorporation into the [*sic*] variety of circum-ambient nature. All devotion and all deflection has a touch of mimicry about it. The ego has been formed in resistance to this mimicry. (Horkheimer and Adorno, 1972: 180–1)

The concept of mimesis is crucial to Adorno's analysis of the culture industry, but also, paradoxically, to his theory of art. Mimesis, as he understands it *vis-à-vis* the art object, is bound up with the concept of autonomy. What Adorno means by autonomy is by no means transparent. He carefully distinguishes autonomous art from the long-standing Western tradition of transcendent art; it is vitally important not to confuse autonomy with transcendence.

> German speculative philosophy granted that a work of art contains within itself the sources of its transcendence, and that its inner meaning is always more than the work itself – but only to demand a certificate of good behaviour from it. According to this latent tradition, a work of art should have no being for itself, since otherwise it would – as Plato's embryonic state socialism classically stigmatized it – be a source of effeminacy and an obstacle to action for its own sake. Killjoys, ascetics, and moralists . . . have no time for aesthetic autonomy. (Adorno, 1980: 192)

Any work of art that has no ulterior motive is 'a reminder of sensual pleasure', and 'no moral terror can prevent the side the work of art shows its beholder from giving him [or her] pleasure, even if only in the formal fact of temporary freedom from the compulsion of practical goals'. Adorno's careful locution here is important, and I want to draw your attention to two aspects of it: first, the pleasure given by art is only one side of it, the side that it shows. On the other side, in an irreconcilable paradox of irresponsibility and responsibility, art is 'the language of suffering'. Adorno insists upon this other side as fundamental to art, and he insists too that it cannot be represented. If suffering is represented, even in committed art with all its good intentions, then it risks rationalization, and the giving of pleasure.

> Victims are used to create something, works of art, that are thrown to the consumption of a world that destroyed them. The so-called artistic representation of the sheer physical pain of people beaten to the ground with rifle butts contains, however remotely, the power to elicit enjoyment out of it. To write lyric poetry after Auschwitz is barbaric, and yet, 'the abundance of real suffering . . . demands the continued existence of art while it prohibits it; it is now virtually in art alone that suffering can find its own voice, consolation, without immediately being betrayed by it.' (Adorno, 1980: 188–9)

Returning now to the phrase 'the side a work of art shows its beholder', the second point I want to stress is that *it* shows that side, that is, the art object as Adorno understands it has intentionality, which is to say that it is a strange and different sort of object that has a life, a being for itself, and a knowledge particular to it. 'Artworks are alive in that they speak in a fashion denied to natural objects and the subjects who make them. They speak by virtue of the communication of everything particular in them' (Adorno, 1997: 5). We typically regard autonomy to be an achievement of the subject, in relation to whom objects are heteronomous, available to appropriation as means, as instruments. In order to understand what Adorno means by aesthetic autonomy, it is crucial to understand that this autonomy does not just refer to the isolation of art, but also that it is an attribute of the art object itself. 'The principle that governs autonomous works of art is not the totality of their effects but their own inherent structure. They are knowledge as non-conceptual objects' (Adorno, 1980: 193). The concept functions to subsume 'a great variety of really existing objects under the same term or thought' (Jameson, 1990: 20). Thus in the artwork as 'knowledge as non-conceptual object', we encounter non-identity, otherness and novelty – a form of knowledge that is fundamentally different than, and that calls into question, that produced by the subject. 'Art completes knowledge with what is excluded from knowledge and thereby once again impairs its character as knowledge, its univocity' (Adorno, 1997: 53–4).

Vis-à-vis the social situation of music Adorno writes:

> Through the total absorption of both musical production and consumption by the capitalistic process, the alienation of music from humanity has become complete. . . . Music is able to do nothing but portray within its own structure the social antinomies which are also responsible for its own isolation. (Adorno, 1978a: 129)

However, music does not reflect or reproduce social antinomies. Rather, these emerge immanently through the musical materials, materials which are not natural, but historical and social, and which therefore inherit certain 'problems'. The music of Schöenberg is important for Adorno not because it is the adequate expression of the alienation and fragmentation of human subjectivity and experience in modernity; nor is its importance located in Schöenberg's oppositional stance toward the tradition he inherited. Rather, Schöenberg's importance lies in his acknowledgement of the demands of the materials themselves, and thereby in his relinquishment of mastery over them. If, dialectically, in Schöenberg's music the domination of the materials becomes complete, it is not a reflection of Schöenberg's practice as such, but expresses the coercive character of the social order, of 'the contradictions and flaws which cut through present-day society' (Adorno, 1978a: 128).

Adorno believed that art constituted the only repository of negation in the administered world of the culture industry. However, it is not fair to accuse him of having taken refuge there. The bulk of the twelve volumes of his collected works deal with music in society, a sociology which examined in detail the production, reproduction and consumption of music. He is often accused of an elitist commitment to canonical classical music. But he is concerned neither with the preservation of great music as such, nor with the ability to listen to it expertly. Rather, his concern is with the structure of experience that music of any type enables or instils.

Autonomy as a problem is the structure at the heart of bourgeois subjectivity and experience, according to Adorno and Horkheimer's recounting of that origin in the *Dialectic of Enlightenment*. The heteronomous would-be subject encounters the other in fear, and responds of necessity with a will to domination, the foundation of instrumental reason. What the hegemony of the latter secures is an unstable autonomy for the subject against the forces of nature, but at the cost of that subject's own nature. Art survives as the repository of a different experience of the encounter of subject and object, and aesthetic comportment encodes an alternative response to fear than that of domination:

> Ultimately, aesthetic comportment is to be defined as the capacity to shudder, as if goose bumps were the first aesthetic image. What later came to be called subjectivity, freeing itself from the blind anxiety of the shudder, is at the same time the shudder's own development; life in the subject is nothing but what shudders, the reaction to the total spell that transcends the spell. Consciousness without shudder is reified consciousness. That shudder in which subjectivity stirs without yet being subjectivity is the act of being touched by the other. Aesthetic comportment assimilates itself to that other rather than subordinating it. Such a constitutive relation of the subject to objectivity in aesthetic comportment joins eros and knowledge. (Adorno, 1997: 331)

In Adorno's notion of aesthetic comportment, mimesis is an activity of the subject in its interaction with the object. As for the expression of the artwork, if Adorno understands the latter to be alive because it speaks, it is important to note Adorno's qualifier: 'they speak in a fashion denied to natural objects and the subjects who make them'. If on a cursory glance Adorno seems to be exploring some sort of phonocentric animism, things are not so simple. The eloquence (*Sprachcharakter*) of the artwork is 'fundamentally distinct from language as its medium'.

> The expressive values of artworks cease to be those of something alive. . . . In their expression artworks do not imitate the impulses of individuals, nor in any way those of their authors. . . . Expression approaches the transsubjective: it is the form of knowledge that – having preceded the polarity of subject and object – does not recognize this polarity as definitive. . . . It becomes what speaks out of the artifact not as an imitation of the subject. . . . Historical processes and functions are already sedimented in them and speak out of them. . . . [Art's] expression is the antithesis of expressing something. . . . What is essentially mimetic awaits mimetic comportment. If artworks do not make themselves like something else but only like themselves, then only those who imitate them can understand them. (Adorno, 1997: 113)

Walter Benjamin designates the subject–object problematic as that of aura, which he described as the gaze of an object: 'To perceive the aura of an object we look at means to invest it with the ability to look at us in return' (Benjamin, 1969a: 188). While Benjamin was ambivalent about the status of aura, in 'The work of art in the age of mechanical reproduction', he evaluates the situation of the artwork in light of the constitutive misrecognitions of commodity fetishism: the imputation of life to the artifacts of human labour endows them with the voice of authority, the disembodied voice of a tradition to which human beings submit as automatons. These circumstances, combined with the specific concepts surrounding artwork of genius and creativity, eternal value and mystery, lead him to evaluate the auratic art object as fascistic. In his view, the mimetic machines – the camera, the phonograph – had the capacity to shatter the hegemony of the auratic object (Benjamin, 1969b).

When Adorno responded to Benjamin's essay in 'On the fetish character in music and the regression of listening', he disregarded the difference in their objects (recorded music as opposed to the photographic and filmic image), concentrating instead upon the effects upon the subject of the saturation of musical experience by the logic of commodity fetishism (Adorno, 1998: 278–9). Beethoven had anticipated the situation more than a century earlier when he attempted, late in his life, some time around 1822, to secure the rights to publish his collected works. He failed to do so, but while he was trying he wrote what would have stood, remarkably, as the preface to his *oeuvre*:

> The legal tomes are fond of sounding phrases about human rights, phrases which the lawyers themselves then trample underfoot. Let me begin with a few sounding phrases. Every author has the right to plan and carry out a revised edition of his works. But there are so many voracious fanciers of the human brain, who love to

devour that food whether it be served pickled or in a stew or fricassee – there are so many cooks ready to pocket up the pennies that the poor author never sees, that it should be stated here and now that the human brain cannot be bought and sold like so many pounds of coffee or like a cheese.

The human brain is not a saleable commodity. . . .[2]

If the final pronouncement sounds defiant, the cynicism of the opening metaphor gives some sense of the effectivity Beethoven attributes to his own bravado, and to the political power of music, with its 'sounding phrases', as ideology. Beethoven, despite his protest, was conscious of the 'fact' that he was becoming coffee, becoming cheese, that he was living in a moment that was seeing exchange value overtake thought itself. In 1938, Adorno saw this situation as having reached completion, writing: 'The liquidation of the individual is the real signature of the new musical situation.' Recorded music 'inhabits the pockets of silence that develop between people molded by anxiety, work, and undemanding docility' (Adorno, 1998: 271, 276).

Of the performance of a Beethoven symphony, Adorno writes:

The new fetish is the flawlessly functioning, metallically brilliant apparatus as such, in which all the cogwheels mesh so perfectly that not the slightest hole remains open for the meaning of the whole. Perfect, immaculate performance in the latest style preserves the work at the price of its definitive reification. . . . The performance sounds like its own phonograph record. The dynamic is so pre-determined that there are no longer any tensions at all. (Adorno, 1988: 284)

Alongside the mimetic taboo, which disciplines the mimetic faculty in the interests of a docile and atomized subjectivity, there persists a mimetic injunction. 'The culture industry is geared to mimetic regression, to the manipulation of repressed impulses to copy' (Adorno, 1978b: 201). Adorno understands this invitation to mimesis, an appeal to the 'mimetic remnants' which inhere in subjectivity, to subtend the contents of any given cultural product, effecting an identification with the apparatus itself. Underneath an apparent freedom of choice and expression with respect to cultural products lies 'man's attempt to make himself a proficient apparatus, similar (even in emotions) to the one served up by the culture industry' (Horkheimer and Adorno, 1972: 167). If one identifies with an apparatus at the centre of which is a mimetic machine like the phonograph, governed by a logic of reproduction and an ideology of high fidelity, then one is in a position to read a script that operates on another level than that conscious, subjective one we normally associate with the processes of reading and writing. With respect to the illegible scribbles that are presented to the eye on the surface of a phonograph record, an inscription written by sounds and read by a needle in a process that operates independently of human audition, Adorno writes: 'if . . . notes were still the mere signs for music, then, through the curves of the needle on the phonograph record, music approaches decisively its true character as writing' (Adorno, 1990a: 59). If the human being identifies with the apparatus in the way that Adorno suggests, then 'it' is in a position to read what he elsewhere refers to as 'a priestly hieroglyphic script'.

> But the secret doctrine which is communicated here is the message of capital. . . . When a film presents us with a strikingly beautiful young woman it may officially approve or disapprove of her, she may be glorified as a successful heroine or punished as a vamp. Yet as a written character she announces something quite different from the psychological banners draped around her grinning mouth, namely the injunction to be like her. (Adorno, 1991a: 80–1)

Miriam Hansen argues that whereas Adorno's concept of mimesis with respect to aesthetic experience has an 'individualistic bent', the degraded form of mimetic comportment that he associates with the culture industry, 'however baleful, is a collective one' (Hansen, 1992: 70). Writing on film, Adorno insists that this collectivity inheres in its innermost elements:

> The movements which the film presents are mimetic impulses which, prior to all content and meaning, incite the viewers and listeners to fall into step as if in a parade. In this respect, film resembles music. . . . It would not be incorrect to describe the constitutive subject of film as a 'we' in which the aesthetic and sociological aspects of the medium converge. (Adorno, 1991b: 158)

Unlike Benjamin, Adorno is unwilling to attach emancipatory significance to the *a priori* collectivity generated by film, because, as it operates according to the mechanisms of the unconscious, it 'facilitates the ideological misuse of the medium'. Benjamin, in a letter responding to Adorno's essay 'On the fetish character in music and the regression of listening', whose argument he professed to follow 'without reservations', wrote: '*Ex improviso*, I am unable to decide whether the different distribution of passages of light and shadow in our respective essays derives from theoretical divergences. It is possibly a matter only of apparent differences in point of view, but the fact is that these points of view are brought to bear on different objects and both are equally valid. It may of course not be said that acoustical and optical apperceptions are equally open to revolutionary change' (Benjamin, 1994: 590, 629). Adorno continued to argue with Benjamin for decades after the latter's death, and in a fragment of the posthumously published *Aesthetic Theory* he posed the persistence of aura in the acoustic in this way: 'Music struggles to free itself of the element by which Benjamin, somewhat overgenerously, defined all art prior to the age of its technological reproducibility: aura, the sorcery that emanates from music, even if it were antimusic, whenever it commences to sound' (Adorno, 1997: 339). The sorcery that emanates from music does so whether it is live or recorded. The aural object has the character of an event: whether musical, spoken or noisy, it is temporal, and it emanates from some body, animate or inanimate. The 'sorcery' of the resonating body compounds the regression in listening that results from the rationalization of musical experience with a more ancient sense of fetishism – that to which the etymology of the word fetish itself points, of sorcery.

Andrew Hewitt has noted that in the *Dialectic of Enlightenment* magic is linked to the feminine (Hewitt, 1992: 70). An encounter with the sorceress Circe induces a regression: in her thrall, men become domesticated animals; in the thrall of recorded music, human beings become jitterbugs, radio hams and, as Adorno emphasizes repeatedly, they become not childlike, but childish, craving the repetition of the familiar and recognizable, triumphant in their ability simply to identify the objects they encounter (Adorno, 1998: 286–93). Adorno thinks that women are particularly susceptible to these effects, not on the grounds of their femininity, but 'because of their position in the productive process' (Adorno, 1991a: 79). While on the one hand one can appreciate the Marxist/proto-feminist sensibilities that enable this observation, on the other one hears faint echoes of the Platonic fear of becoming woman, becoming animal.

However, if Adorno thinks that women are particularly susceptible to regressive mimesis, he also imagines (without ever spelling it out) that they are not, in Irigaray's words, simply resorbed in this function. In an early essay on the phonograph, published in 1928 and seductively entitled 'The curves of the needle', he maintains that female voices do not record well. The sentiment is common enough for its time, and is predictably sexist in its alignment with the masculine appropriation of any new technology not specifically geared to housework. Adorno's reasoning is strange, though – out of step with the march toward mastery.[3]

> The female voice requires the physical appearance of the body that carries it. But it is just this body that the gramophone eliminates, thereby giving every female voice a sound that is needy and incomplete. Only there where the body itself resonates, where the self to which the gramophone refers is identical with its sound, only there does the gramophone have its legitimate realm of validity. (Adorno, 1990b: 52)

Here it is specifically the male body that is able to make itself identical to the apparatus. Adorno does not argue the point, he simply asserts what he will not elaborate upon for several decades. The female body remains unidentical to the apparatus, and if this is the consummation at stake, then the neediness and incompleteness Adorno hears represents this non-coincidence. She eludes its injunction to 'be like me'.

If Adorno's analysis is unremittingly pessimistic, it must be said that he does hold out one small hope, and he locates it in the very regressive mimetic tendencies that he deplores:

> In order to become a jitterbug or simply to 'like' popular music, it does not by any means suffice to give oneself up and to fall in line passively. To become transformed into an insect, man needs that energy which might possibly achieve his transformation into a man. (Adorno and Simpson, 1941: 48)

172 Feminism, culture and society

If 'becoming man' is not an agreeable prospect, and not what we here have in mind, nevertheless the hope that is moored in the energies of transformation, in the capacity to become something else, is worth hanging on to, and taking off from.

Notes

1 The phrase is Peter Dews's with respect to Adorno (Dews, 1989: 2).
2 Quoted in liner notes, the Budapest String Quartet, *The Late Quartets by Ludwig van Beethoven* (Columbia, 1962).
3 I have written about this in 'Adorno and the Sirens' (Engh, 1994: 120–35).

References

Adorno, Theodor (1978a) 'On the social situation of music', *Telos*, 35 (Spring): 128–64.
Adorno, Theodor (1978b) *Minima Moralia*, trans. E.F.N. Jephcott. London and New York: Verso.
Adorno, Theodor (1980) 'Commitment', in Ronald Taylor (ed.), *Aesthetics and Politics*. London and New York: Verso.
Adorno, Theodor (1990a) 'The form of the phonograph record', trans. Thomas Y. Levin, *October*, 55 (Winter): 56–61.
Adorno, Theodor (1990b) 'The curves of the needle', trans. Thomas Y. Levin, *October*, 55 (Winter): 49–55.
Adorno, Theodor (1991a) 'The schema of mass culture', in J.M. Bernstein (ed.), *The Culture Industry: Selected Essays on Mass Culture*. London: Routledge.
Adorno, Theodor (1991b) 'Transparencies on film', in J.M. Bernstein (ed.), *The Culture Industry: Selected Essays on Mass Culture*. London: Routledge.
Adorno, Theodor (1997) *Aesthetic Theory*, ed. Gretel Adorno and Rolf Tiedemann, trans. Robert Hullot-Kentor. Minneapolis, MN: University of Minnesota Press.
Adorno, Theodor (1998) 'On the fetish character in music and the regression of listening', in Andrew Arato and Eike Gebhardt (eds), *The Essential Frankfurt School Reader*. New York: Continuum.
Adorno, Theodor with Simpson, George (1941) 'On popular music', *Studies in Philosophy and Social Science*, 9: 17–48.
Benjamin, Walter (1969a) 'On some motifs in Baudelaire', in *Illuminations*, trans. Harry Zohn. New York: Schocken Books.
Benjamin, Walter (1969b) 'The work of art in the age of mechanical reproduction', in *Illuminations*, trans. Harry Zohn. New York: Schocken Books. pp. 217–51.
Benjamin, Walter (1979) 'On the mimetic faculty', in *One-Way Street and Other Writings*, trans. Edmund Jephcott and Kingsley Shorter. London: NLB.
Benjamin, Walter (1994) *The Correspondence of Walter Benjamin, 1910–1940*, ed. Gershom Scholem and Theodor W. Adorno, trans. Manfred Jacobson and Evelyn Jacobson. Chicago and London: University of Chicago Press.
Cahn, Michael (1984) 'Subversive mimesis: Theodor Adorno and the modern impasse of critique', in Mihai Spariosu (ed.), *Mimesis in Contemporary Theory: An Interdisciplinary Approach*, vol. 1. Philadelphia and Amsterdam: John Benjamins.
Derrida, Jacques (1987) 'Women in the beehive', in Alice Jardine and Paul Smith (eds), *Men in Feminism*. New York and London: Methuen.

Dews, Peter (1989) 'Adorno, post-structuralism, and the critique of identity', in Andrew Benjamin (ed.), *The Problems of Modernity: Adorno and Benjamin.* London and New York: Routledge.

Engh, Barbara (1994) 'Adorno and the Sirens: tele-phono-graphic bodies', in Leslie Dunn and Nancy Jones (eds), *Embodied Voices: Representing Female Vocality in Western Culture.* Cambridge: Cambridge University Press. pp. 120–35.

Galilei, Vincenzo (1965) 'Dialogo della musica antica e della moderna', in Oliver Strunk (ed.), *Source Readings in Music History: The Renaissance.* New York: Norton. pp. 112–32.

Hansen, Miriam (1992) 'Mass culture as hieroglyphic writing', *New German Critique*, 56 (Spring–Summer): 43–73.

Havelock, Eric A. (1963) *Preface to Plato.* Cambridge, MA and London: Bellknap Press of Harvard University Press.

Hewitt, Andrew (1992) 'A feminine dialectic of enlightenment?', *New German Critique*, 56 (Spring–Summer): 143–70.

Horkheimer, Max and Adorno, Theodor (1972) *Dialectic of Enlightenment*, trans. John Cumming. New York: Continuum.

Irigaray, Luce (1985) 'The power of discourse and the subordination of the feminine', in *The Sex Which Is Not One*, trans. Catherine Porter. Ithaca, NY: Cornell University Press.

Jameson, Fredric (1990) *Late Marxism: Adorno, or, The Persistence of the Dialectic.* London and New York: Verso.

Lacoue-Labarthe, Philippe (1994) *Musica Ficta (Figures of Wagner)*, trans. Felicia McCarren. Stanford, CA: Stanford University Press.

Plato (1941) *The Republic*, trans. Francis MacDonald Cornford. London, Oxford and New York: Oxford University Press.

9   Mimesis, Dwelling and Architecture: Adorno's Relevance for a Feminist Theory of Architecture

Hilde Heynen

The feminist critique of architecture presently covers a wide range of themes and strategies. Several approaches have been tried out on a very serious level, but there is not yet a consensus as to what the most important topics are or what strategies deserve to be elaborated. Topics range from a study of 'gendered spaces' (Spain, 1992) to a deconstructive critique of the discipline of architecture as being a 'mechanism of domestication of women' (Wigley, 1992). Strategies also involve a direct criticism of design projects in terms of their emancipatory value (addressing issues of safety, distribution of space according to gender, accessibility of services and the like) (Kanes Weisman, 1992), as a focus on the work of women architects (Hughes, 1996) or present a more general reflection on power relationships in architecture.[1] Within this rather heterogeneous field I would like to show how one could possibly draw some inspiration from the work of T.W. Adorno in order to develop a gender-sensitive critical approach to architecture. I will focus on the idea of 'mimesis' which is of central importance for Adorno, and which bears very interesting gender connotations.

Art as criticism

Adorno himself has only rarely written on architecture. In the few texts that exist he does link architecture's critical potential with its autonomous, mimetic moment.[2] *Mimesis* is a crucial concept in Adorno's work, especially in his *Aesthetic Theory*.[3] It is a concept that he rarely describes in precise terms, but which definitely has a much broader connotation in his work than do the traditional notions of art as an imitation of nature. Adorno's interpretation of this concept is undeniably indebted to Walter Benjamin and his mimetic theory of language (see Benjamin, 1978). Benjamin distinguishes two dimensions in language. Next to the communicative dimension, which resides in the conventional relationship between signifier and signified, there is also a mimetical dimension which has to do with similarities and correspondences. This mimetical dimension of language is valued very highly by Benjamin, and he mourns the fact that it is becoming atrophied because of modernity's preference for rationality and clarity.

In *Aesthetic Theory* Adorno refers to 'mimesis' as meaning a non-conceptual affinity between things and persons which is not based on rational knowledge and which goes beyond the mere antithesis between subject and object (Adorno, 1973a: 86–7; 1997: 54). The mimetic moment of cognition has to do with the possibility of approaching the world in a different way than by rational-instrumental thinking. Mimesis, however, is not simply equivalent to a visual similarity between works of art and what they represent. The affinity Adorno refers to lies deeper. It can be recognized, for example, in an abstract painting which, in mimetic fashion, depicts something of reality's alienating character.

According to Adorno, it is characteristic of art that it endeavours to create a dialectical relation between both moments of cognition: mimesis and rationality. A work of art comes into being on the basis of a mimetic impulse that is regulated by a rational input. Rationality and mimesis however are opposed to each other in a relation that is antithetical and paradoxical: the two moments of cognition cannot easily be reconciled. The work of art therefore is not able to resolve the contradiction by simply mediating between rationality and mimesis, because they are in a way incompatible and this incompatibility cannot be denied. The value of a work of art in fact depends on the extent to which it succeeds in highlighting the antithetic moments of both rationality and mimesis, without eliminating their opposition through some kind of unity that purports to reconcile the two (Adorno, 1973a: 87; 1997: 54–5). This is why Adorno regards tensions, dissonances and paradoxes as basic attributes of modern works of art.

Adorno is convinced that art entails a form of criticism. The critical character of art is in several respects related to its mimetic quality. In the first instance, art is one of the few realms of society where the mimetic principle is still privileged. Generally speaking society tends to forbid mimesis, and social practice is increasingly dominated by instrumental rationality. In view of this situation, the existence of art as a domain which is not totally permeated by rationality provides in itself a critique of the domination of rationality. Adorno argues that the uselessness of art, its refusal to be 'for-something-else', unmistakably implies a form of criticism with regard to a society where everything is forced to be useful (1973a: 336–7; 1977: 227).

Against the prevailing dominant mode of thought – identity thinking – that constantly subsumes the heterogeneous under the heading of sameness, the thought that, in Adorno's words, is 'schooled in exchange' (1973b: 107; 1964: 91), against this thought the principle of mimesis embodies a 'resemblance to itself' that makes room for the non-identical and the opaque (1977: 104; 1973a: 159). Art is thus perceived by Adorno as one of the last refuges where real experience, the experience of the non-identical, is still possible. He concurs with Benjamin in his opinion that modernity has provoked a crisis of experience by increasingly destroying the conditions that allow individuals to develop their capacity for genuine experience. Modern art, he states, provides a way to deal with this crisis and to express it (1973a: 57; 1977: 34).

The very modernity of art in fact depends on how it relates to this crisis. Art cannot escape this condition: '*Il faut être absolument moderne*', says Adorno, thus repeating Rimbaud's maxim. For Adorno, however, the statement does not mean that one should simply accept one's historical condition; it also implies a need to resist the historical trend. Adorno interprets Rimbaud's phrase as a categorical imperative that combines an honest assessment of social reality with an equally consistent opposition to its continuance. If one wants to resist repression and exploitation, one should not ignore them but recognize them as the actual conditions of existence; only by doing so can one take action against them. From an artistic point of view, this means that modern art needs to employ advanced techniques and methods of production; it also means that it is obliged to incorporate contemporary experiences (1973a: 50; 1997: 34). At the same time, however, the implication is that art contains a significant degree of criticism and opposition to the existing system.

It is this shading that gives Adorno's aesthetic theory its specific character: Adorno says modern art *as art* is critical. The critical value of a work of art is not embodied in the themes it deals with or in the so-called 'commitment' of the artist, yet on the contrary, is typical of the artistic process as such. Adorno is convinced that the mimetical potential of art, if it is rightly applied – 'right' not in political, but in disciplinary, artistic-autonomous terms – vouches for its critical character, even apart from the personal intention of the artist. Works of art yield a kind of knowledge of reality. This knowledge is critical because the mimetical moment is capable of highlighting aspects of reality that were not perceivable before. Through mimesis art establishes a critical relation with social reality (Cahn, 1984: 49).

In his dealings with architecture, he also stresses this aspect. He argues for example that the matter-of-fact approach of functionalism implies a correct understanding of the social situation, but states that its truth value is primarily dependent on the way that it treats function mimetically. The danger is not inconceivable that this mimetic element will be lost, so that the architecture does not have any critical bite: when *Mimesis an Funktionalität* is reduced to *Funktionalität* pure and simple, every critical distance from the dominant social reality disappears and functional architecture no longer plays anything but an affirmative role.[4]

In functionalism Adorno recognizes the effects of the dialectics of the Enlightenment. This movement too was characterized by an intertwining of progressive and regressive moments. By giving reason priority over myth, the Enlightenment aspired towards emancipation and liberation, but this very aspiration reverts to myth when its goal is forgotten and 'reason' is reduced to pure instrumental rationality. The same dialectics plays a part in functionalism: inasmuch as its aim was to fulfil genuine 'objective' human needs, one can only see it as a progressive moment, one moreover that contains a critique of a social situation whose whole effect is to deny these genuine needs; when however functionalism is integrated in a social dynamic that employs 'functionalism' as an end in itself, with an absence of reference to any goal beyond it, it represents a regressive position:

> The antinomies of *Sachlichkeit* confirm the dialectic of enlightenment: that progress and regression are entwined. The literal is barbaric. Totally objectified, by virtue of its rigorous legality the artwork becomes a mere fact and is annulled as art. The alternative that opens up in this crisis is: either to leave art behind or to transform its very concept. (Adorno, 1997: 61)[5]

The first alternative – the renunciation of every claim to be art – is precisely the charge that Adorno levels at functionalism in practice. This can clearly be seen in 'Functionalism today', an essay where he is unsparing in his critique of the renunciation of the autonomous moment. In his view it is precisely this reduction that is responsible for the dullness and superficiality of so much postwar architecture.

Today it is no longer functionalism that is at stake in the architectural discourse. Nor is there any longer any dispute over the existence of an 'autonomous moment' in architecture. What interests us here, however, is if and how this autonomous moment can be made productive in terms of a feminist critique of architecture. To answer that question, we turn again to the notion of mimesis, which brings us close to some issues which are relevant for a 'philosophy in the feminine'.[6] As Lacoue-Labarthe has pointed out, following the lead of Luce Irigaray, there are some curious clues, which relate mimesis to the feminine.

Mimesis and the feminine

In 'Typographie', Lacoue-Labarthe's contribution to the book *Mimesis. Desarticulations* (1975/1989), the argument pivots round what he calls the 'constitutive undecidability' of mimesis. The starting point is Plato's treatment and condemnation of mimesis in the *Republic*. In this book Plato explicitly states that poets, writers, actors and artists should be excluded from the ideal state because their work makes no contribution whatsoever to truth and goodness. Their exclusion is first formulated in the chapter that deals with education. According to Plato the spiritual education of small children must not be determined by listening to stories (as is usually the case), because stories are largely based on fantasy and are therefore untrue. The state should keep a careful eye on the production of texts, only permitting those that serve the truth and propagate elevated principles. This means amongst other things that a writer can only tell his tale in indirect speech because the use of direct speech means that he is pretending to be another and that results in confusion and a disguising of truth. For the same reason actors are also not welcome in Plato's *Republic* and music is required to be restrained and lacking in emotion.

Only in a much later chapter about art and censorship is the fundamental reason for this exclusion stated. Here Plato compares the making of a painting or sculpture with the way that reality is reflected in a mirror. The image that appears in a mirror is not real; it is clear that what is involved is a derivative form, a copy of the truth. Plato concludes from this that works of art are far removed from the truth and that the wise man should be on his guard against them.

Lacoue-Labarthe points out that something quite curious is going on in this passage. Apparently Plato is only able to defend his rejection of mimesis by way of the trope of the mirror – in other words, by means of a comparison, by a mimetic gesture. The exclusion of mimesis, the control of mimesis can only be achieved by appealing to a means that is proper to mimesis:

> It remains fragile. And, in fact, if the entire operation consists in trying to go one better than mimesis in order to master it, if it is a question of circumventing mimesis, though with its own means (without which, of course, this operation would be null and void), how would it be possible to have even the slightest chance of success – since mimesis is precisely the absence of appropriate means, and since this is even what is supposed to be shown? How do we appropriate the improper? How do we make the improper appropriate without aggravating still further the improper? (Lacoue-Labarthe, 1989: 95)[7]

We are faced with a crucial dimension of mimesis here – its connection with the conflict between the self and the other, between the authentic and the inauthentic, between the proper and the improper. If one does not succeed in unambiguously separating the categories of truth and mimesis – without, that is, making an appeal to comparisons or metaphors – then it is indeed difficult to determine what it is that is 'proper' about the truth. When mimesis is brought in to help achieve an understanding of the distinctive features of certain entities, the specific character of this operation consists in the fact that these features can only be highlighted by means of a comparison with something else, something different. One can only succeed therefore in grasping the 'proper' by way of the 'improper', something that inevitably complicates one's notion of the proper.

Lacoue-Labarthe relates the anti-mimetic attitude that prevails in the philosophical tradition to the threat that comes from the feminine. Plato associates the mimetic in the first place with the tales that women tell little children. He considers their influence to be dangerous, because in these stories the clear distinction between truth and lies is dissolved. Lacoue-Labarthe argues that a sort of male urge to rebel against the primary control of the mother underlies Plato's text at this point. A child's first surroundings are defined by women who are by consequence always associated with the stage at which the subject is not yet completely developed. As Lacan has shown, a child, an infant (*infans* in Latin means without speech) gradually becomes a subject by making its entry into language, by learning to speak. The human condition is such that the emergence of ego-consciousness does not coincide with physical birth. There is a considerable period in which a child is not yet a subject. The child is not capable of achieving the status of a subject all by itself: it has to go through what Lacan calls the 'mirror stage' (Lacan, 1966). It learns to see itself as an entity and as differing from its environment, due to the fact that it identifies itself with its mirror image and with the name it has been given by its parents. The identity of the subject is in other words not established in a completely autonomous way, but is formed on the basis of elements that come from outside and that are mimetically appropriated.

According to Lacoue-Labarthe here is the ground for the anti-mimetic attitude that one encounters so often in philosophy. Anti-mimesis refers to nothing else than the ultimate Hegelian dream of philosophy, the dream of an absolute knowledge, of a subject that understands its own conception perfectly, thus also controlling it perfectly. The dream of a perfect autonomy is constantly threatened by the confusing plurality that mimesis represents. It is, in other words, threatened by instability, by feminization (Lacoue-Labarthe, 1975: 257–60; 1989: 126–9).

Seen in this light, it is clear indeed that mimesis has secret ties to the 'dark continent' of femininity. It is no coincidence that Luce Irigaray privileges mimesis as a strategy for women to adequately react to the phallocentric discourse from which they cannot escape in any straightforward manner:

> One must assume the feminine role deliberately. Which means already to convert a form of subordination into an affirmation, and thus begin to thwart it. . . . To play with mimesis is thus, for a woman, to try to locate the place of her exploitation by discourse, without allowing herself to be simply reduced to it. It means to resubmit herself – inasmuch as she is on the side of the 'perceptible', of 'matter' – to 'ideas', in particular to ideas about herself that are elaborated in/by a masculine logic, but so as to make 'visible' by an effect of playful repetition, what was supposed to remain invisible: recovering a possible operation of the feminine in language. (Irigaray, 1985: 76)[8]

This proposal stems from the observation that women are not controlling their own identity – they are not able to directly experience their own being since this experience is always already mediated through a system of representation which is established by men and for men, and in which the woman is reduced to mirroring the man. In such circumstances mimesis offers a valuable tactic, because it enables women to subvert – by the double gesture of assimilation *and* displacement – the identification imposed upon them.

We owe to Adorno precise descriptions of what mimesis can bring about in works of art and how it can be the carrier of art's critical import. Adorno argues that art is obliged to enter into a relation of similarity with reality, in order not to fall back into useless consolation. If art wants to serve as genuine critique, it must become '*Mimesis an ihr Widerspiel*' (mimesis of its opposite):

> Art was compelled to this by social reality. Whereas art opposes society, it is nevertheless unable to take up a position beyond it. It achieves opposition only through identification with that against which it remonstrates. (Adorno, 1997: 133)[9]

This is also why Adorno states that works of art can only exercise a critique of the dominant thought inasmuch as they have in part at least made this dominant thought their own:

> The opposition of artworks to domination is mimesis of domination. They must assimilate themselves to the comportment of domination in order to produce something qualitatively distinct from the world of domination. (Adorno, 1997: 289)[10]

The mimetic impulse, according to Adorno, has to do with a gesture of negation: the work of art does not produce a positive image of reality or a positive image of what a utopian, ideal reality might be. On the contrary, the image it produces is a thoroughly negative one, showing as it does the negative aspects of what is called reality. With the gesture of negation that it uses in order to reflect societal reality mimetically, it reveals something about that reality that usually remains hidden. This hidden essence of reality is exposed as something that is unacceptable, a non-essence, while at the same time the need for something else, for a real essence, is suggested:

> Even while art indicates the concealed essence, which it summons into appearance, as monstrous, this negation at the same time posits as its own measure an essence that is not present, that of possibility; meaning inheres even in the disavowal of meaning. (Adorno, 1997: 105)[11]

Adorno firmly insists on giving the negative a privileged status, because he is convinced that only by a gesture of negation does one have the right to appeal to the 'other', to the 'utopian'.[12] To him the objective of modern art is to make people aware of the terrifying character of everyday reality. Under these circumstances, negativity is the only way to keep the idea of the utopian alive. Indeed, the utopian is inconceivable in a positive form, for no image is powerful enough to illustrate the utopian in a positive way without making it appear ridiculous and banal. The utopian element in Adorno's work is essentially negative – utopia after all means 'nowhere'. While it still refers to the notion of the existence of the 'other', this other cannot and must not be named, because then it runs the risk of no longer remaining the 'other' but becoming 'the same'. Utopia then can only acquire form in a negative manner, by as it were continually confronting reality with that which it is not:

Insofar as we are not allowed to cast the picture of utopia, insofar we do not know what the correct thing would be, we know exactly, to be sure, what the false thing is. That is actually the only form in which utopian thinking is given to us at all. (Adorno in Bloch, 1987: 12)

This complex interplay of mimesis, negativity and utopia can be regarded as productive for feminist thought too. It opens up the possibility of reflecting on issues of identity and difference while avoiding the pitfalls of traditional identity thinking. It moreover makes it possible to critically engage oneself with long-established and institutionalized disciplines such as architecture, and to question them from a feminist perspective.

Mimesis in architecture: Adolf Loos

One instance of the way mimesis can be at work in architecture is to be found in the work of Adolf Loos. According to Massimo Cacciari (1985), Loos's architecture displays a feminine grandness which distinguishes it from that of his contemporaries. Cacciari locates this quality in the sensitivity about the difference between interior and exterior that permeates his work. Here resides Loos's affinity with 'Lou's buttons' – the metaphor Cacciari relies upon to mark the difference between what is exchangeable and what is not. Cacciari's text starts with a discussion of Lou Andreas-Salomé's reminiscence of the 'buttons', which represent for her the inalienable and the non-productive (they stand for the collection of memories, more specifically the memory of her mother). Lou's buttons are described by Cacciari as the opposite of money, which is completely exchangeable and stands for a cycle of permanently productive equivalency. His intuition is that the interior in Loos's work stands to the exterior as buttons to money – the first thematizing the idea of collecting memories and storing inalienable things, the second playing its part in the world of exchange and production. This difference is given form in Loos's architecture because Loos refuses to establish a transparency between inside and outside. His exteriors are mute and closed; they don't give any clues as to the contents or the meaning of the interior. Thus the outside appearance of his houses is able to protect their interior – the buttons – against the claims of a world which seeks to place everything under the banner of exchangeability.

This can be seen, for example, in the house Moller, built by Loos in Vienna in 1928. This building is an elaborate *Raumplan*-house. The *Raumplan* is a technique of designing in three dimensions that Loos regarded as his most important contribution to architecture (see Figure 9.1) (Loos, 1982: 214–15). Designing for Loos involves a complex three-dimensional activity: it is like a jigsaw puzzle with spatial units of different heights that have to be defined first and fitted into a single volume afterwards. In the Moller house

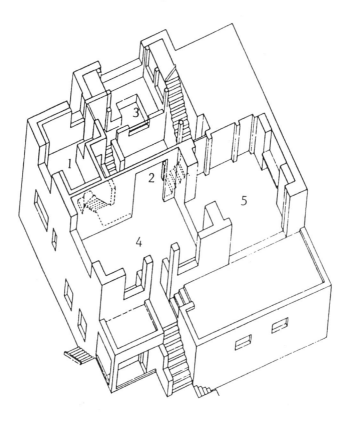

FIGURE 9.1 *Adolf Loos, Moller House, Vienna 1928, axonometric view of the*
Raumplan
1 Entrance with cloakroom
2 Central hall
3 Ladies' lounge
4 Music room
5 Dining hall

the sequence of living areas is built round a central 'hall'. After going
through the small entrance, the visitor has to turn left and mount a flight of
six steps to the cloakroom. After this first stop, one climbs another flight
of stairs – this time with a bend in it – to arrive in the central hall, the heart
of the house. Several rooms are grouped round the periphery of this high-
ceilinged hall: a 'ladies' lounge' (*Damenzimmer*), a music room and a dining
room.

Each room is characterized by different materials and proportions. The
ladies' lounge, which is situated in the bay window above the front door, has
light wood panelling and the fixed benches there are covered with a checked
material (see Figure 9.2). It is like an alcove and has a wide opening on to
the hall. In the music room darker colours prevail and the furnishings are

FIGURE 9.2   *Adolf Loos, Moller House, Vienna 1928, ladies' lounge* (*Photo Albertina*)

largely peripheral: okumé panelling, a polished ebony floor, and blue material for the fixed benches just inside the garden façade. The dining room is a light open room that leads directly to the terrace (see Figure 9.3). It is dominated by the dining table and the Thonet chairs in the middle. Both the dining room and the music room are linked to the garden. The only enclosed rooms on the main floor are the library (*Herrenzimmer*) and the kitchen. An open staircase leads from the hall to the bedroom level.

FIGURE 9.3   *Adolf Loos, Moller House, Vienna* 1928, *dining room seen from the music room* (*Photo Albertina*)

In contrast with the open interior, the dominant impression made by the house's outside appearance is one of closedness and impartiality. The street façade has a severe symmetrical structure and its not too friendly character gives the house the look of an isolated object (see Figure 9.4). The projection containing the lounge juts out at a low level above the front door giving the façade a somewhat unbalanced, almost threatening appearance. The rear of the house, which does not relate to public space, has a clear relation with the garden and conveys rather an impression of openness, due to the interplay of terraces and flights of steps, and to its larger windows (see Figure 9.5).

The house, however, does more than establish the difference between interior and exterior – which in a certain sense could be said merely to reproduce the age-old distribution of space according to which women belong to the inside of the house while men are free to explore public space outside. As Beatriz Colomina (1992) suggests, Loos's houses are elaborated in a very theatrical way – thus staging and framing the play of daily life. This theatricality can be seen in the way Loos creates a choreography of arrivals and departures: through the frequent shifts in direction that oblige one to pause for a moment, and through the transition between the dark entrance and the light living area, one gets a sense of deliberately entering a

FIGURE 9.4   *Adolf Loos, Moller House, Vienna* 1928, *front façade* (*Photo Albertina*)

stage set on which one is being observed, with oneself playing the role of observer.

The spatial layout of the house Moller, for example, brings about a definitely theatrical effect. The route into the house consists of a sequence of spaces and directions that as it were physically prepare one for the actual arrival in the hall. On two occasions visitors are exposed to the controlling view from the ladies' lounge: the first time is when one approaches the front door; the second occurs as one climbs the steps. The ladies' lounge also overlooks the garden via the hall and the music room. All this gives it a privileged position – something that is reinforced by its wide horizontal window and the bay-like projection in the front façade.

Beatriz Colomina (1992) observes that with Loos windows are not normally designed to be looked out of. They function in the first instance as a source of light; what is more they are often opaque or are situated above eye level. Moreover Loos likes placing benches or divans under the windows, something that makes for ideal nooks for sitting and reading in, but where one really has to turn one's head to take a look outside. All this means that the interior is experienced as a secluded and intimate area. Nowhere does the space outside penetrate the house. While partition walls are often absent in the interior, being replaced by large openings between

FIGURE 9.5   *Adolf Loos, Moller House, Vienna 1928, garden façade* (Photo Albertina)

two spaces, every transition to the outside is very clearly defined as a door and not as an opening in the wall. The transition between inside and outside is often modified by a flight of steps, a terrace or a veranda.

Nevertheless the house does not simply reproduce a gender-associated distribution of space. By mimetically enacting this distribution, by framing it as if it becomes a stage for a play, a shift occurs. The house renders visible its own operativity in the construction of subject positions. It no longer silently obeys cultural conventions, but displaces them by making them manifest and by negotiating the direction of the gaze.

Dwelling and the uncanny

In his essay '*Domus* and the megalopolis' Lyotard describes the condition of the *domus* as one that has now become impossible: dwelling as a common-place where a desire to serve and a concern with the community are at work. This domestic community belongs to the past, for the human world has become a megalopolis. The prevailing system orchestrated by the exchange principle is not the least bit concerned with habit, narrative or rhythm. Its memory is dominated by the principle of rationality that tramples tradition underfoot. The *domus* however, concealed behind this system, does leave some trace of itself. This makes it a *fata morgana* for us, the impossible dwelling. Thought that attempts to resist incorporation by the megalopolis appears as the handwriting of these impossible dwellings:

> Baudelaire, Benjamin, Adorno. How to inhabit the megalopolis? By bearing witness to the impossible work, by citing the lost domus. Only the quality of suffering counts as bearing witness. Including, of course, the suffering due to language. We inhabit the megalopolis only to the extent that we declare it uninhabitable. Otherwise we are just lodged there. (Lyotard, 1991: 200)

This impossible notion is for Lyotard what is at stake in thinking, in writing and in works of art. It also forms, in my opinion, what is at stake in architecture: 'To inhabit the megalopolis by declaring it uninhabitable'. This is a way of rewriting Benjamin's formula in which he calls for a new sort of dwelling, a dwelling that is appropriate to the 'hurried actuality' of the present.[13] In addition to the age-old sense of security and seclusion, Benjamin suggests, dwelling takes on a new level of meaning that has to do with porosity and transparency, with adaptability and flexibility. Seen as a transitive verb, dwelling takes on a more active meaning as making an environment for itself and making oneself at home all over again.

Benjamin did not charge his statement with any gender-related connotation, but as women we can make it our own by hearing it as an appeal to transform the meaning of the house. Understanding dwelling as a transitive verb means that the identification with the house which has been imposed upon women by a patriarchal mechanism of domestication, could be subverted by a gesture of mimetical appropriation; instead of being enclosed by the house, enclosing oneself through a new kind of dwelling, which is mobile and active rather than simple and static. Dwelling as permanent quest for an ever new enclosure, because no dwelling can ever be definitive or more than momentary: dwelling as continually permeated by its opposite.

It is not without reason that dwelling is the key metaphor that Freud (1947/1985; cf. Vidler, 1992) uses in his reflection on the uncanny. According to Freud the most uncanny experience occurs in the environment that is most familiar to us, for the experience of the uncanny has to do with the intertwining of *heimlich* (what is of the house, but also what is hidden) and *unheimlich* (what is not of the house, what is therefore in a strange way unconcealed yet concealed). Freud makes plausible in fact that the uncanny is so frightening because it refers to what is one's 'own' but nevertheless must remain hidden. Thus it has to do with that which is repressed. This implies that the figure of repression belongs to dwelling as its other which can neither be completely abandoned nor completely recovered.

Via mimesis and the small shifts and distortions that it generates, architecture is capable of making us feel something of that which is repressed, that which exists beyond the normal and expected, that which lies beyond patriarchal mechanisms of domestication. In this way one could imagine an architecture that would subvert itself and could serve as a guide to a permanent quest for a new dwelling, a dwelling in the feminine.

Notes

1 Several collections of essays appeared which can be helpful for browsing the field. I mention just a few of them: Berkeley (1989); Agrest et al. (1996); Rüedi et al. (1996); Coleman et al. (1996).

2 There is one essay that is explicitly concerned with architecture. It is a lecture that Adorno gave in 1965 at a meeting of the *Werkbund* on the subject of *Bildung durch Gestalt*. The title of the text is 'Funktionalismus Heute' (Adorno, 1977) and it has been translated as 'Functionalism today' (Adorno, 1979). In *Aesthetische Theorie* there is a passage about the dialectics of functionalism (1973: 96–7), in addition to some more passing references. My references to the latter work are to Adorno (1997). The German edition I use is Adorno (1973a).

3 For a detailed analysis of the concept of mimesis in Adorno's work see Früchtl (1986). For a general study of mimesis, see Gebauer and Wulf (1992).

4 I once clarified the difference between *Funktionalität* and *Mimesis an Funktionalität* with reference to Hannes Meyer's design for the Peterschule in Basel. Cf. Heynen (1992).

5 German version: 'Die Antinomien der Sachlichkeit bezeugen jenes Stück Dialektik der Aufklärung, in dem Fortschritt und Regression ineinander sind. Das Barbarische ist das Buchstäbliche. Ganzlich versachlicht wird das Kunstwerk, kraft seiner puren Gesetzmässigkeit, zum blossen Faktum und damit als Kunst abgeschafft. Die Alternative, die in der Krisis sich öffnet, ist die, entweder aus der Kunst herauszufallen oder deren eigenen Begriff zu verändern' (Adorno, 1973a: 97).

6 I refer here to the title of a book by Margaret Whitford: *Luce Irigaray. Philosophy in the Feminine* (1991).

7 French version: 'Cela reste fragile. Et de fait, si toute l'opération consiste à surenchir sur la mimesis pour la maîtriser, s'il s'agit de *contourner* la mimesis, mais avec ses propres moyens (sans quoi, bien entendu, ce serait nul et non-avenu), comment serait-il possible d'avoir la moindre chance de réussir, puisque la mimesis est précisément l'absence de moyens appropriés – et que c'est même ce qu'il s'agit de *montrer*? Comment (s')approprier l'impropre? Comment (s')approprier l'impropre sans aggraver encore l'impropre?' (Lacoue-Labarthe, 1989: 224).

8 Translation adapted by Margaret Whitford (1991: 71).

9 '. . . so zediert sich darin, . . . die Mimesis der Kunst an ihr Widerspiel. Genötigt wird Kunst dazu durch die soziale Realität. Während sie der Gesellschaft opponiert, vermag sie doch keinen ihr jenseitigen Standpunkt zu beziehen; Opposition gelingt ihr einzig durch Identifikation mit dem, wogegen sie aufbegehrt' (Adorno, 1973a: 201).

10 'Die Opposition der Kunstwerke gegen die Herrschaft ist Mimesis an diese. Sie müssen dem herrschaftlichen Verhalten sich angleichen, um etwas von der Welt der Herrschaft qualitativ Verschiedenes zu produzieren' (Adorno, 1973a: 430).

11 'Noch indem Kunst das verborgene Wesen, das sie zur Erscheinung verhält, als Unwesen verklagt, ist mit solcher Negation als deren Mass ein nicht gegenwärtiges Wesen, das der Möglichkeit, mitgesetzt; Sinn inhäriert noch die Leugnung des Sinns' (Adorno, 1973a: 161).

12 This point of view is related to the Jewish tradition of the ban on images. Cf. Koch (1989).

13 Benjamin understands dwelling as an active form of dealing with reality, in which the individual and his surroundings adjust to each other. He refers to the

grammatical connection in German between *wohnen* (dwelling) and *gewohnt* (customary, habitual), a connection that is found in English between 'habit' and 'inhabit'. This connection, he says, gives a clue to the understanding of dwelling as a sort of hurried contemporaneity that involves the constant shaping and reshaping of a casing. For a correct understanding this passage has to be left in the original German: 'Wohnen als Transitivum – im Begriff des "gewohnten Lebens" z.b. – gibt eine Vorstellung von der hastigen Aktualität, die in diesem Verhalten verborgen ist. Es besteht darin, ein Gehäuse uns zu prägen' (Benjamin, 1982: 292).

References

Adorno, Theodor W. (1964) *Jargon der Eigentlichkeit: Zur deutschen Ideologie.* Frankfurt-on-Main: Suhrkamp.
Adorno, Theodor W. (1973a) *Aesthetische Theorie* [1970] (Suhrkamp Taschenbuch Wissenschaft 2). Frankfurt-on-Main: Suhrkamp.
Adorno, Theodor W. (1973b) *The Jargon of Authenticity.* Evanston, IL: Northwestern University Press.
Adorno, Theodor W. (1977) 'Funktionalismus heute' [1965], in *Gesammelte Schriften.* Frankfurt-on-Main: Suhrkamp. pp. 375–95.
Adorno, Theodor W. (1979) 'Functionalism today', *Oppositions*, 17: 39–41.
Adorno, Theodor W. (1997) *Aesthetic Theory.* Minneapolis, MN: University of Minnesota Press.
Agrest, Diana, Conway, Patricia and Kanes Weisman, Leslie (eds) (1996) *The Sex of Architecture.* New York: Harry N. Abrams.
Benjamin, Walter (1978) 'On language as such and on the language of man', and 'On the mimetic fallacy', in *Reflections: Essays, Aphorisms, Autobiographical Writings.* New York: Schocken. pp. 314–36.
Benjamin, Walter (1982) *Das Passagenwerk.* Frankfurt-on-Main: Suhrkamp.
Berkeley, Ellen Perry (ed.) (1989) *Architecture: A Place for Women.* London: Smithsonian Institution Press.
Bloch, Ernst (1987) *The Utopian Function of Art and Literature: Selected Essays.* Cambridge, MA: MIT Press.
Cacciari, Massimo (1985) 'Interieur et expérience: notes sur Loos, Roth et Wittgenstein', *Critique*, 452–3 (January–February): 106–18.
Cahn, Michael (1984) 'Subversive mimesis: T.W. Adorno and the modern impasse of critique', in M. Spariosu (ed.), *Mimesis in Contemporary Theory.* Philadelphia and Amsterdam: Benjamins. pp. 27–64.
Coleman, Debra, Danze, Elisabeth and Henderson, Carol (eds) (1996) *Architecture and Feminism.* New York: Princeton Architectural Press.
Colomina, Beatriz (1992) 'The split wall: domestic voyeurism', in B. Colomina (ed.), *Sexuality and Space.* New York: Princeton Architectural Press. pp. 73–130.
Freud, Sigmund (1947) 'Das unheimliche' [1919], in *Gesammelte Werke*, vol. 12. Frankfurt: Fischer. pp. 229–68.
Freud, Sigmund (1985) 'The "uncanny"' [1919], in *Art and Literature* (Pelican Freud Library, vol. 14). Harmondsworth: Penguin Books. pp. 335–76.
Früchtl, Josef (1986) *Mimesis: Konstellation eines Zentralbegriffs bei Adorno.* Würzburg: Königshausn und Neumann.
Gebauer, Gunter and Wulf, Christoph (1992) *Mimesis: Kultur – Kunst – Gesellschaft.* Reinbek bei Hamburg: Rowohlt.
Heynen, Hilde (1992) 'Architecture between modernity and dwelling: reflections on Adorno's *Aesthetic Theory*', *Assemblage*, 17: 78–91.

Hughes, Francesca (ed.) (1996) *The Architect: Reconstructing her Practice*. London: MIT Press.

Irigaray, Luce (1985) *This Sex Which Is Not One*. Ithaca, NY: Cornell University Press.

Kanes Weisman, Leslie (1992) *Discrimination by Design: A Feminist Critique of the Man-Made Environment*. Chicago: University of Illinois Press.

Koch, Gertrud (1989) 'Mimesis und Bildverbot in Adornos Aesthetik: aesthetische Dauer als Revolte gegen den Tod', *Babylon: Beiträge zur jüdischen Gegenwart*, 6 (October): 36–45.

Lacan, Jacques (1966) 'Le Stade du miroir comme formateur de la fonction du Je', in *Écrits 1*. Paris: Seuil. pp. 89–97.

Lacoue-Labarthe, Philippe (1975) 'Typographie', in Sylviane Agacinski, Jacques Derrida and Sarah Kofman (eds), *Mimesis: Desarticulations*. Paris: Flammarion. pp. 165–270.

Lacoue-Labarthe, Philippe (1989) 'Typography', in *Typography: Mimesis, Philosophy, Politics*. Cambridge, MA: Harvard University Press. pp. 43–138.

Loos, Adolf (1982) *Trotzdem* [1931]. Vienna: Prachner.

Lyotard, Jean-François (1991) '*Domus* and the megapolis', in *The Inhuman: Reflections on Time*. Cambridge: Polity Press. pp. 191–204.

Rüedi, Katerina, Wigglesworth, Sarah and McCorquodale, Duncan (eds) (1996) *Desiring Practices: Architecture, Gender and the Interdisciplinary*. London: Black Dog.

Spain, Daphne (1992) *Gendered Spaces*. London: University of North Carolina Press.

Vidler, Anthony (1992) 'Introduction', in *The Architectural Uncanny: Essays in the Modern Unhomely*. Cambridge, MA: MIT Press. pp. 3–14.

Whitford, Margaret (1991) *Luce Irigaray: Philosophy in the Feminine*. London: Routledge.

Wigley, Mark (1992) 'Untitled: the housing of gender', in Beatriz Colomina (ed.), *Sexuality and Space*. New York: Princeton Architectural Press. pp. 327–89.

Index